T0288203

Praise for *Gun Control in Nazi-Occupied France*

"Stephen Halbrook has done it again, broken new ground with meticulous historical 'gun control' research. This is the harrowing story of Nazi and Vichy government savage repression of French gun owners, in part made possible by pre-war French firearms registration. *Gun Control in Nazi-Occupied France* is an important and highly readable addition to scholarship on how dictators and invaders have disarmed conquered populations."

> —**James B. Jacobs**, Chief Justice Warren E. Burger Professor of Constitutional Law and the Courts; Director, Center for Research in Crime and Justice; New York University; author, *Can Gun Control Work?*

"In the outstanding book, *Gun Control in Nazi-Occupied France*, Halbrook shows that although the French government did not intend to disarm the population when it mandated the registration of firearms, the very existence of registration records made it possible for the Nazis who occupied France during WWII to tighten their bloody grip on the country by hunting down gun owners. The applicable lesson here is that the intentions behind gun control measures aimed at the general population don't matter as much as the inevitable result: subtracting from the people's power to guard their own freedom. His mixture of anecdotes and statistics makes for sobering reading."

> —**Angelo M. Codevilla**, Professor Emeritus of International Relations, Boston University; author, *Informing Statecraft*, *War: Ends and Means* (with Paul Seabury), *The Character of Nations*, and *Between the Alps and a Hard Place: Switzerland in World War II and the Rewriting of History*

"In this detailed and fascinating book, Stephen P. Halbrook gives us a companion volume to his superb *Gun Control in the Third Reich*. Relying on French archival sources and German occupational records as well as a truly illuminating set of eye-witness questionnaire responses and more, Halbrook demonstrates the extent to which modern dictatorship relies on the control and confiscation of weapons and fears what French socialist Jean Jaurès once praised as 'the general arming of the people.' Like Halbrook's study of the Third Reich, *Gun Control in Nazi-Occupied France* greatly expands our historical knowledge about the relationship between private gun confiscation and the Holocaust. As a work of scholarship, the book is— simply put—conclusive. But it is also an intensely interesting and at times inspiring account of how some French people collaborated with dictatorship and occupation, how some complied and just went along, and how some resisted heroically."

> —**T. Hunt Tooley**, Professor of History, Austin College; whose books include *Ethnic Cleansing in Twentieth-Century Europe*, *Battleground and Home Front in the First World War*, and *National Identity and Weimar Germany*

"The theme of *Gun Control in Nazi-Occupied France* is new, and Stephen Halbrook conveys it with laudable precision. In the early 1980s, I spoke to French Resistance fighters who told me how difficult it was to hide weapons during the German occupation. But never before had I read anything about it. We owe Halbrook tremendous gratitude for illuminating a crucial issue that had not been addressed by either the Germans or the French."

—**Wieland Giebel**, Founder and Curator, Berlin Story Museum, Germany; author, *The History of Berlin*, *The Brown Berlin*, *Goebbels's Propaganda*, and *Hitler's Terror in Berlin*

"*Gun Control in Nazi-Occupied France* is an impressive addition to the already vast literature on the Second World War. The book is filled with useful information from primary sources, much of it previously unpublished. Halbrook vividly depicts the terrible years of the occupation of France by German armed forces, in particular from the viewpoint of French owners of firearms, mainly hunting weapons but also miscellaneous military arms retained by the families of soldiers in prior wars. One of Hitler's major objectives was to see France (and other conquered territories) completely firearms-free, and major efforts to this end were expended by the German armed forces and their French collaborators. Two aspects of Halbrook's story are of obvious relevance for contemporary debates about civilian possession of firearms. First, although the Germans collected truckloads of firearms from all over France, they didn't get all of them—or even, perhaps, most of them. Despite threatening the most draconian penalties (including the death penalty, which was carried out in thousands of instances), and despite unlimited powers to search any premises at any time without giving reasons, occupation authorities simply could not successfully disarm a population that was unwilling to cooperate with them. Second, many of the guns that remained in civilian hands found their way to the Resistance, which valued handguns in particular. It is not that people with side arms could credibly threaten to take on organized formations of the German army. But as Halbrook shows, guns played an indispensable moralizing role for the Resistance. Because its members were able to arm and protect themselves, the Resistance was able to survive and grow, and as it grew stronger it did play an increasingly important role in harrying occupation forces, providing vital intelligence to the Allied armies, and preparing the ground for Europe's eventual liberation."

—**Daniel D. Polsby**, Professor of Law, Antonin Scalia Law School, George Mason University

"'Get your guns out of the straw, your stens, your grenades…' These words of the popular 1943 Chant des Partisans, by Joseph Kessel, Maurice Druon and Anna Marly, only make sense if there are hidden guns, sten guns, and grenades to fight against the evil Nazis in the first place. As Stephen P. Halbrook's splendid new book, *Gun Control in Nazi-Occupied France*, makes perfectly clear, the not so-well-intended but comparatively harmless administrative registration of firearms by the French government before World War II made the goal of the Nazis to disarm the liberty-loving people of France much easier. The heroic fight of the resistance against the invader became harder. Until there are no more aggressions—and I fear we still have some distance in front of us until we arrive on that bright sunlit upland of human history—until there are no more wars, a lesson remains: When the battle cry of freedom is heard, people should be well-armed to respond."

—**Jürg F. Stüssi-Lauterburg**, former Director, Library Am Guisanplatz BiG; former President, Foundation Council of the Foundation for Democracy

"Talk of Nazi gun confiscation has long been a staple of American gun debates, but until recently the scholarly work had not been done. In this book, *Gun Control in Nazi-Occupied France*, Stephen Halbrook continues his extensively researched history of Nazi gun controls and gun confiscation, revealing in particular how prewar French gun registration laws made the Nazis' task easier, and how French disobedience to those laws preserved a reservoir of firearms that made the Resistance's task easier. Highly recommended!"

—**Glenn Harlan Reynolds**, Beauchamp Brogan Distinguished Professor of Law, University of Tennessee College of Law

"With *Gun Control in Nazi-Occupied France*, Stephen Halbrook cements his position as one of the leading scholars on the right to bear arms. Halbrook provides us with an important cautionary tale. A seemingly harmless firearms registration measure enacted by France's prewar democratic government would allow a later sinister regime, the forces of the Nazi occupation and its collaborators, to round up firearms and to imprison and execute those who resisted confiscation. Anyone who doubts that disarming a people makes it easier to oppress a people would do well to read Halbrook's well-researched study."

—**Robert J. Cottrol**, Professor of Law, History, and Sociology and Harold Paul Green Research Professor of Law, George Washington University; author, *The Long, Lingering Shadow: Slavery, Race, and Law in the American Hemisphere*

"Stephen Halbrook has done it again. Building on the case he made in *Gun Control and the Third Reich* that gun registration efforts in the Weimer Republic contributed to Hitler's rise to power in Germany, he demonstrates in his newest book, *Gun Control in Nazi-Occupied France: Tyranny and Resistance*, that similar policies in pre-war France facilitated Nazi-occupation of France. Gun registration laws put in place in 1935 by then Prime Minister Pierre Laval made easy pickings of those who failed to surrender their arms under Nazi occupation—a failure whose penalty was execution. But Halbrook also tells the other side of the story—that the many French people who refused to register their firearms in 1935, or who owned hunting guns not subject to the registration laws-were often key cogs in the resistance movement that contributed ultimately to France's restoration of freedom. 'Tis an important lesson that cannot be told too often: Tyrants seek to disarm the citizenry because a well-armed citizenry is the surest defense of freedom."

—**John C. Eastman**, Henry Salvatori Professor of Law and
Community Service, Chapman University; Founding
Director, Center for Constitutional Jurisprudence

"After the conquest of France in 1940, the Germans made intensive efforts to remove guns from French civilians. French civilians took great risks to keep their guns. Secret caches of firearms provided weapons for guerilla bands in the last months of the occupation. They also bolstered the confidence and spirit of a wider range of resisters. Stephen Holbrook's *Gun Control in Nazi-Occupied France* tells this story in vivid detail, drawing on official documents of that era and a range of post-war reminiscences."

—**Jeremy A. Rabkin**, Professor of Law, Antonin
Scalia Law School, George Mason University

"*Gun Control in Nazi-Occupied France* makes evident several inescapable conclusions: first, a disarmed populace is a priority for tyrants; second, disarming a populace is an achievable bureaucratic process done with relative ease over a short span of time; third, once disarmed the populace must choose either submission to tyranny or death; fourth, the natural right to self-preservation is inextricably tied to the natural right to keep and bear arms; and fifth, effective resistance to tyranny does not start at the knock at the door, but at the politicians' call for gun registration. There was a time when most Americans understood these unpleasant truisms. Stephen Halbrook's timely book is an urgent reminder."

—**Marshall L. DeRosa**, Professor of Political Science, Florida Atlantic University; author, *The Ninth Amendment and the Politics of Creative Jurisprudence* and *The Politics of Dissolution and the Rhetorical Quest for a National Identity*

"Stephen P. Halbrook's, *Gun Control in Nazi-Occupied France*, will be received with the same controversy as his previous work, *Gun Control in the Third Reich*. Gun control advocates will hate it and gun ownership supporters will love it. Irrespective of what side of the gun control debate you are on, you should read it. It is meticulously research, but that will not deter critics from saying that an example from occupied France is as irrelevant as that of the Third Reich. But is it? The venerated sociologist Max Weber instructed us to look at the 'extreme case' as a way of understanding social reality, and Halbrook does precisely that. In the aftermath of the Parkland school shooting, do you want to seize guns? Well, even on pain of facing a firing squad, gun owners in Nazi-occupied France largely held on to their weapons. Seizing weapons is not as accessible a social policy as one might assume. An armed populace in Nazi-occupied France formed the foundation for the resistance to the brutality of the occupation. While the resistance could not overthrow the Nazi regime, it undermined it and was able to join the allied invasion force in pushing the Nazis out of France. Critics of Halbrook's earlier work have stated that since Jews were less than 1% of the population of Germany when the Nazis took over, what good would their armed resistance have been? This critique ignores the triumph of the human spirit in its desire to resist oppression, to make the oppression burdensome and odious. In his *Gulag Archipelago*, Alexander Solzhenitsyn argued for resisting the heavily-armed state organs with clubs in the absence of guns because resistance is important. Some of those who seek to join the oppressors will be deterred by the prospect of their own deaths. At a time when the debate over gun control is front and center on the political stage, Halbrook's meticulously researched work on Nazi-occupied France is a welcome contribution to that debate, and one that cannot be easily dismissed."

—**Abraham H. Miller**, Emeritus Professor of Political Science,
University of Cincinnati; Distinguished Fellow, Haym Salomon Center

"The sophisticated analysis in *Gun Control in Nazi-Occupied France* shows how Nazi gun control enforcement was affected by military events, international law, civilian cooperation, and the special situation of the nominally independent Vichy government. Halbrook demonstrates how gun registration laws enacted by a democratic government may later be exploited by a tyranny—with registration leading to confiscation and then to mass murder."

—**David B. Kopel**, Adjunct Professor of Advanced Constitutional Law, Sturm
College of Law, University of Denver; author, *Guns: Who Should Have Them?*;
Research Director, Independence Institute

GUN CONTROL
IN NAZI-OCCUPIED FRANCE

Also by the Author

Gun Control in the Third Reich: Disarming the Jews and "Enemies of the State" (2013)
Translations:
> *Fatales Erbe—Hitlers Waffengesetze: Die legale Entwaffnung von Juden und "Staatsfeinden" im "Dritten Reich"* (2016)
> *Bas les armes! Le désarmement des Juifs et des "ennemis du ille Reich"* (2016)
> *Hitler e o desarmamento—Como o nazismo desarmou os judeus e os "inimigos do Reich"* (2017)

The Swiss and the Nazis: How the Alpine Republic Survived in the Shadow of the Third Reich (2006)
Translations:
> *Schweizer Widerstand gegen Nazi-Deutschland* (2010)
> *La Suisse face aux nazis* (2011)
> *Szwajcaria i naziści* (2015)

Target Switzerland: Swiss Armed Neutrality in World War II (1998)
Translations:
> *Die Schweiz im Visier* (1999)
> *La Suisse encerclée* (2000)
> *La Svizzera nel mirino* (2002)
> *Cel: Szwajcaria* (2003)

INDEPENDENT
I N S T I T U T E

INDEPENDENT INSTITUTE is a non-profit, non-partisan, public-policy research and educational organization that shapes ideas into profound and lasting impact. The mission of Independent is to boldly advance peaceful, prosperous, and free societies grounded in a commitment to human worth and dignity. Applying independent thinking to issues that matter, we create transformational ideas for today's most pressing social and economic challenges. The results of this work are published as books, our quarterly journal, *The Independent Review*, and other publications and form the basis for numerous conference and media programs. By connecting these ideas with organizations and networks, we seek to inspire action that can unleash an era of unparalleled human flourishing at home and around the globe.

100 Swan Way, Oakland, California 94621-1428, U.S.A.
Telephone: 510-632-1366 • Facsimile: 510-568-6040 • Email: info@independent.org • www.independent.org

GUN CONTROL
IN NAZI-OCCUPIED FRANCE
TYRANNY AND RESISTANCE

Stephen P. Halbrook

INDEPENDENT
INSTITUTE
OAKLAND, CALIFORNIA

Gun Control in Nazi-Occupied France: Tyranny and Resistance
Copyright © 2018 by Stephen P. Halbrook
ISBN: 978-1-59813-307-3

Independent Institute
100 Swan Way, Oakland, CA 94621-1428
Telephone: 510-632-1366
Fax: 510-568-6040
Email: info@independent.org
Website: www.independent.org

Cover design: Jeremy Anicete
Cover image: © Media Drum Limited

Library of Congress Cataloguing in Publication Data
Names: Halbrook, Stephen P., author.
Title: *Gun control in Nazi occupied-France : Tyranny and Resistance* / Stephen P. Halbrook.
Description: Oakland, California : Independent Institute, 2018. | Includes bibliographical references and index.
Identifiers: LCCN 2017055816 (print) | LCCN 2018013816 (ebook) | ISBN 9781598133097 (ePub) | ISBN 9781598133103 (ePDF) | ISBN 9781598133110 (Mobi) | ISBN 9781598133073 (hardback) | ISBN 9781598133080 (paperback)
Subjects: LCSH: Firearms--Law and legislation--France--History--20th century. | Gun control--France--History--20th century. | World War, 1939-1945--Law and legislation--France. | France--History--German occupation, 1940-1945. | World War, 1939-1945--Underground movements--France. | BISAC: HISTORY / Military / World War II. | HISTORY / Europe / France.
Classification: LCC KJV5257 (ebook) | LCC KJV5257 .H35 2018 (print) | DDC 940.53/44--dc23
LC record available at https://lccn.loc.gov/2017055816

Contents

Preface

A GERMAN POSTER requiring all people to surrender their firearms within twenty-four hours or face the death penalty is on prominent display at the *Musée de l'Ordre de la Libération* (Museum of the Order of the Liberation) in Paris. The museum has comprehensive information on people and groups inside and outside of France who contributed to the liberation.[1] In one of my visits there in the 1990s, I asked the curator about contact information for the associations of the veterans of the liberation. He provided me with the list.

I then sent questionnaires to each association inquiring about the extent to which the French people had arms before the occupation, the extent to which the population complied with the German decrees to surrender arms or face the death penalty, and the use of arms by the Resistance. The responses, received in the late 1990s and early 2000s, were from younger members of the Resistance who were then still alive and who could be considered as among France's "greatest generation." While not extensive, the responses are worth their weight in gold, and are interspersed in pertinent parts of this book.

But the bulk of this study is based on the records of the German occupation forces from the military archives in Freiburg, Germany (*Bundesarchiv-Militärarchiv Freiburg*). This work would not have been possible without the research assistance of Sebastian Remus, a leading archival expert on the German records of the occupation in France.[2]

---

1. See Musée de l'Ordre de la Libération, *Cinquantenaire de l'Ordre de la Libération* (Paris: Musée de l'Ordre de la Libération, 1990).

2. See Stefan Martens, ed., *Frankreich und Belgien unter deutscher Besatzung 1940–1944. Die Bestände des Bundesarchiv-Militärarchivs Freiburg*, compiled by Sebastian Remus (Stuttgart: Thorbecke, 2002).

Sources also include selected French archival records, which were located with the able assistance of Jean-Paul LeMoigne, who has written on the history of French firearms legislation.[3] Thanks go to Odile Bosch for reviewing countless French newspapers of the time; heavily censored by the Germans, this day-to-day timeline published the names of many French citizens executed for gun possession and the pleas of the Vichy authorities for obedience to the occupation authorities. Selected diaries, which were anything but censored by the Germans, bring to life the actual impositions upon and experiences of real people.

Countless works have been published on the German occupation of France in World War II. Not one focuses on the repression of gun owners. To be sure, many make incidental references to the execution of French citizens for various offenses, including the possession of firearms, and no history of the Resistance is complete without perennial discussion about the shortage of arms. But the alarming threat to the occupation by the mere existence of French civilians who had not surrendered their firearms was expressed in the following German military report: "Illegal weapons possession still represents the core of criminal activities of the French. It appears almost impossible to get rid of it."[4] The Germans demonstrated their frustration on this point by regularly reporting the execution of gun owners and periodically offering amnesty to surrender firearms.

Helping the Nazis get rid of such French transgressions as gun ownership fell to the Vichy government, promoted most vigorously by Pierre Laval. The most notorious collaborator with the Germans, Laval was an opportunist who is perceived as holding perhaps the most sinister place in French history. Forgotten is the fact that as prime minister in 1935, Laval had decreed the registration of firearms. After the French defeat in 1940, and the terms of the armistice specifying that the French police would administer occupied France under the direction of the Germans, how easy it must have been to ferret out registered gun owners who had not surrendered their firearms.

---

3. See Jean-Paul Le Moigne, *Le contrôle administratif de la détention des armes à feu par les particuliers* (Université Reims Champagne-Ardenne, Faculté de Droit et de Science Politique: Mémoire de DEA, 1999–2000).

4. BA/MA, RW 35/1264, Lagebericht des Militärverwaltungsbezirks B, Südwestfrankreich, für die Zeit vom 16. November 1941 bis 15. Januar 1942, 19. Januar 1942.

I am grateful to those who, while not responsible for any deficiencies in this book, helped to make it a better contribution to the literature. Professor Thomas J. Laub, author of the path-breaking study *After the Fall: German Policy in Occupied France, 1940–1944* (New York: Oxford University Press, 2010), critically reviewed the manuscript and made valuable suggestions that greatly improved the factual account and overall thesis of the work. Roy M. Carlisle of the Independent Institute read the manuscript and offered useful pointers for its organization. The encouragement of David J. Theroux, president of the Independent Institute, in moving this book forward is also greatly appreciated. However, I alone am responsible for the interpretations and any errors in this book.

I am greatly indebted to Therese Klee Hathaway for translations from the German occupation records. Odile Bosch is entitled to great appreciation for translations from French. I am further indebted to Lisa Halbrook Hollowell for organizing documents and general research. Jean Blomquist, aided by Cecilia Santini, provided tremendous copyediting in all relevant languages of the manuscript.

A short version of certain topics in this book was published as "Why Can't We Be Like France? How the Right to Bear Arms Got Left Out of the Declaration of Rights and How Gun Registration Was Decreed Just in Time for the Nazi Occupation," vol. 39, *Fordham Urban Law Journal*, no. 5, p. 1637 (October 2012). I am grateful for the comments and suggestions made by the editors.

Introduction

NAZI GERMANY LAUNCHED its blitzkrieg ("lightning war") against France, Belgium, and the Netherlands on May 10, 1940. In every town occupied, Wehrmacht soldiers immediately put up posters warning that civilians who failed to surrender their firearms within twenty-four hours would be shot. French law before the occupation banned "war" weapons and required that firearms be registered. The registration requirement had been decreed in 1935 by Prime Minister Pierre Laval. After its defeat in 1940, France signed the armistice agreeing to administer occupied France on behalf of the Wehrmacht, the German armed forces. The French police could then easily identify citizens who had registered their firearms. Laval returned to power as the chief collaborationist with the Nazis.

Requiring registration of firearms and banning certain firearms was a familiar panacea for crime and violence in Europe and the United States in the 1930s. Street violence between Communist and Nazi thugs prompted a registration decree in 1931 by Germany's Weimar Republic. But the interior minister warned that the registration records must not fall into the hands of extremist elements. That happened in 1933, when Hitler seized power and these very records were used to disarm and repress the Social Democrats and all other "enemies of the state," which later included the entire Jewish population.[1]

In the United States, efforts to repress gun ownership were brewing from long-term efforts to disarm African Americans combined with reaction to organized crime created by Prohibition and Depression-era gangsterism. The

---

1. See generally Stephen P. Halbrook, *Gun Control in the Third Reich: Disarming the Jews and "Enemies of the State"* (Oakland, CA: Independent Institute, 2013).

National Firearms Act of 1934 as originally proposed would have required registration and prohibitive taxation of pistols and revolvers, but—due in part to opposition by the National Rifle Association—was amended only to include machine guns and short-barreled shotguns.[2]

Firearm prohibitions in the United States have always been moderated by the Second Amendment to the U.S. Constitution, which provides that "[a] well regulated militia, being necessary to the security of a free state, the right of the people to keep and bear arms, shall not be infringed." James Madison, draftsman of the Constitution and Bill of Rights, acclaimed "the advantage of being armed, which the Americans possess over the people of almost every other nation," adding that "[n]otwithstanding the military establishments in the several kingdoms of Europe . . . the governments are afraid to trust the people with arms."[3] That certainly applied to the France of Louis XVI and his predecessors, and it applies to the European Union today.

In the months preceding the French Revolution, countless statements of grievances (*cahiers de doléances*) were brought by the Third Estate urging that ordinary French citizens be allowed to keep guns for protection from criminals and from animal predators that destroyed crops.[4] When the Revolution began, one of the first acts of the National Assembly in abolishing feudalism was to declare the right of commoners to hunt.[5]

A draft provision of the Declaration of Rights of 1789—written by le comte de Mirabeau of the Committee of Five (*Comité des cinq*)—would have provided that "every citizen has the right to keep arms at home and to use them, either for

---

2. See Stephen P. Halbrook, "Congress Interprets the Second Amendment: Declarations by a Co-Equal Branch on the Individual Right to Keep and Bear Arms," 62 *Tennessee Law Review* 597 (Spring 1995).

3. James Madison, *The Federalist* No. 46, quoted in Stephen P. Halbrook, *The Founders' Second Amendment: Origins of the Right to Bear Arms* (Chicago: Ivan R. Dee, 2008), 182.

4. Stephen P. Halbrook, "Why Can't We Be Like France? How the Right to Bear Arms Got Left Out of the Declaration of Rights and How Gun Registration Was Decreed Just in Time for the Nazi Occupation," 34 *Fordham Urban Law Journal*, no. 5 (October 2012): 1637, 1652–55. This cites extensively from *Archives Parlementaires de 1787 à 1860: Recueil Complet des Débats Législatifs & Politiques des Chambres Françaises*, Première série (1787 à 1799) (Paris: Librairie Administrative de Paul DuPont, 1867–1879).

5. J. M. Roberts, ed., *French Revolution Documents* (Oxford, England: Basil Blackwell, 1966), 1:152.

the common defense or for his own defense, against any unlawful attack which may endanger the life, limb, or freedom of one or more citizens."[6] Mirabeau explained:

> My colleagues all agree that the right declared in this article is self-evident in its nature, and one of principal guarantees of political and civil freedom; that no other institution can replace it; that it is impossible to imagine an aristocracy more terrible than one which would be established in a state where only a part of the citizens would be armed, and the others would not be; that all contrary arguments are futile sophisms contradicted by the facts, since no country is more peaceful and offers a better policy, than those where the nation is armed.[7]

This provision was not included in the Declaration as adopted, which did however recognize the right of "resistance to oppression."[8] That left France without an explicit constitutional guarantee of the right to keep and bear arms, and created an ambiguity in whether the right to resist oppression included the means to do so by an armed citizenry.

The French Revolution failed to shatter the centralized, authoritarian character of the French state. Perhaps reflecting the distrust of the masses by the new ruling elites, various firearm restrictions of the ancien régime remained in place. Supporters of an American-style republic did not prevail. While Louis XIV was long gone, Napoleon could as well have said, *"L'État, c'est moi,"* as could Pierre Laval almost a century and a half later, albeit in a wholly different context.

While French regimes historically imposed various restrictions on gun ownership, in 1935 Prime Minister Laval issued an unprecedented decree imposing firearm registration. The timing could not have been worse. The German occupation that began in 1940 decreed the death penalty for gun

---

6. *"Tout citoyen a le droit d'avoir chez lui des armes, et de s'en servir, soit pour la défense commune, soit pour sa propre défense, contre toute agression illégale qui mettrait en péril la vie, les membres, ou la liberté d'un ou plusieurs citoyens."* Assemblée nationale, séance du mardi 18 août, Gazette nationale ou le Moniteur universel, n° 42, 18 août 1789, p. 351.

7. *Assemblée nationale, séance du mardi 18 août,* Gazette nationale ou le Moniteur universel, n° 42, 18 août 1789, 351. Available at http://ex.libris.free.fr/mirab170789.html.

8. French Declaration of the Rights of Man and of the Citizen, Art. 2 (1789).

ownership, and the French police—the repository of the registration records—enforced German policy. Laval became the collaborator-in-chief.

Reacting to such occupation policies throughout Europe, shortly before the sneak Japanese attack on Pearl Harbor, the U.S. Congress enacted a law to prohibit "the registration of any firearms possessed by any individual for his personal protection or sport" or "to impair or infringe in any manner the right of any individual to keep and bear arms."[9] A sponsor of the bill explained: "Before the advent of Hitler or Stalin, who took power from the German and Russian people, measures were thrust upon the free legislatures of those countries to deprive the people of the possession and use of firearms, so that they could not resist the encroachments of such diabolical and vitriolic state police organizations as the Gestapo, the Ogpu, and the Cheka."[10] While Hitler came to power legally, he quickly established his dictatorship by various repressive measures, including the disarming of perceived enemies of the state and the arming of his goon squads.

Supporters of firearm registration in the United States were drowned out by the realities of war, not the least of which was the imperative to train the population in marksmanship. The National Rifle Association (NRA) instructed numerous civilians who would go on to use their shooting skills in the Armed Forces to fight the Axis. Not surprisingly, the NRA continued to oppose proposals to restrict firearms, and it needed only to state the obvious to explain why. As the NRA's magazine stated in early 1942:

> From Berlin on January 6th the German official radio broadcast— "The German military commander for Belgium and Northern France announced yesterday that the population would be given a last opportunity to surrender firearms without penalty up to January 20th and after that date anyone found in possession of arms would be executed."
>
> So the Nazi invaders set a deadline similar to that announced months ago in Czecho-Slovakia, in Poland, in Norway, in Romania, in Yugo-Slavia, in Greece.

---

9. Property Requisition Act, Pub. L. 274, 55 U.S. Statutes 742 (1941). See Halbrook, "Congress Interprets the Second Amendment," 618–31.

10. 87 Cong. Rec., 77th Cong., 1st Sess., 6778 (Aug. 5, 1941) (statement of Rep. Edwin Arthur Hall).

How often have we read the familiar dispatches: "Gestapo agents accompanied by Nazi troopers swooped down on shops and homes and confiscated all privately-owned firearms!"

What an aid and comfort to the invaders and to their Fifth Column cohorts have been the convenient registration lists of privately owned firearms—lists readily available for the copying or stealing at the Town Hall in most European cities.

What a constant worry and danger to the Hun and his Quislings have been the privately owned firearms in the homes of those few citizens who have "neglected" to register their guns![11]

Were the above allegations just exaggerations of the "gun lobby"? As will be seen, the same facts were being reported in newspapers such as the *New York Times.* Douglas MacArthur II, nephew of the general, who served in the U.S. embassy in Paris and Vichy in those days, recalled that "[t]he Germans confiscated everything, including shotguns. The Germans let it be known that it was . . . [a] death sentence if you were caught with a weapon in your home, in your place, or anything."[12]

The issue of German occupation policy in World War II arose in the U.S. Congress in 1968 in the context of bills to require the registration of firearms. Opponents raised the specter of the then-more-recent Nazi experience, while proponents denied that the Nazis made any use of records to disarm enemies.[13] A Library of Congress study summarized prewar laws in France and elsewhere, and concluded that it was "unable to locate references to any German use of registration lists to collect firearms."[14] The researchers apparently did not look very far, but at any rate the bills were defeated.

---

11. "The Nazi Deadline," *American Rifleman,* February 1942, 7.

12. "An American Diplomat in Vichy France" (1986), adst.org/2013/07/an-american-diplomat-in-vichy-france/.

13. Rep. John Dingell (D-MI) argued that "sportsmen fear firearms registration. We have here the same situation we saw in small degree in Nazi Germany." *Federal Firearms Legislation: Hearings Before the Subcommittee to Investigate Juvenile Delinquency,* Senate Committee on the Judiciary, 90th Cong., 2nd Sess., 478 (1968). Senator Joseph Tydings (D-MD) disputed "that registration or licensing of guns has some connection with the Nazi takeover in Germany" (478–79).

14. *Federal Firearms Legislation,* Senate Committee (1968), 482–83. See also 487–89.

Fast-forwarding to today, in the United States background checks are required on people who buy firearms from licensed dealers, but once the transaction is approved, the government may not keep records on the identities of the buyers, and gun registration by the federal government is prohibited.[15] A study by the National Institute of Justice stated that with "[u]niversal background checks . . . [e]ffectiveness depends on . . . requiring gun registration. . . ."[16]

By contrast, member states of the European Union (EU) are required to maintain central, electronic registration records of all lawful gun owners. Ironically, Germany was the first state to comply, which was in 2013—the eightieth anniversary of Hitler coming to power.[17]

The advent of terrorist attacks by radical Islamic extremists have kept the issues involving gun ownership and prohibitions in a burning debate. The Paris murders of the satirists of *Charlie Hebdo* magazine and shoppers at a kosher supermarket in early 2015 prompted Rabbi Menachem Margolin, head of the Rabbinical Centre of Europe (RCE) and the European Jewish Association, to plead with the EU states to allow Jews to have guns to protect their institutions.[18] His call went unheeded.

Then Paris again, then San Bernardino, then Brussels, then Orlando, then . . . who knows where else terrorists will attack in Europe and the United States, as they do every day in the Middle East? Prevent terrorist attacks by disarming the citizenry at large or by allowing citizens to arm themselves while fighting back and eradicating the terrorists abroad? The debate will never end.

Other than to acknowledge the perennial nature of the issue of arms and the citizen, historic and current, this book says no more about that broader context. Instead, this work sticks to historical facts concerning French gun control laws in the 1930s, the Wehrmacht conquest in 1940, the armistice

---

15. 18 United States Code §§ 922(t)(2), 926(a).

16. Greg Ridgeway, *Summary of Select Firearm Violence Prevention Strategies* (Washington, D.C.: National Institute of Justice, 2013), http://www.firearmsandliberty.com/PDF-News/nij-gun-policy-memo.pdf (accessed October 25, 2017).

17. "German Weapon Registry to Take Effect in 2013," *Deutsche Welle*, December 18, 2012, www.dw.de/german-weapon-registry-to-take-effect-in-2013/a-16461910 (accessed October 25, 2017).

18. "Prominent Rabbi Calls on Europe to Allow Jews to Carry Guns," www.israelnationalnews.com/News/News.aspx/189932#.VLas7Xtlbm6 (accessed October 25, 2017).

provisions requiring the French police and state to enforce German military dictates, the enforcement of German policies to execute French citizens for possession of firearms, the stubbornness of many French in refusing to surrender their firearms, the threat perceived by the occupiers if even a segment of the population possessed arms, and the tragic impediment of the shortage of arms to the ability of the French Resistance to fight back.

To be sure, "resistance" is a word with many meanings. There was passive, unarmed resistance, from anti-German graffiti to strikes. In the words of Jacques Sémelin, author of *Unarmed Against Hitler*: "Most of those who resorted to unarmed resistance did so for lack of better options, that is, because they had no weapons which remained the principal and ultimate means of those who were trying to oppose the German order."[19] Those who carried guns mostly did so defensively to be able to escape if pursued after an act of sabotage or if identified as a member of an illegal group wanted by the Gestapo (*Geheim Staatspolizei*, secret state police). Only after D-Day did armed confrontation by guerilla organizations become viable, and even then the results could be disastrous.

A Perfect Storm

This book is about a perfect storm of the most extreme form of gun control, in which the risk of facing a firing squad failed to motivate compliance by many French citizens. The failure to comply with the decrees to surrender all arms, made possible by the prewar refusal of many French to register their firearms, was a form of armed resistance that could be passive but had the potential to become active, and did so in many cases. As such, it was a constant source of uncertainty to the occupiers, causing them to devote resources to additional security measures and thereby away from more efficiently pursuing other measures of repression, such as rounding up Jews or conscripting French citizens for forced labor.

There is no reliable data on the number of firearms in France before the Nazi invasion. Handguns and certain rifles were required to be registered

---

19. Jacques Sémelin, *Unarmed Against Hitler: Civilian Resistance in Europe, 1939–1943*, trans. Suzan Husserl-Kapit (Westport, CT: Praeger, 1993), 2.

(those of possible military use were banned), but hunting guns were not. Registered firearms were more likely to be surrendered when the Germans issued decrees to do so, as the owners would have been known due to the registration records.

There were three million hunting guns in France in 1939, according to the Saint Hubert Club de France, a hunting association. During the Nazi occupation of 1940–44, some 715,000 were surrendered by their owners in the occupied zone. In the zone that was not occupied until 1942, 120,000 hunting guns were turned in to French authorities. The hunting guns not surrendered were, if not lost or stolen, hidden by their owners and in some cases used by the Resistance.[20]

That means that only 835,000 of three million hunting guns—less than one-third—were turned in by the French threatened with the death penalty for not doing so. While not every French citizen caught with a gun was shot, the very real threat of the firing squad was not enough to induce every gun owner to comply, leading the Germans repeatedly to declare amnesties. Yet many remained incorrigible and let the deadlines pass. That is an incredible testament to the inefficacy of gun control in the most extreme circumstances.

While the brutality of Nazi occupation varied in different countries, with the most vicious in the East, the general policy that all subjects must be disarmed was the same in all. Whether France's nightmare in this regard in World War II has any lessons for today is for the reader to decide. To be sure, there is no denying that disarming a populace may be a form of repression that will be resisted even under the threat of the death penalty, and that the threat of imprisonment in less troubled times may be an even less effective panacea to rid society of what may be perceived as a retrogressive gun culture. In this context, history may speak louder than rhetoric. If nothing else, it is fitting to remember and pay tribute to the French gun owners who resisted, as well as those who were executed for defying orders to surrender their revolvers and hunting guns, and who thereby contributed in one way or another to the Resistance.

---

20. *Le Saint-Hubert*, n°1, janvier–février 1945, 1.

I

Crisis in the Third Republic

FRANCE IN THE mid-1930s experienced conflict between political factions and the collapse of governments. The most volatile disturbances rocked Paris on February 6, 1934, in which police and the Mobile Guard (*garde mobile*)—helmeted horsemen wielding pistols and sabers—opened fire on civilians, killing eighteen, while one policeman was killed.[1] Among other repressive measures, clamping down on civilian gun ownership appeared to politicians to be a remedy.

This was the era of the Third Republic, born at the defeat of France in the Franco-German War in 1871, and now nearing its death throes, finalized by its subsequent defeat by Nazi Germany in 1940. The 1932 elections brought the *Cartel des Gauches* (Leftist Coalition) government to power. The Great Depression struck France hard in 1933, and the resulting lower wages and unemployment sparked violent strikes and political unrest. The French Communist Party (*Parti Communiste Français*, or PCF) welcomed the opportunity for insurrection.

A scheme involving false bonds in large amounts by a swindler named Alexandre Stavisky, who had connections in high places and who died mysteriously after the scandal broke, led to allegations of corruption and the replacement of the prime minister by Édouard Daladier, the leader of the Radical-Socialists, on January 27, 1934. *Action français* and other rightist groups prepared to take to the streets.

---

1. William L. Shirer, *The Collapse of the Third Republic: An Inquiry into the Fall of France in 1940* (New York: Simon & Schuster, 1969), 214–19. See also Robert Soucy, *French Fascism: The Second Wave, 1933–1939* (New Haven, CT: Yale University Press, 1995), 30–33.

The pot boiled over just days later, after Daladier dismissed the right-leaning Police Prefect Jean Chiappe from office. On February 6, some 4,500 members of the *Croix de Feu* (Cross of Fire) marched in front of the Ministry of the Interior, proceeding from the Madeleine to the Arc de Triomphe, when the Mobile Guard assaulted them at the Place Beauvau.[2] Self-described as a patriotic veterans' organization, *Croix de Feu* included anti-Communists, far-rightists, and French-style fascists.[3]

Demonstrators rushed onto the bridge of the Concorde to storm the passage that led to the Chamber of Deputies. Soldiers shot machine guns over their heads into the air, but one bullet found its mark in the head of a woman.[4] One account described riots by Communists leaving twelve dead and hundreds wounded,[5] while the police prefecture said ten demonstrators were killed and up to 700 were injured.[6] It was later estimated that 1,664 were injured, mostly by use of stones, broken glass, sticks, and hand weapons.[7]

The *Croix de Feu* did not carry arms. Private possession of firearms was highly regulated, and military arms were banned to civilians, but the group hoped to obtain them from like-minded military commanders if needed to meet a Communist threat.[8]

The Daladier government was accused of provoking a civil war by shooting demonstrators, while Minister of Justice Eugène Penancier announced an investigation into the plot against national security, incitation to murder, assault and battery, and arson. The *Croix de Feu* placed posters all over Paris asserting that "[a] government controlled by the red flag attempts to enslave you. . . . Sectarian dictatorship is trying to establish itself here."[9]

2. "Le 'Croix de Feu' ont manifesté hier devant le ministère de l'intérieur," *L'Echo de Paris*, February 6, 1934, 1.

3. See Soucy, *French Fascism*, Chapter 4 and p. 136.

4. "Hier en fin d'après-midi et dans la soirée de graves bagarres se sont produites à l'Hôtel-de-Ville, rue Royale et à la Concorde," *L'Homme Libre*, February 7, 1934, 1.

5. "Une soirée d'émeute a Paris," *Le Figaro*, February 7, 1934, 1.

6. "Le bilan des émeutes de mardi," *L'Homme Libre*, February 8, 1934, 1.

7. Henri Barbier, *Le Délit de Port D'Armes Prohibées* (Paris: Éditions Littéraires de France, 1939), 30.

8. Soucy, *French Fascism*, 109, 167.

9. "Les Croix de Feu parviennent aux grilles du Palais-Bourbon," *L'Echo de Paris*, February 7, 1934, 3. See also "Une proclamation de M. Edouard Daladier," *L'Homme Libre*, February 7, 1934, 1.

The next day, February 7, a delegation of veterans petitioned the president of the Republic, complaining that they marched unarmed and peacefully, but were attacked without provocation with sabers and revolvers by the Mobile Guard on the order of the minister of the interior and of the police chief. They demanded a new government.[10] Daladier resigned at 1:00 p.m. that same day. Communists demonstrated that day and the next, provoking riots that resulted in injuries to both police and demonstrators.[11] A run on every gun shop in Paris sold out firearm inventories.[12]

Pierre Laval acted as head of a group made up of members of parliament and Parisian municipal councilors in a visit to President Albert Lebrun urging the appointment of ex-president Gaston Doumergue. Doumergue formed the National Union government of rightists and Radical-Socialists. (The Radical-Socialists were moderate leftists, but the far left saw them as a bourgeois party that was neither radical nor socialist.) Laval was appointed minister of colonies, and Philippe Pétain was appointed minister of war.[13] Pétain and Laval would later head Vichy France, the puppet government of Nazi Germany.

Pétain, known as the Lion of Verdun for halting the German advance there in 1916, was a national hero. After the Great War, his urgent proposals to enhance military service and to build strong air and tank forces came to naught. He would try again as minister of war, but the Great Depression, now in full swing, frustrated his plans. By contrast, Laval was a professional politician who had been a socialist during the war and was now what might be described as an independent opportunist. His drift from left to right as a populist would be politically expedient as he served in various legislative and ministerial roles.

10. "Une adresse des anciens combattants au chef de l'Etat," *L'Homme Libre*, February 8, 1934, 1; "Les émeutes d'hier," *L'Homme Libre*, February 8, 1934, 3.

11. "Les émeutes ont repris hier, mais cette fois uniquement provoquees par les communistes," *L'Echo de Paris*, February 8, 1934, 1; "Les communistes ont manifesté sur plusieurs points de Paris," *L'Homme Libre*, February 9, 1934, 3.

12. Shirer, *Collapse of the Third Republic*, 221.

13. Geoffrey Warner, *Pierre Laval and the Eclipse of France* (New York: Macmillan, 1968), 56–57.

Prohibiting the Carrying and Sale of Arms

On February 7, invoking an 1834 law, the government decreed a ban on the carrying of pistols and revolvers of all models, calibers, and sizes, together with edged and blunt weapons.[14] On February 8, the new Police Prefect Adrien Bonnefoy-Sibour issued this proclamation: "The sale of arms and ammunition is prohibited in Paris and in the Seine department."[15] The proclamation began by reciting as authority a litany of firearm restrictions dating from 1790 through 1885, including decrees as far back as the French Revolution and the Napoleonic era.[16] Asserting a need to prevent private individuals from obtaining arms, it proclaimed:

> Article One. — The sale of arms and ammunition of any kind shall be prohibited from this day on, and until further notice, in Paris and in the Seine department.

> Article Two. — The gunsmiths shall be closed, and the arms and ammunition shall be kept in a locked place, and shall not be accessible to the public.

> Article Three. — Arms and ammunition shall be removed from the existing gunsmith department in department stores, bazaars and cutlery shops, etc.

> Article Four. — The Superintendent of the City Police, the colonel head of the Republican Guard, the colonel head of the Gendarmerie of the Seine, and the officers placed under their command are in charge of carrying out this order.

---

14. Barbier, *Le délit*, 30.
15. "Après les manifestations," *L'Homme Libre*, February 9, 1934, 1.
16. It recited the following:
    1. The laws of 16–21 August 1790 and 19–22 July 1791;
    2. The consuls' [the three heads of the executive branch under the Consulat Regime (1799–1804), the first was Bonaparte] orders of 12 messidor (10th month of the Revolutionary Calendar = July), in the year VII, and 3 brumaire (2nd month of the Revolutionary Calendar = November), in the year IX, and the law of June 10, 1873;
    3. The law of August 14, 1885, article G.

On February 9, the Communists demonstrated again, clashing with the police. Allegedly armed provocations prompted armed reaction by the police, and blood flowed again in the streets of Paris.[17] Citizens wishing to obtain arms to protect themselves still could not do so ten days later, when pleas were made to allow the reopening of the gunsmith shops.[18]

Former President Daladier denied any government order to shoot during the February 6 disorders, and the Chamber of Deputies named a commission of inquiry to find those responsible.[19] The *Croix de Feu* and others wrote to Council President Doumergue that they had peacefully demonstrated and did not carry weapons, as the police prefect admitted. They considered themselves patriotic workers who were not to be confused with looters, robbers, and enemies of the nation.[20]

Seizing Arms from Alleged "Communists"

A bill to ban associations whose leaders advised their members to violate the law by carrying arms or committing other crimes was introduced in mid-March. Existing penalties for manufacture or sale of illegal arms under an 1834 law were revised to impose incarceration of ten months to two years and a fine of 500 to 5,000 francs if the arms were carried in a group or at a public meeting.[21]

On March 28, Paris newspapers blared with sensational reports of arms seizures. *L'Echo de Paris* carried this headline: "Searches Lead to Weapons Caches in Paris and Suburbs: Arms Owner, Husband of a Communist Teacher Is Arrested."[22] Rumors had spread about arms caches for extremist groups, and the commission of inquiry of the February 6 events invited the government to take the necessary police measures. Police Prefect Roger Langeron instructed

---

17. "Empêchés de manifester place de la République, les communistes out livre aux policiers de sanglantes batailles de rues," *L'Echo de Paris*, February 10, 1934, 1.

18. "La réouverture des armureries," *L'Homme Libre*, February 20, 1934, 2.

19. "A la Chambre une commission d'enquete pour les événements du 6 février," *L'Echo de Paris*, February 20, 1934, 1.

20. "Une lettre des 'Croix de Feu' à M. Doumergue," *L'Echo de Paris*, February 23, 1934, 5.

21. "Informations politiques contre les groupements armés," *Le Figaro*, March 14, 1934, 5.

22. "Des perquisitions font découvrir des depots d'armes a Paris & en Banlieue," *L'Echo de Paris*, March 28, 1934, 1.

the *Renseignements Généraux Department* (the RG, or Police Political Security Branch) to conduct searches for arms.

State Prosecutor Gornien brought an indictment under the 1834 law, which made it unlawful to manufacture, sell, or even possess a "war weapon" or ammunition therefor. A communiqué from the justice minister announced an investigation about arms caches and possession of war weapons. Four judges led searches beginning at 7:00 a.m. on March 28. Further, the justice and interior ministers submitted a regulatory decree to the Council further restricting arms sales.

One search warrant was executed by Judge Roussel, along with Police Superintendent Pradier, at the home of a Mr. Léopold Dancart, an apartment at 25, rue Godillot in St-Ouen. The dining room was an immense aviary where hens, finches, and other birds were feeding and flying from one piece of furniture to another. The search revealed about fifty military rifles, shotguns and Lebel carbines, Mauser rifles, German parabellum pistols, Brownings and other automatic arms and cartridges hidden under the bed and in the armoires.

Mr. Dancart declared himself to be a nonpolitical collector with no intent to harm anyone. He added that he did not even vote and had never been to an electoral meeting. As he spoke, his wife walked in, criticizing her husband for his hobby, which put her job at risk. She was a schoolteacher supposedly affiliated with the French Communist Party.

Dancart, who was born in 1879, had previously been convicted for an illegal arms cache. On this occasion, he was interrogated by Police Superintendent Pradier, who arrested him under a warrant issued by Judge Saussier. In searches elsewhere, police confiscated clubs, sword canes, bayonets, and cartridges. Some war weapons were confiscated at the homes of people who otherwise were licensed to sell arms.[23]

L'Homme Libre published an editorial lauding the searches for caches of arms in private homes, which had increased since February 6.[24] The regime was based on freedom and majority rule, the editorial argued, and should avoid dictatorship based on force, as had occurred in neighboring states. Re-

---

23. "Les saisies d'armes," *L'Echo de Paris*, March 28, 1934, 3.
24. "L'autre désarmement," *L'Homme Libre*, March 28, 1934, 1.

grettably, gunsmiths allegedly made a gold mine in sales the day after February 6. Ignoring that law-abiding people may have been arming for defense, the editorial continued that extremists, whether from left or right, would be able to prepare for civil war. It praised the judicial proceedings and the introduction of a decree to the Council of State severely limiting the sale and possession of arms.

Le Figaro published the same communique by the justice department prefaced with this commentary: "Finally the government takes care of the war weapon caches set up by Communist organizations!"[25] It provided more details on the raid at the home of Léopold Dancart, described as a former mechanic and race-car driver who now was a flea market vendor. "Mr. Dancart has a small hobby, which is collecting weapons, can you imagine! For this reason, the police searched his home yesterday, and confiscated 48 rifles and shotguns, 86 revolvers and pistols, a few clubs and daggers, and about a thousand cartridges."

The article alleged that Dancart had provided war weapons to Colonel Francesc Macià when he was preparing his Catalan plot,[26] for which Dancart had been imprisoned for four and a half months. He now "acts as an innocent angel," stating that "collecting guns is no more reprehensible than merely collecting stamps, and moreover he was not hiding anything since we can see from the street the arms hung up on nails in his bedroom."

Describing Dancart as "a bird catcher," the article continued: "When one knocks on his door, a concert of chirping sounds answers, and from the street, one can see cages more than display of guns."[27] Turning to his wife, it added that "Mrs. Dancart is an elementary school teacher precisely at the school on Rue du Château . . . where subversive theories seem to have been favored at times." Under the subtitle "Bolshevik agent?" it asked, "Could the bird

25. "Plusieurs dépôts d'armes de guerre découverts à Paris et en banlieue," *Le Figaro*, March 28, 1934, 1.

26. The leftist-Republican Catalanist Francesc Macià had proclaimed an independent Catalan state from Spain in 1931, but compromised with a provisional regional government. "Francesc Macià," http://www.catalangovernment.eu/pres_gov/government/en/president/presidents/macia.html.

27. "Plusieurs dépôts d'armes de guerre découverts à Paris et en banlieue," *Le Figaro*, March 28, 1934, 5.

catcher–flee market vendor be one of those agents named by the Communists to carry out their plan of secret armament, which has been indubitable over the past few days?" Hopefully, the police search at his house, resulting in his arrest under Article 3 of the 1834 law forbidding arms caches, would only be the beginning of operations against others preparing for revolution.

After the above operation, investigating Judge Roussel and Police Superintendent Pradier proceeded to Number 47 of the rue Ordener, the shop of another flea market vendor named Gruyer. His wife opened the door, explaining that he was at a scrap metal fair. Police confiscated twenty-seven revolvers, some automatic pistols, eight military rifles of different calibers, and two large bags filled with cartridges. The load was transported to the *Renseignements Généraux Department* (the RG, or police political security branch).

Other searches were carried out by investigating Judges Saussier, Cuenne, and Verdier, assisted by Police Superintendents Oudard, Noetz, and Gianvilti from the RG Department. At Mr. Burgeroux's home at 52 rue du Vert-Bois—Burgeroux was also a flea market vendor—investigators confiscated a German military rifle and some cartridges. They went to several other businesses but found no violations.

Keeping Track of Gun Buyers

Details on the proposed new law punishing the carrying and sale of prohibited arms were reported by *L'Echo de Paris*.[28] At the general assembly on March 28 presided over by Théodore Tissier, the Council of State passed a decree bill proposed by the minister of justice and the minister of interior revising the law of May 24, 1834, Article I of which punished the manufacture, sale, or transfer of prohibited arms with imprisonment of one month to one year and a fine of 16 to 200 francs. The law would be amended as follows:

> Article 1 of the decree reported by Mr. Peyromaure-Debord, in charge
> of petitions, lists all arms for which the above Article 1 sanctions shall
> be applied: any models of pistols or revolvers, daggers, dirks [*couteaux-*

---

28. "Une nouvelle réglementation du port et de la vente des armes," *L'Echo de Paris*, March 29, 1934, 3.

poignards], clubs, sword canes, leaded and steeled canes (at one tip only), as well as any object liable to constitute an arm dangerous to public safety.

In addition, in Article 2, the decree-law enacts that anyone involved in the commerce of arms prohibited to be carried and the ammunition thereof, must have a special register, each page of which shall be numbered and signed by the Prefect or his delegate, and without blanks or alterations. For each arm sold, it must include its features, as well as the full name and home address of the buyer, with an indication of the picture identification document provided by the said buyer to demonstrate his identity.

A further proposed law considered by the Chamber of Deputies on May 17, 1934, provided that the sale, transfer, or trade of weapons of unregulated models or designs would require the presentation by the purchaser of a written, approved authorization prepared after an investigation by the prefect or the subprefect.[29] The bill did not pass, but the subject would be addressed again the following year.

Pierre Etienne Flandin was named prime minister on November 8. He proposed a bill to restrict private possession of firearms, which did not pass.[30] His presidency ended on June 1, 1935, after which Pierre Laval took over.

After serving in the Parliament, Laval would head the French government three times during the 1930s, and would assume a primary leadership role during the Vichy regime in the 1940s. In all four of these periods, he would serve as prime minister, minister of foreign affairs, and at times other positions. His policies were French-style socialism and fascism.

---

29. Doc. Parl., Chambre, 1934, p. 571, in Barbier, *Le délit*, 116.

30. Projet de loi du 20 décembre 1934 concernant l'importation, la fabrication, le commerce, la vente et la détention des armes, présenté au nom de M. Albert Lebrun, Président de la République française, par M. Pierre-Étienne Flandin, président du Conseil. Chambre des députés, 2e séance du 20 novembre 1934, J. O., Documents parlementaires, annexe n° 4143, pp. 128-129. J. O., 24 octobre 1935. Cited in Jean-Paul Le Moigne and Stéphane Nerrant, "Commentaire critique et comparé de la Proposition de loi n°2773 du 30 juillet 2010," *Gazette des Armes*, 14 août 2010, http://www.armes-ufa.com/spip.php?article678.

A Conscripted Army or a People in Arms?

As France experienced internecine conflict, Hitler was preparing for war. On March 15, 1935, the Führer announced the creation of the Luftwaffe and the introduction of conscription of young men into the armed forces. That same day, the Chamber of Deputies debated whether to require young Frenchmen to serve for two years in the military. The Socialists and Communists voted against it.[31]

However, Socialist leader Léon Blum noted, "Jaurès declared here, twenty-two years ago, that the true military protection of a country lies not in permanent strong forces, or in numerous troops in barracks, serving as the basis of defensive strategy. Rather that it is to be found in what Revolutionaries have called the levying of the masses, in what our old master Vaillant called the general arming of the people. . . ."[32]

Blum was referring to Jean Léon Jaurès, who in 1910 had proposed a bill in the Chamber requiring all able-bodied citizens from age twenty to forty-five to provide military service.[33] Besides promoting widespread rifle practice, the plan proposed that "[i]n the departments of the Eastern region, each soldier will keep his arms at home."[34] As he explained elsewhere, this was a scaled-down version of the democratic Swiss militia army in which all citizens served and kept their arms at home. Responding to those who may have feared a revolution of the proletariat, Jaurès stated, "I do not believe that the universal arming of the citizens, everyone keeping at home their sabers and their rifles, has the social consequence that one imagines."[35] The Swiss experienced no upheaval from having citizen soldiers keep their arms at home.[36]

---

31. Paul Reynaud, *In the Thick of the Fight, 1930–1945* (New York: Simon & Schuster, 1955), 43.

32. Reynaud, *Thick of the Fight*, 105.

33. Jean Jaurès, *L'Armée Nouvelle* (Paris: l'Humanité, 1915), 549.

34. Jaurès, *L'Armée Nouvelle*, 552. "Dans les départements de la région de l'Est, chaque soldat aura ses armes à domicile."

35. Jaurès, *L'Armée Nouvelle*, 223. "A vrai dire, je ne crois pas que l'armement universel des citoyens, ayant chacun à domicile leur sabre et leur fusil, ait la conséquence sociale qu'on imagine."

36. Jaurès, *L'Armée Nouvelle*, 224–25.

Indeed, the editors of an English edition of Jaurès's book would write during the Great War that "[t]he rapidity and ease with which Switzerland mobilized all her active forces in August, 1914 was noted by all critics; and it has more than once been suggested that this accounts for Germany's decision to attack through Belgium rather than through Switzerland."[37] But fear of social revolution made it inconceivable that the ruling parties in France, both before and after World War I, would trust the people at large with arms.

To be sure, the French Communist Party advocated armed insurrection, and extremists on the far right reciprocated. For those in power, the potential risks of such upheavals—however unrealistic—outweighed the potential benefits of a universal militia.

That is why such policy was not even raised in the above debates in 1935 over conscription. But another issue loomed large. Before the proceedings in the Chamber, Paul Reynaud met with Lieutenant Colonel Charles de Gaulle, who had been advocating an armored corps that could be rapidly deployed. Arguing in support of such armaments programs as well as conscription, Reynaud noted, "When Switzerland imposes on herself new sacrifices, is she joining in the armaments race? Yes, but only to ensure peace. . . ."[38] Switzerland was indeed building up its armaments in response to the Nazi threat.[39]

The Chamber voted for the conscription measure. However, de Gaulle's proposals for an armored corps fell on deaf ears. The static defense of massive concrete fortifications making up the Maginot Line, under construction since 1930, would become the losing strategy. And instead of arming the people as in the Swiss model, restrictions were about to be decreed to make it more difficult than ever before for citizens to obtain and keep arms.

---

37. Jean Jaurès, *Democracy and Military Service: An Abbreviated Translation of the* Armée Nouvelle, ed. C. G. Coulton (London: Simpkin, Marshall, Hamilton, Kent & Co., 1916), Chapter 7, n.3, http://www.marxists.org/archive/jaures/1907/military-service/index.htm.

38. Reynaud, *Thick of the Fight*, 104–5.

39. Stephen P. Halbrook, *Target Switzerland* (New York: Sarpedon, 1998), 35–37.

2

Pierre Laval Decrees
Firearm Registration

PIERRE LAVAL NOW returned to power in his third ministry, which would last from June 7, 1935 to January 24, 1936. As always, he was both prime minister and minister of foreign affairs. On June 8, the Chamber of Deputies passed an enabling act granting Laval power to rule by decree. In opposition to groups such as the *Croix de Feu*, the Radicals joined with the Socialists and Communists in the *Front Populaire*.[1]

By fall, the leftist press warned that the *Croix de Feu* was planning to seize power. The alarm was at high pitch at the Radical Party conference meeting on October 24–27. On October 23, Laval took advantage of the panic by issuing three decree-laws (*décret-lois*) without legislative action, under the enabling act of June 8. The power of the government would be strengthened to restore public order.[2]

First, the size of the Mobile Guard, which could be used to suppress dissent, was increased from 15,000 to 20,000 members.[3]

Second, people who wished to organize an assembly were required to register several days in advance with the police, who could prohibit the demonstration if it might "disturb public order."[4]

---

1. Warner, *Pierre Laval*, 86, 88.

2. Warner, *Pierre Laval*, 112, citing *Journal Officiel* [J.O.], *Lois et Décrets*, 25 October 1935, pp. 11202-4, 11214.

3. Décret ayant pour objet d'augmenter les effectifs de la garde républicaine mobile, 23 octobre 1935, lecahiertoulousain.free.fr/Textes/decret_1935_effectif.html.

4. Décret-loi du 23 octobre 1935 portant réglementation des mesures relatives au renforcement du maintien de l'ordre public, https://www.legifrance.gouv.fr/affichTexte.do?cidTexte=LEGITEXT000006071320&dateTexte=vig.

Third, people who wished to obtain a firearm had to register with the police. Proposed under the previous government, this had been introduced by Georges Chauvin as "a bill concerning demonstrations on public streets, and commerce, import and possession of arms."[5] It was now proposed by Léon Bérard, minister of justice, and Joseph Paganon, minister of the interior,[6] the pertinent cabinet members, and given final approval by Pierre Laval.[7]

As a member of the Senate when the Nazis were overrunning France in 1940, Bérard, a member of the liberal *Union républicaine*, would cast his vote on July 10 to give full powers to Philippe Pétain. He thereafter served the Vichy regime as an ambassador.[8] Paganon, a Radical-Socialist who had served in previous cabinets, would die in 1937.[9]

The Laval decree defined "war weapons" as arms so designated by the ministers of the land, sea, and air forces.[10] Military arms, including small arms and ammunition therefor, were already banned to civilians, with punishment of up to two years' imprisonment, under an 1834 law.[11] The new decree also restricted importation of firearms, extended record-keeping requirements, including the keeping of daily registers by firearm manufacturers and dealers, and prohibited the sale of firearms by flea market vendors.[12] Its most radical provisions required registration of firearm owners and of their firearms, and

---

5. "Au Conseil de Cabinet, Un project pour réprimer les tentatives de désordre 'd'où qu'elles viennent," *L'Echo de Paris*, October 23, 1935, 2; "Décret-loi portant réglementation des mesures relatives au renforcement du mainten de l'ordre public," *L'Echo de Paris*, October 24, 1935, 1.

6. "Au Conseil des Ministres, De nouveaux décrets-lois ont été adoptés hier," *L'Homme Libre*, October 24, 1935, 1.

7. Décret portant réglementation de l'importation, de la fabrication, du commerce et de la détention des armes, *Journal Officiel*, 24 octobre 1935. The decree was widely publicized, for example, "Trois décrets-lois relatifs au maintien de l'ordre," *Le Figaro*, October 24, 1935, 1; "Le commerce et le port des armes," *Le Figaro*, October 24, 1935, 3; "Le décret-loi relatif au renforcement du maintien de l'ordre," *L'Homme Libre*, October 24, 1935, 3; "Décret-loi relatif à l'importation et à la vente des armes," *L'Echo de Paris*, October 24, 1935, 3.

8. "Léon Bérard," www.assemblee-nationale.fr/sycomore/_fiche_14-19.asp?num_dept =650.

9. "Troisième République," www.histoire-france-web.fr/republique_3/lebrun.htm.

10. Article 1. Décret portant réglementation de l'importation, de la fabrication, du commerce et de la détention des armes, *Journal Officiel*, 24 octobre 1935.

11. Barbier, *Le délit*, 104.

12. Articles 2–8. J.O., 24 octobre 1935.

punished violators without regard to any evil intent. Specifically, Article 9 stated:

> Each person in possession of a firearm at the enactment of the present decree must make a declaration of it to the prefect or the sub-prefect of the place of his residence within the time limit of one month.
>
> Anyone after the enactment of the present decree who receives a firearm must make a declaration of it to the prefect or the sub-prefect of the place of his residence within the time limit of 8 days.
>
> Receipts of the declarations referenced in the two previous paragraphs will be delivered to the concerned parties.
>
> Each violation of the requirements of the first two paragraphs of the present article shall be punishable by a fine of 100 to 1,000 Francs. The court in addition will order the forfeiture of the weapon. . . .
>
> Failure to comply with this order shall be punishable with imprisonment of from six months to two years. . . .[13]

However, the registration requirement did not apply to hunting guns or to historic or collectable firearms.[14]

Prominently publicized was that the decree "requires anyone in possession of arms to declare his place of residency to the prefect or his assistant." It was further published that people involved in the manufacture and commerce of arms were required to declare them to the police prefecture within a month, and that owners of firearms (other than hunting arms, historic arms, and collectible arms) had to make a declaration to their neighborhood or district police superintendent within a month. The deadline would expire on November 24, 1935.[15]

For the first time in the history of modern France, the Laval decree mandated the registration of firearms. It also enhanced existing prohibitions on the sale of ordinary military arms, such as bolt-action rifles. To be sure, something needed to be done about the very real violence in the streets and subversive threats by extremist groups on the left and the right. Successive governments

---

13. Article 9. J.O., 24 octobre 1935.

14. Article 10. J.O., 24 octobre 1935.

15. "Le décret-loi relatif au renforcement du maintien de l'ordre," *L'Homme Libre*, October 24, 1935, 3.

of differing political stripes would not repeal the Laval decree, suggesting that it had considerable support. But it was naively aimed at firearm owners at large and did not focus on those responsible for fomenting political violence.

The decree also had potential for disaster if an extremist group seized power or if France was conquered by a foreign enemy. As it turned out, the registration records would be highly useful five years later when France fell to Nazi Germany, which sought to confiscate all firearms under the threat of the death penalty, with the help of French collaborationists led by none other than the same Pierre Laval.

Authorized and Unauthorized Weapons

Regulations to implement the decree-law were promulgated on November 22, 1935.[16] Apparently the bureaucrats in charge were unable formally to implement the requirements until two days before the deadline to register. Registration of a firearm included one's name, date and place of birth, nationality, profession, domicile, and description of the firearm—type, caliber, manufacturer, and serial number, if one existed. The declarations were to be made at police stations or city halls, and passed on to the prefecture, to be filed in the departmental file registering all people in possession of arms.[17]

Excepted from the registration requirement were governmental agents—various officials, the police, and people required to possess firearms. Exceptions, as included in the regulation of December 16, 1935, included hunting, competition, salon, and gallery guns. Antique and obsolete rifles and carbines were excepted, including percussion weapons 6 mm and lower, and—for people in approved associations—two obsolete service rifles, the Fusil Gras and the Lebel.[18] The Fusil Gras Modèle 1874 M80, a single-shot blackpowder cartridge rifle, had been replaced by the now equally obsolete Lebel bolt-action rifle in 1886.[19]

---

16. J.O., 23 novembre 1935. See summary in Barbier, *Le délit,* 104–7.

17. Articles 2–4. J.O., 24 octobre 1935.

18. See summary in Barbier, *Le délit,* 104–07.

19. Ian V. Hogg and John Weeks, *Military Small Arms of the 20th Century* (Northfield, IL: DBI Books, 1985), 128–29.

The decree-law distinguished authorized and unauthorized weapons. Unauthorized weapons were designated by the minister of war on January 16, 1936, to include "[p]istols, automatic and military pistols, and revolvers of a higher caliber than 6.5 mm, or of which the barrel length is over 10 centimeters, as well as all other rifled firearms of 6 mm caliber and above."[20] Handguns and rifles thought to be of military usefulness were thus banned.

To what extent did the population comply with the decree-law to register firearms within the one-month deadline of November 24? Would urban dwellers have complied more than rural people? Perhaps, but the percentage who complied was probably low. Those who did so may have been people who were either compulsively law-abiding in every respect or naive people who could not foresee negative consequences. Those who failed to comply perhaps saw little use in an unprecedented diktat, yet another one of the endless bureaucratic mandates that had the potential for confiscation to boot.

Information on the extent of compliance or noncompliance may be gleaned from police reports in the various departmental archives of the period. As discussed below, archival records from the Ardennes reflect that few complied in that department.

Last Gasp of Laval

Meanwhile, back in Paris, the politicians were at it again. In debate in the Chamber of Deputies on December 6, 1935, rightist deputy Jean Ybarnégaray offered on behalf of the *Croix de Feu* that all groups should disarm and that carrying a firearm be punished with imprisonment for one to three years.[21] Socialist Léon Blum replied that the "self-defense" Socialist groups would do so if the paramilitary leagues would. Maurice Thorez agreed for the Communists, as did Ybarnégaray for the *Croix de Feu*. Pierre Laval noted "with satisfaction this triple declaration, which does honour to the Chamber and from which the government will draw the necessary conclusions."[22] Since he would issue decrees on the same subjects, Laval then tabled bills abolishing

---

20. J.O., January 16, 1936, cited in Barbier, *Le délit*, 100.
21. 1ère séance du 6 décembre 1935, J.O. débats parlementaires, 7 décembre 1935, 2391.
22. J.O. débats parlementaires, 7 décembre 1935, 2389–92 (comments of all four).

paramilitary units, banning the bearing of arms in public, and increasing penalties for inciting murder in the press. Some 351 deputies (including 76 Radicals) gave him a vote of confidence over 219 votes against.[23]

The same day, Laval proposed a prohibition on carrying restricted arms as a decree, which was issued in two parts on January 10, 1936. The law on the carrying of prohibited arms (*loi sur le port des armes prohibées*) punished the carrying of a weapon, openly or concealed, in a demonstration or meeting, with imprisonment of three months to two years and a fine of 100 to 1,000 Francs.[24] The law on combat groups and private militias (*loi sur les groupes de combat et sur les milices privées*) empowered the president of the Republic and the Council of Ministers to decree the banning of what they deemed to be paramilitary groups and the confiscation of arms used or intended to be used by such groups.[25]

On that same day, the Popular Front published its program, criticizing rule through decree-laws. The Front included the Radical Party, then headed by Edouard Daladier. Within days, key ministers resigned and then Laval himself did so.[26] A new government would come to power.

During 1936–37, the *Comité secret d'action révolutionnaire* (Secret Committee of Revolutionary Action), which has been described as both socialist and fascist, sought to organize armed groups to support the army in the event of a Communist revolution. Named *La Cagoule* (The Hooded Cloak) by the press, it planted a bomb in the office of a business association and engaged in political violence. In October 1937, police in Paris raided one of its arms caches, finding large quantities of explosives and grenades, sixteen submachine guns, and a dozen rifles. Interior Minister Marx Dormoy announced that seized documents revealed a plot to overthrow the Republic.[27]

Not surprisingly, weapons depots of this subversive organization were weapons of war smuggled into France, not civilian arms bought in commerce. Nonetheless, the plot would prompt in part the decree-law of April 18, 1939, which further restricted firearms.[28] That will be discussed further below.

---

23. Warner, *Pierre Laval*, 114–15.
24. J.O., 12 janvier 1936.
25. J.O., 12 janvier 1936.
26. Warner, *Pierre Laval*, 128–29.
27. Robert Soucy, *French Fascism*, 46–53.
28. Dominique Venner, *Les Armes de la Résistance* (Paris: Pensée Moderne, 1976), 148, n.10.

• • •

Low Registrations in the Ardennes

In the Ardennes department, in northern France, archives from the period reflect that few paid any attention to the registration decree. A rural, forested area with plenty of wild game, its population included numerous hunters who would not necessarily comply, not knowing which guns had to be registered or even knowing about yet another useless decree coming from Paris.

On November 21, 1935, the commissioner of police in Sedan reported that, despite the publicity in the newspapers, only nineteen persons had registered firearms, while an estimated 300 should have registered.[29] The commissioner of Givet thought it striking that so few had registered.[30] Police in Vouziers just said that registrations were coming in.[31]

A month after the deadline passed, on December 22, the Charleville commissioner reported 220 declarations of possession of firearms, without speculating on how many failed to comply.[32] But the commissioner of Mohon counted only 45 registrants, adding that "there is certainly in Mohon more than 500 people in possession of firearms."[33] By the end of the year, he lamented, only 52 people registered firearms.[34]

As discussed earlier, in this period the leftist and rightist parties accused each other of secretly arming. For instance, the commissioner of Charleville, in

29. Commissariat de police de Sedan, 21 novembre, 1935. Archives des Ardennes, Fonds du Cabinet: Rapports des RG sur la situation générale du département, 1M14/3, Rapports mensuels décembre 1934–1935. Exécution de la circulaire du Ministre de l'Intérieur du 26 novembre 1934.

30. Commissariat de police de Givet, 21 novembre, 1935, Archives des Ardennes, 1M14/3, Rapports mensuels décembre 1934–1935.

31. Sous-Préfecture de Vouziers, 22 novembre, 1935, Archives des Ardennes, 1M14/3, Rapports mensuels décembre 1934–1935.

32. Commissariat de police de Charleville, 22 décembre, 1935, Archives des Ardennes, 1M14/3, Rapports mensuels décembre 1934–1935.

33. Commissariat de police de Mohon, 22 décembre, 1935, Archives des Ardennes, 1M14/3, Rapports mensuels décembre 1934–1935.

34. Le commissaire de police de Mohon, 22 janvier, 1936, Archives des Ardennes, Fonds du Cabinet: Rapports des RG sur la situation générale du département, 1M14/4, Rapports mensuels 1936.

the Ardennes, reported on September 19, 1936, that following the heightened state of alert, the different parties mutually admitted to possession of arms and munitions depots.[35] A month later, after investigation, the various accusations of the import or depots of arms alleged by the opposite parties were revealed to be without foundation, although surveillance would be intensified.[36]

So what use was being made of the decree criminalizing the failure to register firearms? Examination of the Ardennes archives revealed no record of extremist groups with depots of unregistered arms. The only record discovered was one indicating that at the end of 1936, Madam Benvenutti, a grocer living on the rue Gambetta in Mohon, was charged for not registering her revolver, and the case was referred to the public prosecutor.[37]

On the Alert for Violations

In 1937, police were still on high alert for violations of the arms decree, but they reported virtually no incidents. Suspicion existed that some hunting guns without import permits were being brought across the border into France. Despite the awareness that only a small number of firearms possessed had been registered, only three arrests for unregistered firearms, all in Sedan, were reported[38]—probably because the crime of keeping a gun at home without papers was hard to detect.

Charleville reported that its intense surveillance on the clandestine commerce in arms revealed nothing, similar to earlier fruitless investigations based on anonymous letters. Four unusable German military rifles that had been

---

35. Le commissaire spécial de Charleville, 19 septembre, 1936, Archives des Ardennes, Fonds du Cabinet: Rapports des RG sur la situation générale du département, 1M14/4, Rapports mensuels 1936.

36. Le commissaire spécial de Charleville, 18 octobre, 1936, Archives des Ardennes, 1M14/4, Rapports mensuels 1936.

37. Le commissaire de police de Mohon, 22 décembre, 1936, Archives des Ardennes, Fonds du Cabinet: Rapports des RG sur la situation générale du département, 1M14/4, Rapports mensuels 1936.

38. Le commissaire de police de Sedan, 21 Mai, 1937, 20 septembre, 1937, and 20 Octobre, 1937, Archives des Ardennes, Fonds du Cabinet: Rapports des RG sur la situation générale du département, 1M14/5, Rapports mensuels 1937.

kept since the armistice in 1918 had been discovered. A brewer in Gespunsart was denounced by a former employee for possession of war weapons, but this was rejected when the informer admitted that he gave a false statement to get revenge.[39]

In this period, an open investigation by the police against the rightist *Comité secret d'action révolutionnaire* was reported by Charleville to have prompted people to get rid of war weapons left by the Germans in the Great War. The January 1938 report noted that the weapons were mostly unusable, but their discovery had been exploited for political ends. During one month, fewer than ten old rifles, several missing parts, and some ammunition had been found abandoned in bushes or hedges.[40]

A special commissioner of Saint-Étienne-à-Arnes reported that nothing was discovered from the rumors and anonymous denunciations, other than some unusable arms and ammunition from the Great War, nor was any clandestine arms trade found among the regional gunsmiths.[41] Similarly, the Ardennes prefect reported increased denunciations but no discoveries.[42]

Out of numerous Ardennes files for the entire year of 1938, just two incidents could be found of citations for failure to register a firearm. A wine salesman from Paris named Alexandre Levy was issued a summons to appear in court for an unregistered Unique automatic pistol.[43] The criminal court in Charleville fined railway employee Armand Fox sixteen francs for possession of an unregistered firearm.[44]

---

39. Le commissaire spécial de Charleville, 21 décembre, 1937, Archives des Ardennes, 1M14/5, Rapports mensuels 1937.

40. Le commissaire spécial de Charleville, 21 janvier, 1938, Archives des Ardennes Fonds du Cabinet: Rapports des RG sur la situation générale du département, M14/6 Rapports mensuels 1938.

41. Le commissaire spécial de Saint-Etienne, 23 février, 1938, Archives des Ardennes, M14/6, Rapports mensuels 1938.

42. Le prefet des Ardennes, 29 mars, 1938, Archives des Ardennes, M14/6, Rapports mensuels 1938.

43. Commissariat de police de Mézières, 22 avril, 1938, Archives des Ardennes, M14/6, Rapports mensuels 1938.

44. Commissariat de police de Mohon, 21 juin, 1938, Archives des Ardennes, M14/6, Rapports mensuels 1938.

For the entire year, only Mohon police reported that two firearms had been registered and the information transmitted.[45] Either no one was registering firearms, or the information was not considered worthy of reporting.

It continued to be "all quiet on the Western front" for gun violations as reported in the Ardennes for 1939 through April of 1940. For all of 1939, only trivial matters were reported. Marcel Piron was convicted by the Charleville criminal court of possession of an unregistered automatic pistol of a model used in the army.[46] Fumay reported just two gun registrations in February and March,[47] and Mohon reported three registrations in March.[48] Weapons from the Great War were discovered in a house that was sold in Thilay.[49]

The Ardennes was a rural department, and compliance with the registration requirements may have varied in urban areas or in regions with differing social, political, and religious cultures. Research into the relevant archives would be a study of its own and is beyond the scope of this work, but the experiences of regimes in various countries to the present does not suggest a large percentage of voluntary compliance with registration decrees in general populations.

Meanwhile, Hitler launched World War II by invading Poland on September 1, 1939. Poland fell quickly, and the Phoney War with France and England lasted over the next half year until the blitzkrieg hit. The only report from Mézières was that the only licensed gun shop was closed since hostilities began.[50] At the end of the year, Mohon reported that a single gun had been registered.[51]

---

45. Commissariat de police de Mohon, 21 novembre, 1938, Archives des Ardennes, M14/6, Rapports mensuels 1938.

46. Commissariat de police de Mézières, 21 février, 1939, Archives des Ardennes, Fonds du Cabinet: Rapports des RG sur la situation générale du département, 1M14/7, Rapports mensuels janvier 1939 à avril 1940.

47. Commissariat de police de Fumay, 24 mars, 1939, Archives des Ardennes, 1M14/7, Rapports mensuels janvier 1939 à avril 1940.

48. Commissariat de police de Mohon, 21 mars, 1939, Archives des Ardennes, 1M14/7, Rapports mensuels janvier 1939 à avril 1940.

49. Le prefet des Ardennes, 28 juillet, 1939, Archives des Ardennes, 1M14/7, Rapports mensuels janvier 1939 à avril 1940.

50. Commissariat de police de Mézières, 23 décembre, 1939, Archives des Ardennes, 1M14/7, Rapports mensuels janvier 1939 à avril 1940.

51. Commissariat de police de Mohon, 22 décembre, 1939, Archives des Ardennes, 1M14/7, Rapports mensuels janvier 1939 à avril 1940.

A Veteran's Perception

Around the turn of the twentieth to the twenty-first century, I sent questionnaires to veteran Resistance organizations seeking information on gun ownership before the war and reaction to German disarming policies when the occupation began in 1940. One respondent was Louis Charmeau, who was born in 1923 and lived in the Saône-et-Loire department in the region of Bourgogne in eastern France.[52]

Before the war, Charmeau recalled that it was easy to obtain firearms, or at least hunting guns: "As long as you did not have any previous police record, it was fine. Arms were sold in catalogs, such as *Le Chasseur Français* (The French Hunter), the most popular one before 1939." However, the extent of ownership depended on the type of gun: "Sporting firearms were reserved for the 'rich.' A few arms from the 1914–18 War were around, but they were owned by veterans of that war who kept them as souvenirs. Quite a few handguns, revolvers in fairly great number." He was apparently referring to veteran ownership, for he added, "Some civilians (few) owned a handgun. We did not live in today's insecurity."

• • •

A Shooting at the German Embassy

While requiring the registration of firearms facilitates the confiscation thereof from people who abide by the law, a timeless truism is that it fails to prevent homicide by a determined individual. This was infamously illustrated on November 7, 1938, by the failure of Herschel Grynszpan, a teenage Polish Jew, to register the revolver he just bought, instead using it to shoot an attaché at the German embassy in Paris. His ostensible motive was to avenge the mistreatment of Polish Jews, including his relatives, who were expelled from Germany. The death of the attaché provided the Nazis with the welcome excuse to mount the pogrom known as the Night of Broken Glass (*Reichskristallnacht*).[53] Weeks

---

52. Louis Maurice Charmeau, président de l'Union Départementale des Combattants Volontaires de la Résistance, Bordeaux, France, letter to author, June 10, 2003.

53. See Gerald Schwab, *The Day the Holocaust Began: The Odyssey of Herschel Grynszpan* (New York: Praeger, 1990), 1–6, 59–76.

before, Nazi Germany had already been disarming German Jews, including those who had registered firearms, and had been taking other actions as if to anticipate the pogrom.[54]

Grynszpan bought a 6.35 mm (.25 caliber) revolver and cartridges from gunsmith M. Carpe at his small store *À la Fine Lame* (The Sharp Blade), 61 rue du Flaubourg St. Martin, Paris.[55] He claimed that he needed it to protect bank deposits he carried for his father. The gunsmith recorded his identity and address from his passport, gave him the registration form, and instructed him to proceed to the police station to register it. Instead, Grynszpan loaded the revolver and went to the German embassy.[56]

When an attaché received Grynszpan, the latter pulled out his revolver and fired, mortally wounding him. Grynszpan was quickly arrested. He still had the registration form that he was supposed to have submitted to the police, and the revolver still had the price tag on the trigger guard.[57]

Was Grynszpan a loner motivated solely by his brooding over Nazi persecution of Jews and a desire for revenge? Was the teenager manipulated by Nazi agents provocateurs to instigate an incident that could be used to inflame anti-Semitism and provoke a massive pogrom?[58] The French International League Against Antisemitism (*Ligue internationale contre l'antisémitisme,* or LICA) published an article suggesting the latter.[59]

At any rate, the affair demonstrated that requiring registration of firearms failed to prevent an individual from procuring one and shooting someone. Those who did register their firearms would be threatened by German occupation authorities just a year and a half later with the death penalty for not turning them in.

54. Halbrook, *Gun Control in the Third Reich*, Chapter 10.

55. Schwab, *Holocaust*, 1. An example of a 6.35 mm revolver was the small Vélodog Francotte made in Liège, Belgium.

56. Schwab, *Holocaust*, 75.

57. Schwab, *Holocaust*, 3, 5.

58. See Friedrich Karl Kaul, *Der Fall des Herschel Grynszpan* (Berlin: Akademie Verlag, 1965), 8–9; Vincent C. Frank, "Neuer Blick auf die Reichskristallnacht," *Neue Zürcher Zeitung*, November 4, 1998, www.hagalil.com/archiv/98/11/pogrom.htm.

59. LICA magazine article "The Truth Behind the Assassination," *Le Droit de Vivre* [*The Right to Live*], cited in Schwab, *Holocaust*, 41.

The 1939 Decree-Law

Alarm over perceived domestic threats such as the *Comité secret d'action révolutionnaire* (Secret Committee of Revolutionary Action), the smuggled arms caches of which had been seized in 1937,[60] and over Germany's widening aggression prompted the even more restrictive decree-law on war matériel, arms, and munitions of April 18, 1939.[61] It listed weapons in eight categories. "War weapons" were in the first category, and they included any firearm that could fire ammunition used in any military weapon. "Defensive arms" were in the fourth category.[62] "The acquisition and possession of weapons or ammunition from the first or fourth category are prohibited unless authorized." Even when authorized, a person had to obtain further permission to possess more than one such arm or more than fifty rounds of ammunition therefor.[63]

Hunting arms and ammunition were in category 5; edged weapons in category 6; target, fair, and salon arms (*armes de tir, de foire ou de salon*) in category 7; and historical and collectable arms in category 8.[64] Category 2 included equipment for use with combat arms, and category 3 was equipment for protection against poison gas.

An implementing decree was promulgated on August 14, 1939. Category 1 war weapons included semiautomatic pistols firing cartridges of the regulation 7.65 mm long or greater caliber, or of which the length of the barrel was 11 mm or longer. Other handguns were category 4 defensive arms, possession of which required authorization of the commissariat of police or the gendarmerie, limited to only one weapon per home.[65]

Dominique Venner, historian of the arms of the French Resistance in World War II, would write about the 1939 decree: "The happy time is no more of the law of 1885 that had practically rendered free the possession of arms of

60. Venner, *Armes de la Résistance*, 148, n.10.

61. *Décret-loi du 18 avril 1939 fixant le régime des matériels de guerre, armes et munitions*, J.O., 13 juin 1939, 7463–7466. The same law with amendments through 1992 may be viewed at www.securite-sanitaire.org/anciensite/armesafeu/d180439.htm.

62. *Décret-loi du 18 avril 1939*, J.O., 13 juin 1939, 7463–7466, articles 1 and 2.

63. *Décret-loi du 18 avril 1939*, J.O., 13 juin 1939, 7463–7466, article 15.

64. *Décret-loi du 18 avril 1939*, J.O., 13 juin 1939, 7463–7466, article 2.

65. Venner, *Armes de la Résistance*, 147.

all sorts, expressing confidence in the citizens who had not misused them. In a period of war or unrest, one does not joke with weapons anymore."[66]

At this point, by law French civilians were prohibited from possession of firearms considered "war weapons," and firearms they were allowed to possess, with some exceptions, were supposed to be registered with the police. This regime of gun control would be highly useful to the Nazi occupation authorities when France fell the next year. But few anticipated the hell that would break loose.

---

66. Venner, *Armes de la Résistance*, 147–48.

3

Blitzkrieg, Defeat, and Twenty-Four Hours to Turn in Your Gun or Be Shot

IT WAS NOT yet France's turn, but Hitler and his henchmen were devising what would become a familiar policy of occupation. Czechoslovakia was abandoned by England and France, whose ambassadors agreed with Hitler in the Munich Agreement of September 1938 to cede the Sudetenland to Germany. Police and the Gestapo swiftly moved in, decreeing that "to prevent misuse of arms on the part of 'Marxist elements,' all weapons held by the civil population were required to be surrendered immediately. The only arms-bearers in the Sudetenland will be the army, the police and the Elite Guard members while on active service."[1]

As part of the Austro-Hungarian Empire before World War I, what became Czechoslovakia in 1918 had been governed by the Austrian Firearms Act, which required a permit, renewable every three years, to possess a firearm. A local district office administered the law, and its records of firearms licenses constituted a registration system.[2] The Nazis could thereby readily identify gun owners.

The Dominos Start to Fall

That was just the beginning. In the wee hours of the morning of March 15, 1939, Hitler intimidated Dr. Emil Hácha, president of Czechoslovakia, into

---

1. "Czech to Shape Tie with Berlin Today," *New York Times*, October 13, 1938, 6.
2. Karel Novak, *Vzoroo ve vecech honebniho prava, zbrojniho patentu a rybolovu Kempas* (Prague, 1934), 151–52; Czechoslovakian Firearms Act §§ 17–40. See *Federal Firearms Legislation*, Senate Judiciary Committee (1968), 482.

agreeing that his country would become a protectorate of the Reich. Hácha ordered his military forces to disarm and not resist.[3] The London *Times* reported:

> Immediately a proclamation, bordered in red and bearing the German eagle and swastika which is now familiar to every Czech town and village, was posted on the hoarding. Under this proclamation no one was allowed in the streets after 8 p.m. . . .; all popular gatherings were forbidden; and weapons, munitions, and wireless sets were ordered to be surrendered immediately. Disobedience of these orders, the proclamation ended, would be severely punished under military law.[4]

It is still generally remembered today that, on the first day of the occupation, the Nazis put up posters in every town ordering the inhabitants to surrender all firearms, including hunting guns. The penalty for disobedience was death. The Nazis were able to use local and central registration records of firearms owners and hunters to execute the decree. Lists of potential dissidents and other suspects were already prepared, and those people disappeared immediately.[5]

In Prague, motorized units descended to conduct house searches for weapons, leading to numerous arrests.[6] "Inside the Rathaus citizens complied with a military order requiring them to surrender all armaments. Revolvers, old muskets and antique weapons of all sorts were carted into the building and turned over to the authorities, who gave receipts in return."[7]

Suspicious that many firearms had not been surrendered, in August the protectorate again ordered that they be turned in, threatening the death penalty for those who did not comply.[8] A revolt erupted the following month. People who did not own any firearms were said to have somehow armed themselves. In Prague, female workers reportedly attacked some Germans with poles

---

3. *The Times* (London), March 15, 1939, 14a.

4. *The Times* (London), March 16, 1939, 16b. See also *Neue Zürcher Zeitung*, March 15, 1939, 1.

5. Milan Kubele (Uherský Brod, Czech Republic), in discussion with author, March 16, 1994.

6. "Berhaftungen in Prag," *Neue Zürcher Zeitung*, March 17, 1939.

7. "Nazis Bar Violence on the Czech Jews," *New York Times*, March 19, 1939, 39.

8. *New York Times*, August 11, 1939, 6.

with nails sticking out. Numerous executions ensued in the brutal repression that followed.[9]

Hitler launched World War II by attacking Poland on September 1, 1939. The blitzkrieg overwhelmed the Polish army in short order as it awaited help from its supposed allies, Britain and France. The most brutal occupation followed with the expected decree from the military commanders, enforced with the most severe punishment: don't be in the street after six o'clock, turn in all of your weapons, and don't carry metal objects which could be used to injure or kill.[10]

Simha Rotem, who was Jewish and who would later join the Resistance, recalled that the Germans "searched from house to house, from apartment to apartment, and naturally did not neglect the Jews. Under the pretext of looking for weapons, they searched our house thoroughly, even rummaging in the oven."[11] Josef Sadowski, an American citizen who returned to his native country of Poland, was executed in Warsaw after a court martial convicted him of "having concealed a considerable quantity of arms and ammunition in violation of German regulations."[12]

France and Britain declared war on Germany on September 3, but they waged only a Phoney War, as they never took action. Since Hitler and Stalin were now pals, the Communist parties in Europe endorsed the Russo-German pact. The French Communist press advocated defeatism and disobedience to orders in the French military, and was banned by the French government.[13]

The Führer's Orders

But Hitler was planning his next move, this time against the West. Blitzkrieg was repeatedly ordered but then canceled due to bad weather. As part of the

9. *Neue Zürcher Zeitung*, September 21, 1939, 1.

10. *Der Bund* (Bern), September 29, 1939, 3.

11. Simha (Kazik) Rotem, *Memoirs of a Warsaw Ghetto Fighter and the Past Within Me* (New Haven, CT: Yale University Press, 1994), 10.

12. *New York Times*, November 4, 1939, 5.

13. Henri Michel, *The Shadow War: European Resistance 1939–1945*, trans. Richard Barry (New York: Harper & Row, 1972), 55, 183; Thomas J. Laub, *After the Fall: German Policy in Occupied France, 1940–1944* (New York: Oxford University Press, 2010), 112.

planning, on November 14, 1939, Army Group Command B issued orders for the administration of territories to be occupied in the future.[14] That included Belgium and Holland, despite Hitler's feigned promises to respect their neutrality and the references in the orders strictly to respect international law.

The first item regarding decrees to be imposed read: "The appeal of the Führer to the population and the decree by the Army High Command regarding weapons possession in the occupied territory will be made known by way of proclamations put up on walls when the troops invade." The local commanders would proclaim where firearms were required to be turned in, after which they would have to be secured or destroyed.

The directive distinguished guerrillas from uniformed soldiers, from militia members who wear insignia and carry arms openly, and even from people in a not yet occupied territory who resist on their own initiative, carry arms openly, and observe the laws and customs of war. If a guerrilla was captured, he would be judged by a summary court-martial and sentenced to death. A sample judgment form recited that on a certain date the defendant shot at German troops with a firearm and was therefore sentenced to death as a guerrilla. It ended that the judgment had to be executed immediately by shooting the defendant.

While the above reflected the international law of war, the same rules would later be applied to civilians who were not guerrillas for mere possession of firearms. The proclamations posted on walls during the invasion in 1940 announced the death penalty for any person who did not surrender all firearms within twenty-four hours. International law and the Hague Convention allowed an army of occupation to exercise sovereign authority, but it did not explicitly countenance the execution of a farmer for having a shotgun to control predators or an urbanite for having an old revolver in the attic.

Orders issued for Army Group A on December 20, 1939, concerned possession of weapons in the territories to be occupied.[15] For Luxembourg, the decree on weapons would not be published unless needed, with the intent that

---

14. Bundesarchiv-Militärarchiv (BA/MA), RH 19II272, Geheime Kommandosache, Heeresgruppenkommando B, Erst besondere Anordnungen für die Verwaltung und Befriedung der besetzen Gebiete, 14. November 1939.

15. BA/MA, RH 19II217, Anlage zu Heeresgruppe A O.Qu., Besondere Anordnungen für die Verwaltung und Wirtschaft der besetzten Gebiete, 20. Dezember 1939.

the population could keep their arms. In Belgium, unusable weapons kept as souvenirs would not have to be turned in, but hunting guns would need to be tagged with the owner's identity and turned over to the mayor for safekeeping. Troop leaders could allow ethnic Germans to keep their weapons.

"The Führer has given the order to cross Holland, Belgium, and Luxembourg in order to gain final victory over our enemies England and France," stated Army Group Command B on January 15, 1940. "Any kind of resistance, even the armed resistance of the civilian population, must be broken with armed force." It repeated earlier jargon about "the appeal of the Führer and the decree about weapons possession," which had been distributed to all the army commands. As before, hunting guns had to be turned in to the mayors for safekeeping.[16]

A directive issued on April 3 by the Army High Command, General Staff, detailed how the military administration would issue decrees by wall posters, newspapers, and broadcast on a variety of subjects, including the introduction of German criminal law, distribution of food, prohibition of price increases, and possession of arms.[17]

A directive by Army Group A, issued on April 9, stated that in Belgium, unusable weapons kept as souvenirs need not be turned in. Hunting rifles had to be marked with the owner's name, profession, and residence, and turned over to the mayor who was responsible for their safekeeping. That would leave the option later to return the weapons in general or in individual cases to their owners if the owners' behavior and the general situation allowed. Further, if the population did not resist, police, customs, and forest service officers could serve with firearms, which could be confiscated and then returned. Finally, troop leaders were authorized to let ethnic Germans keep their firearms.[18]

On April 9, 1940, the Wehrmacht occupied Denmark and invaded Norway. Denmark capitulated immediately. The German weekly news showed

---

16. BA/MA, RH 19II272, Heeresgruppenkommando B, Befehl für das Verhalten des deutschen Soldaten im besetzten Gebiet, 15. Januar 1940; BA/MA, RH19II272, Geheime Kommandosarche, Heeresgruppenkommando B, Besondere Anordnungen Nr. 2 für die Verwaltung und Befriedung der besetzten Gebiete, 15. Januar 1940.

17. BA/MA, RH 19II272, Oberkommando des Heeres, Generalstab des Heeres, Besondere Anordnungen für die Militärverwaltung, 3. April 3 1940.

18. BA/MA, RH 19I/217, Heeresgruppe A Oberquartiermeister, Zusätze der Heeresgrupe A zu den Bestimmungen des OKH für die Militärverwaltung, 9. April 1940.

Danish police surrendering their arms, taking an oath to obey the Germans, and then the arms being given back to the police.

In Norway, the German High Command ordered that civilians surrender all weapons and threatened that civilians found with weapons or instigating resistance would be shot on the spot. Despite such measures, guerrilla war began to spread.[19] In one incident, marksmen from a local rifle club beat back German paratroopers. An attempt to mobilize the weak military forces collapsed when the Germans seized the weapons depots before arms could be distributed to the Norwegian soldiers; reservists and volunteers were turned away because there were no arms to give them.[20] A British expeditionary force with some French support briefly sought to intervene, but quickly withdrew without materially helping the Norwegians. Norway would surrender on June 10.[21]

It would next be France's turn.

Posters for the Blitzkrieg

On May 10, Germany launched its blitzkrieg attack on France, avoiding the Maginot Line and crashing through Belgium, Luxembourg, and the Netherlands. The military forces of these three neutral countries were quickly crushed, and the German Wehrmacht soon penetrated France. The Germans came with a supply of posters with proclamations and regulations that they nailed up on entering the towns and villages. Most prominent was a poster threatening the civilians with the death penalty unless they immediately surrendered all firearms and radio transmitters. It was dubbed the Decree of May 10, 1940, on the Possession of Arms in the Occupied Territory, and it stated:[22]

---

19. "Warnung der deutschen Militärbehörden," *Neue Zürcher Zeitung*, April 21, 1940; "Die deutsche Occupation in Norwegen," *Neue Zürcher Zeitung*, April 24, 1940.

20. François Kersaudy, *Norway 1940* (Lincoln, NE: University of Nebraska Press, 1990), 80, 100–101.

21. Kersaudy, *Norway 1940*, 159–224.

22. Verordnung über den Waffenbesitz im besetzten Gebiet, vom 10.5.1940, Verordnungsblatt (des Militärbefehlshabers) in Frankreich (VOBIF), MA 75 168, S. 4; Ordonnance du 10 mai 1940 sur la détention d'armes en territoire occupé, Verordnungsblatt für die besetzten französischen Gebiete, n° 1, 4 juillet 1940, 4; "Tout détenteur d'armes non déclarées sera puni de la peine de mort," *Le Matin*, June 27, 1940, 1. See Hans Umbreit, *Der Militärbefehlshaber in Frankreich 1940–1944* (Boppard am Rhein: Harald Boldt Verlag, 1968), 119–20.

1. All firearms and ammunition, hand grenades, explosive devices and other war matériel are to be surrendered.

   The delivery must take place within 24 hours at the nearest German military administrative headquarters or garrison, provided that other special arrangements have not been made. The mayors (heads of the district councils) must accept full responsibility for complete implementation. Commanding officers are authorized to approve exceptions.

2. Anyone who, contrary to this decree, possesses firearms, munitions, hand grenades, explosives and other war matériel will be sentenced to death or forced labor or in lesser cases to prison.

3. Anyone who commits any acts of violence whatsoever against the German army or its members will be punished with death.

The Commander in Chief of the Army[23]

The incredible victories were vividly depicted on the silver screen, with all the embellishments of Goebbels's propaganda, in the German Weekly Newsreel (*Die Deutsche Wochenschau*) for May 15.[24] In the newsreel, the instant Wehrmacht troops and tanks cross a border and enter a town, soldiers nail up a poster about two and a half by three feet feet in size. The camera scans the top of the double-columned poster, written in German on the left and Flemish on the right, with an eagle and swastika in the middle:

---

23. The text stated in French:

1° Toutes les armes à feu et munitions, grenades à main, explosifs et autres matériel de guerre sont à remettre.

La remise doit s'effectuer dans l'espace de 24 heures auprès du prochain commandement de place ou de camp, à moins qu'il n'y ait d'autres prescriptions d'ordre local. Les maires (préposés aux communes) sont tenus pleinement responsables de la mise en exécution exacte. Les Chefs de troupes sont autorisés à accorder des dispenses.

2° Toute personne possédant des armes à feu, munitions, grenades à main, explosifs ou autres matériel de guerre, à l'encontre de la présente ordonnance, sera puni de mort ou de travaux forcés, en cas plus légers de prison.

3° Toute personne commettant des actes de violence, quels qu'ils soient, contre l'Armée Allemande ou l'un de ses membres sera punie de mort.

Le Commandant supérieur de l'Armée.

24. Die deutsche Wochenschau, no. 506, 15 May 1940, UfA, Ton-Woche. Reproduced by International Historic Films, vol. 2, disk 1 (available at ihffilm.com/22902.html).

Regulations on Arms Possession in the Occupied Zone[25]

1. All firearms and ammunition, hand grenades, explosive devices and other war matériel are to be surrendered.

   The delivery must take place within 24 hours at the nearest German military administrative headquarters or garrison, provided that other special arrangements have not been made. The mayors (heads of the district councils) must accept full responsibility for complete implementation. Commanding officers are authorized to approve exceptions.

The bottom part of the poster, threatening the death penalty for violation, is not shown. Why show that part, given that the happy citizens wave as the artillery and infantry roll through the streets? Scenes then switch to onslaughts against Dutch and Belgian soldiers, and the Führer's message that this great war heralds the thousand-year Reich. A patriotic song mixed with the images and music of artillery barrages, Luftwaffe bombings, and tank assaults compose the Wagnerian grand finale.

Jack van der Geest, a young Dutchman at the time, described how a German convoy of tanks and trucks entered his town. Some soldiers raided the food shops, while others took over government offices and radio stations. He wrote:

> The soldiers confiscated all our guns. It wasn't hard to do. By a Dutch law passed in 1938, gun owners had to register their weapons at City Hall. The Queen had left the list behind in her rush to safety.
>
> Our own weapons were taken away late that Thursday afternoon. A knock sounded on our apartment door. . . . When Ma opened the door, we stared right into the barrel of a machine gun. A second soldier held a list which indicated the registration numbers of the guns each family possessed. I got our two weapons and handed them over without a word. People who were unable or unwilling to turn over their weapons were immediately dragged to the street and shot. We heard intermittent gunfire all evening. From our window I saw bloody bod-

---

25. *Verordnung über Waffenbesitz im besetzen Gebiet.*

ies lying in the street where soldiers left them as a reminder that they meant business.[26]

Holland capitulated on May 14 following the indiscriminate bombing of Rotterdam. The Germans broke through at Sedan, rushing through France. On May 26, the British Expeditionary Force and other Allied troops were evacuated from the beaches of Dunkirk. Belgium surrendered the next day.

In the onslaught, when Wehrmacht troops prevailed, the first order of business was to set up the *Kommandantur*, the German commander's office, and to search for and seize arms. The *Völkische Beobachter*, Hitler's newspaper, provided this explanation:

> Right after the occupation forces have moved on and the enemy forces have pulled back, the headquarters arrive. The field police is deployed, clears the area of criminal elements that are potentially still present or of snipers, establishes what booty was left behind, searches apartments and other buildings for weapons or explosives located there, closes off areas that are dangerous because of unsafe buildings or blind shells and in particular makes sure that easily recognizable road signs are set up in central locations.[27]

In June, as the French army retreated and the occupation expanded, Wehrmacht soldiers pasted large posters at major intersections. In the left column, in small print, were meticulous explanations designed to regulate conformity of the army of occupation and the population to the international law standards of the Hague Convention. In the right column, in large characters, appeared what has been called "the major focus of the army of occupation: arms."[28] Issued on June 20, the order stated:

---

26. Jack van der Geest, *Was God on Vacation? A WWII Autobiography* (Highlands Ranch, CO: Van der Geest Publishing, 1999), 10. "Dutch Shoot at Nazi," *New York Times*, November 22, 1940, 6, reported: "Because a potshot was taken at a German sentry Tuesday night, the Chief of Police today ordered all inhabitants of this famous university town [Leyden] to turn over all firearms by 10 p.m. Anyone found in possession of arms after that hour will be shot on sight, said the official decree. . . ."

27. "Das Leben in den besetzten Gebieten kehrt wieder," *Völkische Beobachter*, June 23, 1940.

28. Venner, *Armes de la Résistance*, 144.

1. All firearms, munitions, hand grenades, explosives and other war matériel must be immediately surrendered.
2. The surrender must be made within 24 hours at the nearest office of the headquarters of the line or the stage [*l'état-major de ligne ou d'étape*]. Mayors will have full responsibility for its immediate execution.
3. Anyone who, contrary to this decree, possesses firearms, munitions, hand grenades, explosives and other war matériel will be punished with either death or hard labor.
4. Anyone who commits acts of violence against the German army or its members in the occupied territory will be punished with death.
5. This decree does not apply to keepsake arms without practical use. Hunting guns must be delivered to the responsible mayor for safekeeping under the designation of the owner's name, profession, and address. Anyone who disregards this act of surrender is guilty of sabotage and will be punished with death.[29]

The decree was signed by the commander in chief of the army. It recognized a provision of the Hague Convention as applied to French soldiers by imposing the death penalty for violent resistance only in the occupied territory, not territory where combat continued. However, nothing in the Hague Convention explicitly authorized the death penalty for civilians who merely possessed arms without using them in any manner for resistance. Surrendering hunting guns and recording the owners' identities implied that they would be kept safely and returned after the war, which would turn out to be a false inducement. No reference was made to other civilian arms, which presumably would be confiscated by the Wehrmacht as spoils of war, even though they were private property.

Surrendering Guns

Northern and eastern parts of France occupied by Germany in 1914 had been subjected to similar confiscations, and the firearms were never returned. Now,

---

29. Venner, *Armes de la Résistance*, 144.

firearms were surrendered en masse in the town halls, police stations, and the *Kommandanturen*. They were not labeled by owners, who received no receipts, other than in Paris and a few other localities. Given the threat of capital punishment, there was no time to do so.[30] Many would not have left their identities for fear of being identified as a gun owner who could be accused of not surrendering all of their firearms.

But those who had registered their arms would be known to the authorities. To be sure, as seen earlier regarding experiences in the Ardennes, admonitions to register only had mixed results. As for those who had done so, some French police were already cooperating with the Germans. In Charleville, in June, the Germans enlisted a former police officer to run the police station, and he would spend the next year helping to discover and arrest escaped prisoners of war and members of intelligence networks.[31] He would have been fully cognizant of the need to conduct the far easier task of opening the files with the gun registration records.

The turning in of hunting guns at a town hall is shown in a rare photograph.[32] In the foreground, a French man shoulders a long-barreled gun as he walks and talks with another shouldering a double-barreled shotgun and carrying a bag perhaps filled with ammunition. A German soldier watches them intently. A dozen more soldiers with helmets and gear mill around near a troop transport truck, with no apparent concern. Another group of soldiers looking relaxed sit or stand on some stairs in the direction of where the French are walking. No danger is expected from a couple of complacent French citizens coming to turn in their hunting guns.

There is no way to know how many French people owned firearms or how many they owned before the war, how many turned in all of their firearms during the occupation, how many turned in some but not all, and how many turned in none. While German situation reports often included numbers of firearms turned in and seized, it would be impossible to construct an accurate

---

30. "La restitution des armes de chasse déposées aux autorités allemandes," Le Saint-Hubert, organe officiel du Saint-Hubert-Club de France, n° 4, 40e année, juillet-août 1941, 37.

31. Philippe Lecler, "Les auxiliares français de la police allemande: L'exemple du département des Ardennes," in Patrice Arnaud and Fabien Théofilakis, eds., *Gestapo et Polices Allemandes: France, Europe de l'Ouest 1939–1945* (Paris: CNRS Éditions, 2017), 76.

32. Venner, *Armes de la Résistance*, 146.

summary. Members of resistance groups would later complain of the shortage of arms, but prewar French law had banned firearms that would have been more useful for military purposes and no certain data exists on the numbers confiscated during the occupation, except to say that they were extraordinarily numerous.

The following personal accounts by people who became members of resistance groups reflect their observations that many did not turn in their firearms, implying the guns were for potential resistance, and their attitude that some who did turn in their arms were "cowards." An obvious reason exists for these impressions or biases. I solicited responses from then-elderly people who were veterans of the Resistance and members of their latter-day organizations. It would have been impossible to ask for information from people who identified as complacent or collaborationist. Needless to say, they had no association to keep their spirit alive after the liberation.

• • •

Yves Lenogré witnessed the surrender of arms in 1940, and would later become a member of both the FFC (*Forces Françaises Combattantes*, or Fighting French Forces) and the FFL (*Forces Françaises Libres*, or Free French Forces). Responding to my questionnaire to organizations of veterans of the Resistance in 2000, he wrote:[33]

> I noticed your announcement in issue #308 of our magazine *France Libre* [*Free France*]. I can tell you what I remember of the disarmament of civilians by the occupying forces in 1940. I was young then, but I knew that according to the decree-law of 1936, the Third French Republic prohibited the possession of arms of the first class, including of course rifles, pistols, revolvers, and other arms that were part of the regulatory equipment of armies around the world.[34] This therefore did indeed contribute to a significant restriction in the possession of arms.
>
> At that time, I lived in Quimperlé, in Brittany, which would become, in the next few years, a forbidden area, and of strategic impor-

33. Yves Lenogré of Périgueux, France, letter to author, January 15, 2000.
34. While the decree-law was imposed in 1935, the actual banned arms were specified in 1936. J.O., January 16, 1936, cited in Barbier, *Le délit*, 100.

tance with the construction of a submarine base in Lorient 15 km from us as the crow flies, and of the construction of the Lann Bihoué airport. It would become the future Luftwaffe center for observation and attack raids on the Allied convoys. This meant a huge military presence by the occupying forces. This, therefore, was our geographic location, part of the important section of territory dedicated to the future battle of the Atlantic.

According to my memories, the Feldgendarmerie [German military police], most likely under the watch of the Abwehr [German military intelligence service] attached to the armies, presided over operations to disarm civilians. After the formal notice to surrender arms was announced on posters and in newspapers, it took place in a big room of the courthouse. It seems to me that there was not a great number of Feldengendarmes present. There were also a few French gendarmes to set up the lists.

I could see that all hunting guns had to be turned in. There probably were guns of great value (some with flint and fulminate cap), all with black powder. I remember a Chassepot rifle from 1870, an old-fashioned arm indeed, but one that was loaded through the breech, with black powder.[35] I also saw different pistols, some of which were French small calibers from 1892,[36] and possibly some Browning automatics of varied calibers. There were also many bayonet sabers and varied daggers. All these made up a very diverse group of items, a little like a fair with a lot of curious objects, nothing very dangerous. Only the hunting guns could be of a certain danger.

I am telling you this, because I accompanied my mother to this depot to turn in a 6 mm single-shot rifle, an arm of little effect.

I don't have to tell you that in the stupor caused by our defeat, the manner in which the Werhmacht carried out this confiscation was only a small operation of little importance, since many citizens were taking great efforts to grease their arms and hide them in safe places.

---

35. The Chassepot, official name *Fusil modèle 1866*, was a bolt-action, breech-loading rifle used in the Franco-Prussian War of 1870–71.

36. The Modèle 1892 revolver, which chambered the weak 8 × 27 mm cartridge, was issued to French officers in World War I.

My father did so for his long 7 mm MAB 1938,[37] and a Model 35 6 mm automatic.[38] My father eventually registered at the BCRA (*Bureau Central de Renseignements et d'Action,* or Central Bureau of Information and Action), taking my mother and myself into the resistance movement for the Cohors-Asturies network, in 1943 and '44.[39]

• • •

Pierre Michel, born in 1922, was a student in Paris when the occupation began. From 1942–44, he was in charge of an information network in Normandy, went to Great Britain, and parachuted back into France three times. He would attend the École Spéciale Militaire de Saint-Cyr (ESM, or Special Military School of Saint-Cyr), France's preeminent military academy, and become a general.[40]

General Michel recalled that prewar French law made it difficult for civilians to obtain firearms. They mostly had hunting weapons in great numbers, but also souvenirs (mostly handguns) from the Great War, target arms in clubs, and arms obtained for professional reasons. He estimated that about 715,000 hunting arms were surrendered to the Germans, but many arms were hidden, often buried in yards, in oiled wraps.

Asked whether he was aware of people who possessed firearms in violation of the German decrees, he replied, "Yes, my parents—as an instinctive reaction against the occupying forces, in the hope they could use them someday. People hid their arms in varied caches depending on whether they lived in the city or the countryside."

• • •

---

37. The M91 Mannlicher-Carcano Modello 38 (the rechambered 7.35 mm version) was made by MAB (Manufacture d'Armes de Bayonne).

38. The Modèle 1935A was the French military sidearm at this time, which was actually in 7.65 mm.

39. This was a resistance network associated with General de Gaulle. See "Réseau Cohors-Asturies," sgmcaen.free.fr/resistance/reseau-cohors-asturies.htm; "Cohors-Asturies," https://fr.wikipedia.org/wiki/Cohors-Asturies.

40. Général Pierre Michel, Paris, response to author's questionnaire, October 18, 1999.

"Only the Cowards Complied"

Louis Charmeau, born in 1923, lived in the Saône-et-Loire department in the region of Bourgogne in eastern France, which would be divided between the occupied zone and Vichy France during the war. Regarding the German decree to surrender firearms, he said, "Few were turned in to the *Kommandatur*. . . . Only the cowards complied." In the department of Saône-et-Loire where he lived, houses were not searched for arms except upon denunciations. What about the fact that the Germans had access to French police records of licenses for firearms? "Of course, but a good hunter owns more than one arm. So . . . [h]e would turn one in, and, if possible, make it unusable or damage it with acid."[41]

Asked if he was aware of people who possessed firearms in violation of the German occupation decrees, Charmeau replied, "Yes. Why? Just as a reaction against the ban. . . . Underground caches were numerous, well protected in the countryside, where it was much easier to find many possible hiding places. Many [guns] were not turned in." But the consequences could be severe: "Persons who owned weapons from the 1914–18 World War could get in trouble . . . usually they were deported or taken hostage in the event of serious sabotages." Yet, he added, "One of my friends in 1941 was reported and shot after he flaunted a revolver while in town—it was more an act of defiance than of patriotism."

• • •

André Marchiset was born in 1925 at Raddon in the Haute-Saône department, located east of Paris, near the German border. In 1940, he was a pharmaceutical assistant in nearby Villersexel. He recalled the orders to surrender firearms: "These decrees were not taken all that seriously. At this time, in 1940, the Germans behaved properly, which was not the case later on. Those who obeyed these decrees were cowards, in my opinion."[42]

---

41. Louis Maurice Charmeau, président de l'Union Départementale des Combattants Volontaires de la Résistance, Bordeaux, France, letter to author, June 10, 2003.

42. André Marchiset (born January 25, 1925), Raddon, Haute-Saône, France, response to author's questionnaire, no date.

However, he added, "A few hunters had several guns; they never handed over the best one." Others did not comply at all. "My father, a brigadier for the forestry department, supervised six wardens. None of them turned in his revolver to the Germans." The types of arms kept by civilians and by members of the Resistance included 6.35 and 7.65 mm revolvers, hunting guns, and military rifles from the Great War.

• • •

A Defeatist Mentality

French authorities acted as agents of the Wehrmacht to discourage resistance and confiscate firearms. Bernard Lecornu, the prefect for Châteaubriant in northwest France, was confronted by an old colonel, the president of the local veterans group, who demanded, "Do you have arms to distribute to us? Not only that, but you will bring your hunting guns and will block the road with plows, tractors, and all of the heavy obstacles that you can find." Lecornu objected, "But we will be considered illegal snipers (*francs-tireurs*)!" The colonel replied, "No, because we will prepare armbands for you!"[43] If captured, *francs-tireurs* could be shot on the spot, while uniformed soldiers were entitled to be treated as prisoners of war. Whether armbands would have sufficed was problematic.

The prefect thought resistance to be laughable. Instead, he busied himself facilitating a smooth occupation, seeing to the quartering of the troops, putting up signs, coordinating the movement of vehicles and pedestrians, blacking out windows and lights, banning gatherings, enforcing curfews, and—naturally—administering the confiscation of hunting guns.[44]

Variations of the Nazi gun decrees would be made throughout the years of occupation. One such poster is on display today at the Museum of the Order of the Liberation in Paris.[45] Unlike the above decree, this version adds radio

43. Bernard Lecornu, *Un Préfet sous l'Occupation allemande: Chateaubriant, Saint-Nazaire, Tulle* (Paris: France-Empire, 1984), 19–20.

44. Lecornu, *Préfet sous l'Occupation allemande*, 30–31.

45. *Ordonnance concernant la détention d'armes et de radio-émetteurs dans les territoires occupés*, on display at the *Musée de l'Ordre de la Libération*, Paris. Photograph of poster in author's possession.

transmitters to the list of verboten objects, and does not exempt keepsake arms or provide that hunting guns would be tagged with the owner's identity:

Decree Concerning the Possession of Arms and Radio Transmitters in the Occupied Territories

1. All firearms and all sorts of munitions, hand grenades, explosives and other war matériel must be surrendered immediately.

   Delivery must take place within 24 hours to the closest *Kommandantur* [German commander's office] unless other arrangements have been made. Mayors will be held strictly responsible for the execution of this order. The [German] troop commanders may allow exceptions.

2. Anyone found in possession of firearms, munitions, hand grenades, or other war matériel will be sentenced to death or forced labor or in lesser cases prison.

3. Anyone in possession of a radio or a radio transmitter must surrender it to the closest German military authority.

4. All those who would disobey this order or would commit any act of violence in the occupied lands against the German army or against any of its troops will be condemned to death.

The Commander in Chief of the Army

This poster is relatively small and may not have been sufficiently conspicuous to be seen. It has no information on the time or even date of its issuance. The French would have had no idea when the twenty-four-hour clock started ticking—a firearm surrendered a day or even an hour late would have subjected its possessor to the death penalty. To be sure, in this early period of total French defeat before a resistance movement was organized, the threat of the death penalty was more bark than bite, carried out more often to frighten gun owners into submission than to execute them.

Hiding Guns

While many complied with the orders of the German authorities, others hid their arms for multiple reasons. Besides those contemplating resistance, these recalcitrant gun owners were attached to their property, which had value for collecting and for hunting. They buried guns in gardens, and concealed them ingeniously behind cupboards and under sheds.[46] Historian Henri Michel noted:

> The "occupied" were careful to keep such personal weapons as they had; a revolver, a sporting rifle or some trophy of the 1914–18 war was easy to conceal in a barn or granary. When the occupying power issued orders to hand them in, the acquiescent or fearful minority obeyed but many more refused to comply.[47]

In the Haut-Marnais, a department in the Champagne-Ardenne region of northeastern France, there were plenty of hunting guns—about ten thousand hunting licenses were issued annually before 1939—as well as a number of war souvenirs in good condition. How many were surrendered is unknown, but a great deal of weapons were secreted. A Maxim machine gun was found in a stream in the early 1980s.[48]

• • •

Hiding guns from the Germans could be a cat-and-mouse game, and rust would prove to be a formidable enemy. Resistance member Jacques Demange wrote to me about his experiences in the village of Mont-sur-Meurthe, located in northeastern France.[49]

> The first priority for the Germans was to collect all the arms scattered in the homes as soon as possible. Of course, it was difficult to escape it. As far as I am concerned, my father was a hunter, and owned two shotguns, one of which was old. Of course, it is the latter that I registered at the City Hall. We had a very short time to act.
>
> The way the Germans operated was simple, and as follows: They went to the city hall and demanded the names of the residents of the village who were hunters, and then threats followed. However, a great

---

46. Venner, *Armes de la Résistance*, 148.

47. Michel, *Shadow War*, 82.

48. Colonel Henry Dutailly, "Les armes des maquis Haut-Marnais," *Revue de la Société des Amis du Musée de l'Armée*, n° 109, juin 1995, 20.

49. Jacques Demange, vice-président de l'association d'anciens combattants du village, Mont-sur-Meurthe, France, letter to author, June 3, 2003.

number of arms were hidden. For my part, I greased and oiled my father's shotgun, as well as a collection of Arab daggers and a G-35 revolver. I carefully wrapped everything before placing them in a wooden box, which I buried in the cow pasture.

Capitulation

The reasons why the French forces were defeated are numerous. Germany's superior infantry and panzers could simply go around the bunkers of the Maginot Line, and France's air force was no match for the Luftwaffe. French intelligence failed dramatically to anticipate how Germany would wage this blitzkrieg.[50] Among countless other reasons, one soldier exclaimed, "We had the guns but the wrong ammunition! . . . They expected men with rifles to hold up tanks."[51]

The situation was looking bleak when the French war cabinet met on May 24, 1940. Prime Minister Paul Reynaud asked General Louis-Antoine Colson whether more young men should be called up. "The General replied that there would be neither arms, clothes, nor blankets for these young recruits." About existing troops that were being reorganized, he added, "Not even enough rifles were available; at the outside there were five thousand, and they were of an old pattern."[52] While Reynaud wanted to fight on, already General Maxime Weygand, commander of the French armies, and Marshal Philippe Pétain began to demand an armistice.[53]

The Luftwaffe bombed Paris on June 3, the government fled to Tours on the 10th. The Wehrmacht entered the city on the 14th, and its victory march under the Arc de Triomphe was filmed and widely shown. Three out of five million inhabitants had fled in panic, and there was no resistance.[54] Because

50. Stephen A. Schuker, "Seeking a Scapegoat: Intelligence and Grand Strategy in France, 1919–1940," chap. 3 in Jonathan Haslam and Karina Urbach eds., *Secret Intelligence in the European States System, 1918–1989* (Stanford, CA: University Press Scholarship Online, 2014).

51. Ninetta Jucker, *Curfew in Paris: A Record of the German Occupation* (London: The Hogarth Press, 1960), 53.

52. Reynaud, *Thick of the Fight*, 380.

53. Reynaud, *Thick of the Fight*, 382.

54. David Pryce-Jones, *Paris in the Third Reich: A History of the German Occupation, 1940–1944* (New York: Holt, Rinehart & Winston, 1981), 3.

of the Nazi-Soviet nonaggression pact, the French Communist Party had opposed the war and encouraged friendship with the Germans when they occupied Paris.[55] While patriots of both left and right would later create resistance movements, the majority adopted a wait-and-see attitude.

Meanwhile the government had moved on to Bordeaux. On June 11, Churchill flew in to meet with the war cabinet, urging that they "wage a kind of guerilla warfare in various parts of France, if co-ordinated war became impossible." Pétain replied that the result would be "the destruction of the country." Reynaud resigned, and on the 16th Pétain was appointed in his place. Pierre Laval reemerged to join the new government and to assist with negotiating an armistice.[56]

On June 17, Pétain broadcast to France: "With a heavy heart, I am telling you today that it is necessary to bring fighting to an end."[57] As the newspaper *Le Matin* put it: "Marshal Pétain, the new Prime Minister of the Council of the French Republic, announces in a radio broadcast to the French people that France must give up her arms."[58] Jean Guéhenno, a Parisian man of letters who kept a copious diary, wrote, "There, it's over. At half past noon an old man who doesn't even have the voice of a man anymore, but talks like an old woman, informed us that last night he had asked for peace."[59]

A few hours after the broadcast, General Alphonse Joseph Georges complained that Pétain had "broken the last resistance of the French army." Colonel Passy (codename for André Dewavrin) noted that near Brest "the ditches along the roads [are] strewn with arms lamentably abandoned by men shouting: 'The war is over! Pétain has just said so. Why get killed when the war is over?'" The general commanding the eighteenth military district at Bordeaux issued this order: "Disarm everyone. . . . Consign officers and men to quarters. Remain where you are, without firing. Officers who do not

55. Shirer, *Collapse of the Third Republic*, 849.

56. Shirer, *Collapse of the Third Republic*, 848; Reynaud, *Thick of the Fight*, 486.

57. Reynaud, *Thick of the Fight*, 558.

58. "A France Doit Mettre Bas Les Armes déclare le maréchal Pétain," *Le Matin*, June 18, 1940, 1.

59. Jean Guéhenno, *Diary of the Dark Years, 1940–1944: Collaboration, Resistance, and Daily Life in Occupied Paris*, trans. David Ball (New York: Oxford University Press, 2014), 1.

execute these orders will be hauled before a court-martial!" A soldier who said, "I had never fired a rifle before," shot an officer who wanted to fight.[60]

"Order and Security"

In Munich that same day, Hitler told Mussolini that the French would more readily obey the occupier's orders if executed indirectly by their own countrymen.[61] The strategy for collaboration was set.

It was still June 17 when General Johannes Blaskowitz was appointed as the military commander in France (*Militärbefehlshaber in Frankreich*, or MBF), which headquartered itself in the luxurious Hotel Majestic in Paris. That was on the Avenue Kléber, a five-minute stroll from the Arc de Triomphe at the head of the Champs-Élysées. He would be replaced by General Alfred Streccius on June 30.[62] Regional commanders (*Bezirkchefs*) in Saint-Germain, Dijon, Angers, Bordeaux, and most significantly greater Paris (*Groß-Paris*) served under the MBF. Under each of these were field commanders (*Feldkommandanten*), who exercised administrative supervision over the prefect of the department, which in turn formed the backbone of the French administration. At the local level were town commanders (*Ortskommandanten*).[63]

SS-Brigadeführer Werner Best was appointed chief of the departmental administration (*Abteilung Verwaltung*) of the administrative staff (*Verwaltungsstabs*) under the MBF, where he would serve through mid-1942. He supervised fifteen bureaus, such as General Administration, Propaganda, Police, and Justice, these last two being key to the repressive apparatus.[64] Best had gained notoriety in Germany in 1931 before Hitler came to power as author of plans for the seizure of power by the storm troopers (*Sturmabteilung* or

60. Shirer, *Collapse of the Third Republic*, 854–56, 876.

61. Michel, *Shadow War*, 197.

62. Laub, *After the Fall*, 41, 43.

63. Werner Best, "Die deutsche Militärverwaltung in Frankreich," *Reich, Volksordnung, Lebensraum* (1941) 1:29, 55–57.

64. Best, "Die deutsche Militärverwaltung," 54. See generally Ulrich Herbert, *Best: Biographische Studien über Radikalismus, Weltanschauung und Vernunft, 1903-1989* (Bonn: J. H. W. Dietz Nachfolger, 1996), Chapter 4; Ahlrich Meyer, *Die deutsche Besatzung in Frankreich 1940–1944: Widerstandsbekämpfung und Judenverfolgung* (Darmstadt, Germany: Wissenschaftliche Buchgesellschaft, 2000), Chapter 1.

SA) in which anyone failing to surrender firearms within twenty-four hours would be shot on the spot.[65] As chief legal adviser to the Gestapo in 1935, he forbade police from issuing firearm licenses to Jews.[66]

Best would write a description of the German military administration in France in which "order and security" was foremost. The list of decrees under that category began with the ban on possession of weapons of May 10, 1940, followed by the imposition of German criminal law, surrender of radio transmitters, ban on public assemblies, measures against Jews, restrictions on hunting, and other repressive measures.[67] After helping oversee the policy in occupied France to execute people who neglected to hand in their firearms, in 1942 Best would be appointed German Reich plenipotentiary in Denmark, where he again implemented a decree threatening execution for anyone not turning in their guns in twenty-four hours.[68]

Charles de Gaulle began broadcasting from London on June 18, 1940.[69] Seeming like wishful thinking, his appeal on the BBC proclaimed that "France has lost a battle, but she has not lost the war, for this is a world war."[70] Jean Guéhenno wrote, "Last night the voice of General de Gaulle on London radio. In the midst of this vile disaster, what a joy to hear a voice with some pride in it at last: 'I, General de Gaulle, I am asking . . . The flame of French resistance cannot go out. . . .'"[71]

---

65. Martin Loiperdinger, "Das Blutnest vom Boxheimer Hof," in Eike Hennig, ed., *Hessen unterm Hakenkreuz* (Frankfurt am Main: Insel Verlag, 1983), 435.

66. Betr.: Erteilung von Waffenscheinen an Juden, preußische geheime Staatspolizei, B.Nr. I G - 352/35 (16. Dezember 1935). DCP 0072, Bundesarchiv Lichterfelde, R 58/276. See Halbrook, *Gun Control in the Third Reich*, 111–13.

67. Best, "Die deutsche Militärverwaltung," 64–65.

68. Harold Flender, *Rescue in Denmark* (Princeton University Press, 1963; repr., Washington, DC: Holocaust Library, n.d.), 40–41; Werner Best, *Dänemark in Hitlers Hand: Der Bericht des Reichsbevollmächtigten Werner Best*, ed. Siegfried Matlok (Husum, Germany: Husum Druck GmbH, 1988), 52–53.

69. Pryce-Jones, *Paris in the Third Reich*, 16.

70. Michel, *Shadow War*, 68.

71. Guéhenno, *Diary of the Dark Years*, 1.

The Armistice

For many, the flame was extinguished. On June 19, the French commanding general at La Rochelle issued this order: "Disarm everyone. Collect all arms and ammunition in one place. Consign officers and troops to quarters. Wait where you are without firing or offering resistance of any kind."[72]

Pétain appointed General Charles Huntziger to head the delegation to negotiate the armistice. The Franco-German Armistice Agreement was signed on June 22 at Compiègne, in the same railway car where the Germans signed the armistice ending the Great War.[73] As shown in German newsreels, Hitler made a jubilant appearance, then left to view the Eiffel Tower and other Paris landmarks.

France was largely divided into the occupied zone administered by the German military commander, including northern and western France, and the unoccupied zone, which would be ruled by Pétain from Vichy.[74] The German military commander in Belgium administered two French departments at the northwest border, Italy controlled a small zone in southeastern France, and Alsace and Lorraine were returned to Germany after the armistice. The agreement required French collaboration with the occupation force:

> In the occupied parts of France the German Reich exercises all rights of an occupying power; the French Government obligates itself to support with every means the regulations resulting from the exercise of these rights and to carry them out with the aid of French administration.
>
> All French authorities and officials of the occupied territory, therefore, are to be promptly informed by the French Government to comply

72. Shirer, *Collapse of the Third Republic*, 873.

73. Shirer, *Collapse of the Third Republic*, 864, 878.

74. Articles II and III, "Armistice Agreement Between the German High Command of the Armed Forces and French Plenipotentiaries, Compiègne, France, June 22, 1940," avalon.law.yale.edu/wwii/frgearm.asp. Source: U.S. Department of State, *Documents on German Foreign Policy 1918–1945*, Series D (Washington, DC : U.S. Government Printing Office, 1956), 9:671-76. See also "Les Textes Officiels Des Contrats D'Armistice Franco-Allemand Et Italo-Français," *Le Matin*, June 27, 1940, 1.

with the regulations of the German military commanders and to co-operate with them in a correct manner.[75]

Collaboration, in which the French police and bureaucracy would enforce German commands, would make for an easier occupation. Direct German military rule, such as existed in conquered Poland, was infinitely harsher, involving the physical elimination of entire classes of people.[76] But collaboration would entail its own costs, moral and human, and would enlist the collaborators in the Nazi cause.[77]

The armistice further provided that French armed forces "are to be demobilized and disarmed," excepting "only those units which are necessary for maintenance of domestic order," which Germany and Italy would decide.[78] "Weapons, munitions, and war apparatus of every kind remaining in the unoccupied portion of France are to be stored and/or secured under German and/or Italian control—so far as not released for the arming allowed to French units."[79] In addition to forbidding the French government to allow any of its armed forces to fight against Germany, the armistice provided that "[t]he French Government will forbid French citizens to fight against Germany in the service of States with which the German Reich is still at war. French citizens who violate this provision are to be treated by German troops as insurgents."[80]

That last provision meant that French who resisted with arms would do so "unlawfully," and would not need to be taken as prisoners of war, but could be executed on the spot. No right to defense of the community against tyranny would be recognized.[81] As events would turn out, some members of both the right and the left would join the Resistance, and they well understood the risks if caught or captured. Others of both political spectrums would choose the paths either of passivity or of collaboration.

---

75. Armistice Agreement, Article III.

76. Mark Mazower, *Hitler's Empire: How the Nazis Ruled Europe* (New York: Penguin Press, 2008), 89–96.

77. Mazower, *Hitler's Empire,* 416–45.

78. Armistice Agreement, Article IV.

79. Armistice Agreement, Article VI.

80. Armistice Agreement, Article X.

81. See Peter Lieb, *Konventioneller Krieg oder NS-Weltanschauungskrieg? Kriegführung und Partisanenbekämpfung in Frankreich 1943/44* (Munich: R. Oldenbourg Verlag, 2007), 236–39.

More Death Threats

Neither the armistice nor the Hague Convention explicitly authorized the death penalty for civilians in mere possession of firearms, although both gave great latitude to the authority of the occupying power. Disarming a conquered population for the security of the occupier might be justified under the traditional laws of war, but executing gun owners not acting as *francs-tireurs* (combatants without uniforms) would be hard to justify.

Just five days after the armistice was signed, *Le Matin* published the decree threatening execution of anyone who failed to surrender all firearms within twenty-four hours, some six weeks after its original issuance, under the headline: "Anyone in possession of unregistered arms shall receive the death penalty."[82] This itself was misleading, in that firearms registered under French law were not exempt. The decree stated:

**Decree concerning the possession of arms
in occupied territory, dated May 10, 1940**

1. Any firearms and ammunition, hand grenades, explosives or other material shall be surrendered.

    This surrender shall be done within 24 hours at the next place or camp of command, unless other prescriptions or local orders have been given. The mayors (officials in charge of town districts) shall be held fully responsible to carry out this decree as it is prescribed. Commanders of troops are authorized to give exemptions.

2. Anyone in possession of firearms, ammunition, hand grenades, explosives or other war matériel, counter to the said decree, shall receive the death penalty or hard labor, or, in less serious cases, jail.

3. Anyone committing any acts of violence against the German army or any of its members shall be put to death.

The Army High Command

---

82. "Tout détenteur d'armes non déclarées sera puni de la peine de mort," *Le Matin*, June 27, 1940, 1.

A footnote to the above requirement that firearms be turned in within twenty-four hours stated: "That is to say from the publication or announcement of this decree." However, no certain way existed to know what time or even the date the decree was published or announced, meaning that a person who sought to surrender a firearm days, hours, or even minutes late was subject to the death penalty.

The *New York Times* reported from Paris on the same day that "German Army Decrees Death for Those Retaining Arms and Radio Senders."[83] The article stated:

> Two severe orders were issued this morning by the military authorities; one, signed by General Walther von Brauchitsch, commander in chief of the German armies, demands that all radio sending apparatus, even that made by amateurs, be turned over to the nearest German military post. . . .
>
> The other order, signed by the Army High Command, concerns firearms. All firearms, hand grenades, explosives and other war material must be turned over to the military authorities. Any one not obeying the order is liable to death, hard labor or a prison term.

Such orders were widely disseminated in public places. But as Agnès Humbert, a member of the Resistance, noted, "[A]s fast as German posters are put up in Paris they are slashed and torn down again. The people of Paris are rebelling already."[84] But that was wishful thinking. Slashing some posters in a few parts of town expressed defiance, but hardly constituted rebellion in a manner that would threaten the occupation. "Resistance" is a word that would have many meanings, and it would be a long road ahead to liberate France.

About "those gray men I begin to pass in the streets," Guéhenno wrote, "[a]n invasion of rats."[85] The *New York Times* observed:

> The best way to sum up the disciplinary laws imposed upon France by the German conqueror is to say that the Nazi decrees reduce the

83. "German Army Decrees Death for Those Retaining Arms and Radio Senders," *New York Times*, July 1, 1940, 3.

84. Agnès Humbert, *Résistance: A Woman's Journal of Struggle and Defiance in Occupied France*, trans. Barbara Mellor (New York: Bloomsbury, 2008), 8.

85. Guéhenno, *Diary of the Dark Years*, 2.

French people to as low a condition as that occupied by the German people. Military orders now forbid the French to do things which the German people have not been allowed to do since Hitler came to power. To own radio senders or to listen to foreign broadcasts, to organize public meetings and distribute pamphlets, to disseminate anti-German news in any form, to retain possession of firearms—all these things are prohibited for the subjugated people of France, as they have been verboten these half dozen years to the people of Germany.[86]

Ambiguities of International Law?

Even with the glorious victory over France, the German people were not fully behind the Führer, as the negative answer to the following rhetorical question made clear: "[W]ill Hitler now abolish the Gestapo and set up a free press?"[87]

To be sure, Hitler was at the height of his popularity for undoing the results of the Great War and getting revenge for the Versailles Treaty. But the propaganda films of cheering crowds could not hide the years of repression and dictatorship.

Nazi aggression violated numerous tenets of international law. Did the seizure of civilian firearms under threat of the death penalty violate international law?

The Hague Convention Respecting the Laws and Customs of War on Land of 1907 was signed by Germany and most powers. It includes several provisions pertinent to possession of arms. Article 1 of the convention provides that the laws and rights of war apply not only to armies, but also to militia and volunteer corps under a command. Members needed to have "a fixed distinctive emblem recognizable at a distance" and to "carry arms openly."[88] Under Article 2, inhabitants of a territory "who, on the approach of the enemy, spontaneously take up arms to resist the invading troops without having had time to organize themselves in accordance with Article 1" are regarded as belligerents if they carry arms openly.[89]

86. "Topics of the Times: Their Common Fate," *New York Times*, July 2, 1940, 4.

87. "Topics of the Times," *New York Times*, 4.

88. Charles I. Bevans, comp., *Treaties and Other International Agreements of the United States of America 1776–1949* (Washington, DC: U.S. Government Printing Office, 1968), 1:643.

89. Beavens, *Treaties and Other International Agreements*, 644.

If a territory is occupied, the occupier does not have unlimited power, and in particular must respect "the lives of persons" and cannot confiscate private property.[90] Article 53 of the convention provides:

> An army of occupation can only take possession of cash, funds, and realizable securities which are strictly the property of the State, depôts of arms, means of transport, stores and supplies, and, generally, all movable property belonging to the State which may be used for military operations.
>
> All appliances, whether on land, at sea, or in the air, adapted for the transmission of news, or for the transport of persons or things, exclusive of cases governed by naval laws, depôts of arms, and, generally, all kinds of ammunition of war, may be seized, even if they belong to private individuals, but must be restored and compensation fixed when peace is made.[91]

Under the first paragraph above, the occupying force may seize government property, including "depôts of arms." Under the second, "depôts of arms" and "all kinds of ammunition of war" may be seized from private individuals. It is unclear that these terms would include single or small numbers of arms, especially hunting and target arms, and ammunition that is not of a military type. Moreover, the power to "seize" depôts of arms in no manner suggests a duty of the civilian voluntarily to surrender arms or a power under the convention to execute the owner thereof after the seizure. Indeed, soldiers engaged in hostilities who are captured and disarmed cannot be executed because of their prior possession of arms. What would justify execution of a nonbelligerent civilian for mere possession of an arm?

To be sure, the Hague Convention included an ambiguous preamble declaring that "in cases not included in the Regulations adopted by them, the inhabitants and the belligerents remain under the protection and the rule of the principles of the law of nations, as they result from the usages established among civilized peoples, from the laws of humanity, and the dictates of the

---

90. Beavens, *Treaties and Other International Agreements*, Article 46, 651.
91. Beavens, *Treaties and Other International Agreements*, Article 53, 652–53.

public conscience."[92] This clause had been introduced by Fyodor Fyodorovich Martens, the Russian delegate at the Hague Peace Conference of 1899, as a compromise between the Great Powers such as Russia and Germany, who deemed civilians who take up arms to be treated as *francs-tireurs* subject to execution, and the small states like Belgium and Switzerland, who saw them to be patriots doing their duty and entitled to be treated as prisoners of war.[93]

Despite the humanistic phrases in the Martens Clause, historically occupying powers have disarmed civilians and severely punished those who fail to obey diktats of all kinds. That is the very nature of what it means to be an occupied country. The dilemma faced by the Germans would be how to repress the French population to keep them subjugated without doing so to such extremes that would spark resistance.

92. Beavens, *Treaties and Other International Agreements*, Preamble to Convention, 633.

93. Jeffrey Kahn, "'Protection and Empire': The Martens Clause, State Sovereignty, and Individual Rights," *Virginia Journal of International Law* 56:1, 23–25 (2016).

4

Occupation and Collaboration

THE MOST PROMINENT French collaborator with the Nazis would be none other than former Prime Minister Pierre Laval, who had decreed firearm registration in 1935, and who joined the government as minister of state and deputy prime minister in late June 1940.[1] Laval spearheaded the destruction of parliamentary democracy and the Republic, introducing a dictatorship with Pétain at its head and Laval as the real power and successor behind him. This dictatorship was supported both by the Socialists and by the rightist parties.[2] Laval told French senators that the constitution must be "modeled upon the totalitarian states," including the introduction of concentration camps.[3] Laval wielded power until December when he would be fired, but he made a comeback later.

Jean Guéhenno quipped in his diary, "Pétain and Laval do not speak for us. Their word does not commit us to anything and cannot dishonor us."[4]

On July 14, Winston Churchill spoke these words: "This is no war of chieftains or of princes, of dynasties or national ambition; it is a war of peoples and of causes. There are vast numbers, not only in this Island but in every land, who will render faithful service in this war, but whose names will never be known, whose deeds will never be recorded. This is a War of the Unknown

---

1. Warner, *Pierre Laval*, 428–29; Pierre Laval, *The Diary of Pierre Laval* (New York: Charles Scribner's Sons, 1948), 63.

2. Shirer, *Collapse of the Third Republic*, 903–11, 919–46.

3. Warner, *Pierre Laval*, 197.

4. Guéhenno, *Diary of the Dark Years*, 3.

Warriors. . . ."[5] A "shadow army" of resistance groups rose all over occupied Europe, and it would contribute to the final victory.[6] Countless unknown French citizens in the coming years would pick up arms and form the Resistance.

• • •

Forms of Resistance

Resistance did not, and could not, begin with armed actions, but took many individual forms. In July, Marcel Demnet began acting as a human smuggler in Vierzon-Forges (Cher), the only city in France to be bisected by the demarcation line between occupied France and Vichy France. A young man employed at the town hall at the time, he responded to my questionnaire in 2002. In Demnet's experience, before the war those who possessed firearms were mostly hunters, and the acquisition of a hunting gun was not regulated. Only members of shooting clubs could acquire revolvers and pistols after authorization by the prefect. There was a shooting club in Vierzon.[7]

Regarding the German decrees to surrender firearms, Demnet noted, "It doesn't seem to me that in general the French in the occupied zone overwhelmingly obeyed these orders. The French are rebellious by nature and do the opposite of what one asks them to do. With the coming of the Germans, it was well within their temperament to engage in passive disobedience."

What arms were kept by civilians and the Resistance? Demnet's response: "Hunting guns and military rifles recovered after the debacle by farsighted French!" He added, "When the decrees appeared, some surrendered them to the occupation authorities but the others, certainly the most numerous, took care to grease them thoroughly, to slip them into protective cases, and to bury them or to hide them in places where they were more or less sure that the Germans would not be going to look for them—maybe with the hope that one day it would serve a good cause!"

---

5. Guillain de Bénouville, *The Unknown Warriors*, trans. Lawrence G. Blochman (New York: Simon & Schuster, 1949), 8.

6. Michel, *Shadow War*, 15.

7. Marcel Demnet, response to author's questionnaire, November 13, 2002.

For the next two years, Demnet worked for the Resistance to help as many as nine hundred people move clandestinely across the border. A favorite ruse for smugglers was to stage fake funeral convoys between the church (in the occupied zone) and the cemetery (in the free zone) over the Cher bridge.[8] Then he was arrested by the Gestapo. He eventually would be released but went underground when he was about to be drafted as a forced laborer for the Germans, only to reappear to fight for the liberation of Vierzon in 1944.

This pattern repeated itself countless times. The Paronnaud family, farmers from Annezay in southwestern France, handed in their hunting weapons but tried to hide their new rifle. The mayor, already collaborating, threatened to denounce them to the occupation authorities. Their teenage sons, Yves and Robert, joined with others to form the nucleus of a resistance group. Before long their activities consisted of recovering hunting weapons, cutting Wehrmacht cables, hiding wanted people, collecting information on German troops, and writing anti-Nazi graffiti. They fought for the Resistance through the end of the war.[9]

• • •

Only Germans May Hunt

Meanwhile, the Germans were settling in for a comfortable stay. From Paris, on July 31, the *Chef der Militärverwaltung in Frankreich* (MVF, or head of the military administration in France), decreed that the French could not hunt because they could not possess firearms, but that German soldiers could pursue game. Hunting would use the country's resources to help meet the needs of the Wehrmacht and the German war economy.[10]

The way was thus paved for the plunder not only of the natural resources of the occupied country—its wild game—but also of its citizens' firearms. Firearms of all kinds were confiscated not only to prevent any resistance, but

---

8. See histoire-en-questions.fr/vichy et occupation/ligne de demarcation/vierzon.html.

9. "Paronnaud Yves," Mémoire et Espoirs de la Résistance, Association des Amis de la Fondation de la Résistance, www.memoresist.org/resistant/paronnaud-yves/.

10. BA/MA, RW 35/326, Oberbefehlshaber des Heeres, Vorschriften für die Jagdnutzung im Bereich des Chefs der Militärverwaltung in Frankreich, 31. Juli 1940.

also to be transferred to German soldiers for hunting and other purposes. Such orders were only a more organized form of the same kind of looting that took place by warring aggressors in ancient times. In the years of occupation, it was German policy to loot everything that could be looted, art and wine being conspicuous examples,[11] but most prominent being labor and economic resources. As would be found in the Nürnberg (Nuremberg) trials, the pillaging of private property in all of the occupied countries was unlimited.[12]

However, such organized theft was not yet taking place as occupation authorities still observed some semblance of international law. An August 11 order of the Army High Command, General Staff of the Army, applicable in occupied France, Netherlands, and Belgium provided for "Weapons Confiscated from Private Citizens" as follows:

> Pursuant to the Military Administration in France, in addition to captured weapons, Local and District Military Administrative Headquarters have turned over to military police staff weapons and ammunition confiscated from private citizens (mostly hunting rifles). These weapons will probably be returned to their owners later because they are not captured property. They must be separated from the captured property and held for pickup by Local and District Military Administrative Headquarters. Make sure that any documents showing ownership remain with these weapons.[13]

However, such registration of private property would prove illusory. A Nazi organization known as the *Einsatzstab Reichsleiter Rosenberg* (ERR) was at work registering Jewish cultural assets supposedly to protect them, but with the proviso that the Führer would decide their disposition. Historian Thomas Laub relates, "They described the registration of art as a measure comparable to military decrees ordering Frenchmen to register arms that could be used in

---

11. Lynn H. Nicholas, *The Rape of Europa* (New York: Random House, 1994), 119–51; see Don and Petie Kladstrup, *Wine & War: The French, the Nazis, and the Battle for France's Greatest Treasure* (New York: Random House, 2001).

12. *United States v. Goering*, 6 Federal Rules Decisions 69, 120 (International Military Tribunal in Session at Nürnberg 1946–47).

13. BA/MA, RW 35/544, Oberkommando des Heeres, Generalstab des Heeres, Generalquartiermeister, Sichergestellte Waffen aus Privatbesitz, 11. November 1940.

a future conflict."[14] Such registration was just the first step to the confiscation of all such property.

Not foreseeing the harsh occupation to come, gun owner organizations promoted measures to identify people who had surrendered their firearms so they could be returned when peace came. The *Saint-Hubert-Club de France*, a hunting association, and *l'Union Fédérale des Sociétés de Tir aux Armes de Chasse*, a society of target shooters and hunters, supported the sending of questionnaires nationwide to do so. Monsieur Glandaz of the Saint Hubert Club met with Jean Chiappe, president of the municipal council of Paris, to implement the plan, which spread to departments throughout the occupied zone.[15] Events would prove the scheme to be naive indeed.

Le Matin repeatedly published a communiqué from the prefecture of police headlined "Possession of Arms in Occupied Territory" beginning on August 13. It recited the German decrees of May 10, ordering the surrender of firearms, and June 20, ordering that hunting guns be included, and noted that the orders had been published in the *Moniteur des ordonnances du commandant d'armes de Paris* (Bulletin of Orders from the Military Commander of Paris), July 4, 1940. The communiqué concluded: "Following the return of many people to their homes, it is important once again to turn the population's attention to their obligation to surrender their firearms, while reminding everyone that the offenders shall face serious punishments according to the *Moniteurs des ordonnances* provisions."[16]

The duty to surrender arms was repeated in an edict dated August 20 of the MVF, who added that firearms must be turned in to the German authorities, while hunting guns must be surrendered to the mayors, who would keep them in custody. This applied to both usable and unusable firearms. All hunting guns and ammunition would then be transferred to the district military administrative headquarters, which would set up hunting-gun depots.[17]

---

14. Laub, *After the Fall*, 78.

15. "À nos adhérents," in *Le Saint-Hubert*, organe officiel du Saint-Hubert-Club de France, n°4, 39e année, décembre 1940, 33.

16. "La Detention D'Armes Dans La Region Occupee," *Le Matin*, August 13, 1940, 1. Reprinted in issues dated August 27, September 3 and 10.

17. BA/MA, RH 36/430, Erlass des Oberbefehlshabers des Heeres, Chef der Militärverwaltung in Frankreich, über die Verwaltung der Jagdwaffen und Jagdmunition in dem Bereich des Chefs der Militärverwaltung in Frankreich, vom 20. August 1940.

The deadline for reporting the central registration of hunting guns and locations of depots would be extended from October 1 to November 10. Usable hunting guns were to be categorized as rifles, shotguns, or combination rifle/shotguns. The rounds of ammunition were to be counted.[18]

Along with enjoying French wine, women, and song, German soldiers wanted to try their luck at hunting. For the French, hunting was ended. As reflected in an August 29 order, the MVF repeated that "the local population in the occupied territory must surrender all hunting guns. Only members of the German Army may hunt." The soldiers were admonished strictly to abide by the German hunting rules of the *Reichsjagdgesetzes* (Reich Hunting Laws) dated July 3, 1934.[19]

A Disregarded Decree

In the chaos, the decrees were not enforced uniformly. An August 21 report from the commune of Maisons-Lafitte noted secret field police (*Geheime Feldpolizei*) intelligence that "[w]eapons in the possession of civilians have not been surrendered in a consistent way. For example, one military office did not request the surrender of more than 30 rifles and shotguns, as well as several pistols, stored in the open in the office of a mayor. In some towns, surrendered weapons were apparently returned to their owners."[20]

Similarly, the August 22 order of the day (*Tagesbefehl*) from Dijon observed that the surrender decree "has been repeatedly disregarded, mostly by people who are returning. The population must be reminded to observe the decree of May 10 conscientiously and of the penalties in case of violations."[21] Countless civilians had fled the German invasion and were now coming home.

In this early period, death sentences were by no means automatic for mere possession of a firearm. For instance, on August 26 a student named Pierre

18. BA/MA, RH 36/430, Tagesbefehl Nr. 47 des Bezirkschefs C Qu./Ia in Dijon, 12. Oktober 1940.

19. BA/MA, RW 35/135, Div. Nachschubführer 157, Antrag zu den "Besonderen Anordnungen," 29. August 1940.

20. BA/MA, RW 35/1195, Tätigkeitsbericht der GFP [Geheimen Feldpolizei] bei den Militärverwaltungen, 21. August 1940.

21. BA/MA, RH 36/430, Tagesbefehl Nr. 22 des Bezirkschefs C, Qu./Ia in Dijon, 22. August 1940.

Lebelle in Rennes was sentenced to four years' imprisonment for flight and possession of weapons, and three student accomplices got eighteen months.[22] As resistance activities escalated over time, death sentences became more common.

The French police assisted the Germans in all aspects of occupation policy. The situation report of the MVF for August reflected this: "The activity of the military police at District and Local Military Administrative Headquarters was limited to weapons searches, supervision of French police regarding surrender of weapons, search for and arrest of British citizens, searches for German emigrants, night watch, price control, and putting up of flyers against sabotage."[23] Aside from such provisions of occupation policy, German military law applied in the occupied zone to crimes where a German was the perpetrator or victim, and French law otherwise applied.

Service of the French police to the Germans was noted with contempt by Agnès Humbert: "At the Palis-Royal Métro station I notice a Paris gendarme saluting a German officer with obsequious servility. Rooted on the spot, I watch as he repeats the gesture over and over again for the benefit of every passing officer—stiff, mechanical, German already."[24]

The German authorities trusted the French police with arms, but with reservations. As noted by the MVF, the French criminal police could be armed only with as many pistols as were needed, to include only one magazine with ammunition per pistol. Public notices of the orders banning weapons possession and the introduction of German criminal law were ordered to be provided immediately. As for the reports about weapons openly stored in a mayor's office and mayors returning previously surrendered weapons to their owners, the district military administrative headquarters were reminded to secure surrendered weapons.[25]

The above was followed by an order condemning the unauthorized confiscation by some German officers of weapons from the French police, who were

22. Venner, *Armes de la Résistance*, 144–46.

23. BA/MA, RW 35/4, Lagebericht des Chefs der Militärverwaltung in Frankreich, Kommandostab, für den Monat August 1940.

24. Humbert, *Résistance*, 11.

25. BA/MA, RW 35/1196, Besondere Anordnungen Nr. 32, Chef der Militärverwaltung, Bezirk A, 2. September 1940.

entitled to a sidearm, a rubber truncheon, and one pistol with nine shots.[26] The need to establish a policy for issuance of weapons permits to French authorities and private entities such as banks and guard services was also recognized.[27]

A regular situation report (*Lagebericht*) began to be filed by each of the military administrative districts (*Militärverwaltungsbezirke*) in September 1940. They included District A at Saint-Germain-en-Laye (northwestern France); District B at Angers (southwestern France); District C at Dijon (northeastern France); District Paris; and District Bordeaux.

District Paris reported a raid netting only four illegal weapons.[28] While noting some violations, District A reported that the threats of punishment seemed to have worked.[29]

District B had more substance. Bookstores were searched for illegal books and weapons were confiscated. About reports that weapons had not been surrendered, District B indicates that these mostly concerned farmers who had failed to turn in their hunting guns, which they either hid under hay or straw or did not bother to hide. Sentences ranged from one month to one year in prison.[30] That was pretty lenient given that the death penalty could have been ordered.

A report added that German soldiers were being insulted with taunts of "*boches*" or "German pigs," but admitted that the soldiers had caused the insults by being drunk or fighting with civilians.[31] At least in some areas, the occupation was not going too harshly.

The MVF, which received the above reports, saw progress in disarming civilians with military arms but, given the large number of those who used to

26. BA/MA, RW 35/1196, Besondere Anordnungen Nr. 33, Chef der Militärverwaltung, Bezirk A, 3. September 1940.

27. BA/MA, RH 36/565, Bericht des Chefs des Militärverwaltungsbezirks Paris, Kommandostab, Stabsoffizier der Feldgendarmerie, Tgb. Nr. 51/40 betreffend Genehmigung zum Waffenbesitz, 12. September 1940.

28. BA/MA, RH 36/565, Monatsbericht des Chefs des Militärverwaltungsbezirks Paris, Kommandostab, Stabsoffizier der Feldgendarmerie, Paris, 21. September 1940.

29. BA/MA, RW 35/1196, Lagebericht für die Zeit vom 21. August bis 4. September 1940, Militärverwaltungsbezirk A, St. Germain, 8. September 1940.

30. BA/MA, RW 35/1254, Lagebericht September 1940, Chef des Militärverwaltungsbezirks B, Südwestfrankreich, Gericht, 22. September 1940.

31. BA/MA, RW 35/1254, Durchschrift für den Chef des Kommandostabes, 20. September 1940.

have the right to hunt, few hunting guns were confiscated.[32] French hunters were perhaps not taking the threat of the death penalty seriously, or thought they would not be detected, as hunting guns were not registered.

Registration of the Jews

A German decree requiring the registration of Jews was published on September 30.[33] Vichy quickly fell in line. "The victor is inoculating us with his diseases," wrote Guéhenno on October 19. "This morning the Vichy government published the 'Statute Regulating Jews' in France. Now we're good anti-Semites and racists." On the 22nd, Pierre Laval met with Hitler. "And since then, the whole country is trembling," noted Guéhenno, adding, "What could that horse-trader have done? For what price did he sell us down the river?"[34]

"Through a haze of cigarette smoke we saw a stocky, greasy-faced little man behind the desk," wrote Associated Press correspondent Roy Porter about his interview with Laval during this period. Banging his fist on the desk, Laval shouted, "I hope to God that the Germans smash the hell out of the British until they leave only a grease spot. Then, perhaps, France can take her proper place in European affairs without British domination."[35] His policy of collaboration was unabashed.

By now, military tribunals were hard at work punishing French citizens who had failed to surrender firearms. District A in Saint-Germain reported numerous cases, particularly in an area where house searches took place in retaliation for cut cables, netting old hunting guns and rusty pistols that had not been surrendered out of fear. The only death sentence reported concerned a man who fired a shot at a German soldier.[36] Numerous searches found weapons

32. BA/MA, RW 35/4, Lagebericht des Chefs der Militärverwaltung in Frankreich, Kommandostab, für den Monat September 1940.

33. *Journal Official,* no. 9, September 30, 1940, 92, cited in *Nazi Conspiracy and Aggression* (Washington D.C.: U.S. Government Printing Office, 1946), 1:984; available at https://archive.org/stream/naziconspiracyago1unit/naziconspiracyago1unit_djvu.txt.

34. Guéhenno, *Diary of the Dark Years,* 28–29 (entries for October 19 and 24, 1940).

35. Roy P. Porter, *Uncensored France* (New York: Dial Press, 1942), 10–11.

36. BA/MA, RW 35/1198, Lagebericht für den Zeitraum vom 20. September bis 20. Oktober 1940, St. Germain, 20. Oktober 1940.

possessed by Catholic priests and demobilized soldiers who just returned and were afraid to surrender their weapons.[37]

District A further reported the bringing of 54 cases of illegal weapons possession and the confiscation of 12,085 hunting guns, 115,305 hunting cartridges, and 404 pistols. The low number of prosecutions compared to the quantities seized indicates that most were voluntarily surrendered, either to German military officials or to French mayors or police. Captured property, that is, weapons taken from the French military, included 5,718 rifles and 425 handguns, together with 5 tanks, 42 artillery pieces, 2 mortars, 88 machine guns, and 2,486 sidearms (bayonets and swords).[38]

As reported from District B, hunting guns continued to be found, along with a few pistols seized in a search of ministers' houses. In Châtellerault, 350 rifles, 50 machine guns, and 60 pistols were found in a basement.[39] Besides weapons possession, crimes committed by the French included theft, anti-German demonstrations such as ripping off propaganda posters, currency export violations, illegal border crossings, slander of the German army, and illegal traffic with prisoners of war. Lack of French discipline caused most traffic accidents. Finally, it noted the death sentence against one André Eluau for using a knife to attack a sentry armed with a rifle who was stationed in front of the Hôtel de Paris in Le Mans.[40]

Otto von Stülpnagel, Military Commander

On October 25, General Otto von Stülpnagel replaced General Streccius as the military commander in France (*Militärbefehlshaber*, or MBF).[41] Above all others, Stülpnagel would trust and rely on Werner Best, the central figure

---

37. BA/MA, RW 35/1198, Lagebericht für Zeitraum vom 21. September. bis 20. October 1940, Chef der Militärverwaltung A, St. Germain, 24. Oktober 1940.

38. BA/MA, RW 35/1198, Lage- und Tätigkeitsbericht für die Zeit vom 12. September 1940 bis 12. Oktober 1940, Militärverwaltungsbezirk A, Tgb. Nr. 796/40, 21. Oktober 1940.

39. BA MA, RW 35/1258, Ic Lagebericht für die Zeit vom 21. September bis 20. Oktober 1940, Chef des Militärverwaltungsbezirks B, 23. Oktober 1940.

40. BA/MA, RW 35/1258, Lagebericht, Chef des Militärverwaltungsbezirks B, Südwestfrankreich, Gericht, 23. Oktober 1940.

41. Laub, *After the Fall*, 43.

of the administrative staff.[42] While serving in the next year and a quarter, he would order the execution of numerous French citizens for firearm possession. Earlier that month, the SS security service (*Sicherheitspolizei und Sicherheitsdienst*, or Sipo-SD) began operations to focus on the repression of Jews, religious groups, Communists, and other targeted classes.[43]

The MBF command staff reported appropriate measures taken against several cases of illegal weapons possession, some involving clerics. The military police secured abandoned military ordnance, including heavy weapons together with 160 machine guns and 1,200 handguns. Some 1,500 rifles and pistols and 27,000 hunting guns had been confiscated from civilians, proving that large numbers still lay in the hands of the population. The report noted that two German soldiers were sentenced to over five years' imprisonment—one for rape, another for desertion—while a French citizen was sentenced for five years, and another for seven years, for weapons possession, and a third to ten years for demoralization of the troops.[44]

The military police of the District Paris filed a report for October 13 to November 12 that included an extraordinary number of arms confiscated or taken into custody by district military administration headquarters (HQ) #758,[45] including a large number of rifles to be scrapped, 6,612 hunting guns, 1,034 shotguns and *teschings* (small caliber parlor rifles), 622 handguns, 10,555 hunting cartridges, and 10,000 hunting cartridge cases. Yet only 22 cases of illegal weapons possession were reported from HQ 758, suggesting that almost all of the confiscated arms were turned in voluntarily. Numerous firearm confiscations were also reported from other HQ sectors.

District A reported a decrease in illegal weapons possession in one area after a military court suggested new warnings to the prefect, who passed it on to the public. But in another area where arrests increased, to counter claims by

42. Allan Mitchell, *Nazi Paris: The History of an Occupation, 1940–1944* (New York: Berghahn Books, 2010), 6, 42.

43. Laub, *After the Fall*, 65.

44. BA/MA, RW 35/4, Lagebericht des Militärbefehlshabers in Frankreich, Kommandostab, für den Monat Oktober 1940.

45. BA/MA, RH 36/565, Lage- und Tätigkeitsbericht des Chefs des Militärverwaltungsbezirks Paris, Kommandostab, Stabsoffizier der Feldgendarmerie, für die Zeit vom 13. Oktober bis 12. November 1940, 19. November 1940.

many French that they failed to surrender their arms because they hid them too well, the court offered an amnesty for arms surrendered by November 20.[46]

"Cooperation with French Police Is Good"

"Cooperation with the French police is good," reported District B. The search of a cave in Saumur based on confidential information yielded nothing, but weapons were found in a forest on the coast.[47] The next monthly report noted 45 cases of illegal weapons possession and confiscations of 356 rifles, 65 pistols, 158 hunting guns, 1,121 rounds of hunting ammunition, and five kilograms of gunpowder.[48]

Similarly, District Paris reported, "We have a good relationship with the French gendarmes and police. Our cooperation with both of them is excellent. . . . They are fully at the service of the German offices." This cooperation would have included ferreting out "illegal weapons possession," of which only a dozen or so were reported. However, of "confiscated or secured objects," all districts reported rifles and pistols and sizable quantities of ammunition (ranging up to 30,000 rounds in one district), and one district reported 850 hunting guns. "Captured property" included 1,300 rifles, 35 pistols, and 53 slashing and thrusting weapons.[49]

The fall hunting season was in full swing, about which various directives were issued. District B in Angers reiterated that hunting guns could only be issued to holders of army hunting permits. Useable and quality hunting guns stored in depots had to be maintained by workers paid by the mayor.[50] Major General Karl-Ulrich Neumann-Neurode, head of District B, ordered that the depots be cleaned out of old guns, such as flintlocks without practical

---

46. BA/MA, RW 35/1199, Lagebericht für den Zeitraum vom 20. Oktober bis 20. November 1940, Chef der Militärverwaltung A, 21. November 1940.

47. BA/MA, RW 35/1258, Ic Lagebericht für die Zeit vom 21. Oktober bis 20. November 1940, Chef des Militärverwaltungsbezirks B, Südwestfrankreich, Gericht.

48. BA/MA, RW 35/1258, Lage- und Tätigkeitsbericht, Chef des Militärverwaltungsbezirks B, Südwestfrankreich, 21. Dezember 1940.

49. BA/MA, RH 36/565, Lage- und Tätigkeitsbericht des Chefs des Militärverwaltungsbezirks Paris, Kommandostab, Stabsoffizier der Feldgendarmerie, Tgb. Nr. 454/40. für die Zeit vom 13. November bis 12. Dezember 1940, 19. Dezember 1940.

50. BA/MA, RW 35/1257, Der Chef des Militärverwaltungsbezirks B, 21. November 1940.

use as weapons for which ammunition was unavailable, and of old sabers and swords. They were to be returned to their owners either directly or through the prefect or mayor.[51]

The same directive clarified that no distinction existed between hunting guns surrendered by private citizens and those surrendered by dealers—both had to be transferred to hunting-gun depots immediately if they had not been already. Besides disarming the populace, this would ensure a bountiful supply for German hunters. The directive ordered a count of the number of hunting permits issued by the army as of the year's end as well as the number of hunting guns issued to German soldiers, guns that did not need to be returned.

The MBF issued a comprehensive report covering four months from late 1940 to early 1941.[52] French citizens were sentenced to over five years' imprisonment for illegal weapons possession, assault on a soldier, and distribution of flyers favoring the enemy. The number of cases of illegal weapons possession was as follows:

| Period | Total | Military Administrative District | | | | |
		A	B	C	Paris	Bordeaux
Sept. 13–Oct. 12	197	?	?	?	?	?
Oct. 12–Nov. 11	279	134	51	59	22	13
Nov. 11–Jan. 10	358	113	83	93	28	41

However, the number of confiscated weapons was far higher, suggesting that large quantities were surrendered to the Germans directly, or to the French authorities and then confiscated from them (see chart on next page):

As can be seen, 13,398 hunting guns were surrendered in Bordeaux, followed by 3,685 in District A at Saint-Germain-en-Laye (northwestern France), 1,391 in District C at Dijon (northeastern France), 920 in Paris, and only 103 in District B at Angers (southwestern France). Except for the latter two—nine times more hunting guns were surrendered in Paris than in District B—these figures may have reflected the prominence of hunting guns in rural France. However, more rifles were surrendered in District A than in Bordeaux, with far more pistols confiscated in Bordeaux than District A. The countless human realities behind the statistics were not recorded.

---

51. BA/MA, RW 35/1256, Der Chef des Militärverwaltungsbezirks B, 18. Dezember 1940.
52. BA/MA, RW 35/4, Lagebericht für die Monate Dezember 1940 und Januar 1941.

Confiscated Weapons	Military Administrative District				
	A	B	C	Paris	Bordeaux
Heavy machine guns	1	1	3	1	15
Light machine guns					6
Rifles of all kinds	3,920	903	273	24	3,042
Pistols of all kinds	885	240	90	39	3,740
Sidearms [bayonets, swords] of all kinds	1	104	380	–	1,007
Hunting guns	3,685	103	1,391	920	13,398
Hunting ammunition		1,240		2,840	13,036
Rounds of various ammunition	4,160	2,436	14,697	34,696	24,045
Explosives			3.8 tons		
Other explosives	300				

A Flame of Resistance

Those organizing to resist the occupation contemplated using underground publications and acquiring arms. On October 22, Alphonse Juge, representing the Popular Democrats (*Démocrates populaires*), organized a meeting in Montpellier in the living room of Professor Jean-Rémy Palanque. He proposed a plan of action around the review *Temps nouveau*. He was harshly interrupted by one of participants, P-H. Teitgen, who shouted, "Your idea is very well, my dear Juge, but it is not sufficient for us! You must obtain arms to use against enemies and traitors!"[53]

Similarly, in another context, Jewish resister David Knout insisted, "We have but one means of defending ourselves . . . taking up arms against the Germans."[54]

The first arms of the Resistance were typically an old hunting rifle and an obsolete revolver model 1873. This obsolete revolver, which fired an 11 mm

---

53. Henri Noguères, *Histoire de la Résistance : La Première Année, Juin 1940 - Juin 1941* (Paris: Robert Laffont, 1967), 1:162.

54. Anny Latour, *The Jewish Resistance in France (1940–1944)* (New York: Holocaust Library, 1970), 24. The author made arms deliveries for the resistance (p. 10).

black-powder centerfire cartridge, was last produced in 1886, and was no longer a "military" arm banned to civilians by French law. Rifles such as the bolt-action carbine model 1892/16 8 mm Lebel, being "military," had been banned from civilian ownership, but would be highly desirable by the future Resistance members.[55]

A member of the Resistance named Camaret was wanted by the Germans for hiding arms but had been tipped off and narrowly escaped. He crossed the border into the unoccupied zone on December 28, but would be in danger when he returned to Paris. Along with Guillain de Bénouville, he met with an attorney, Jacques Renouvin, who "told us that in addition to the military organizations which were hiding arms from the German commissions, other Resistance groups were already in existence. . . . They were unarmed, because the officers charged with hiding arms from the Germans would give them none."[56]

Most would have to content themselves with unarmed resistance, even if only symbolic. Simone de Beauvoir noted in her diary that she had seen a hawker "selling comic composite pictures of gorillas, pigs, and elephants, each with Hitler's head instead of its own." But shoving a German soldier could be deadly. On the Boulevard Saint-Michel, she saw the following warning in red print: "Jacques Bonsergent, engineer, of Paris, having been condemned to death by a German Military Tribunal for an act of violence against a member of the German Armed Forces, was executed by shooting this morning."[57]

At the end of 1940, France had experienced an occupation for six months that, while traumatic, was not the worst of all possible worlds. Regarding the focus of this study, French citizens who failed to surrender their firearms within twenty-four hours of Wehrmacht presence were threatened with the death penalty, but no instance of imposition thereof for mere firearm possession was reported. Probably thousands of violations were alleged, but incarceration, and not execution, was imposed.

---

55. Venner, *Armes de la Résistance*, 130, 143; Garry James, "French Model 1873 Revolver," *American Rifleman*, November 2012, 120.

56. de Bénouville, *Unknown Warriors*, 13, 16, 18.

57. Simone de Beauvoir, *The Prime of Life*, trans. Peter Green (New York: Lancer Books, 1966), 511 (entry dated December 8, 1940), 570 (entry dated December 28, 1940).

Enormous quantities of personally owned firearms were surrendered to the Germans to be kept in arms depots. This provided a complete supply of hunting guns to happy German soldiers just in time for the fall hunting season. Unknowable but also enormous quantities of firearms were not turned in, prompting the occupiers repeatedly to admonish and threaten the occupied to comply with their orders. The French police received the highest praise for their collaboration with and assistance to the Germans.

To say that times would change for the worse would be an understatement.

• • •

"Laval is Hitler's man, and *collaboration* is merely a fine word for servitude," wrote Jean Guéhenno in early 1941.[58] Major General Neumann-Neurode verified that cooperation with the French police was good, although they were not enthusiastic in enforcing rules about traffic and darkening houses. But illegal weapons, mostly hunting guns and pistols, continued to be found, and owners were sentenced by military courts. He added that churches and the houses of ministers had been searched for weapons, and two ministers had been sentenced for weapons possession.[59]

The above bears out the generalization by historian Henri Michel that "[i]n all occupied countries the Gestapo made use of the national police force, though placing little trust in it and had access to its files and saw its reports; they recruited from it volunteers who were completely at their service."[60] The records of firearm registrations were certainly within this cooperation. Although the Wehrmacht controlled the French police at this time, the tentacles of the Gestapo would increasingly assert themselves.

In the two-month period ending on January 10, some 61 cases of spying, 139 cases of sabotage, and 358 cases of illegal weapons possession were reported. The numbers of confiscated arms, surrendered or otherwise seized, were phenomenal: roughly 8,000 rifles, 5,000 pistols, and 19,000 hunting guns.[61]

---

58. Guéhenno, *Diary of the Dark Years*, 58.

59. BA/MA, RW 35/1260, Chef des Militärverwaltungsbezirks B, Südwestfrankreich, 15. Januar 1941.

60. Michel, *Shadow War*, 258.

61. BA/MA, RW 35/286, 1941 Militärbefehlshaber in Frankreich, Lagebericht Dezember 1940 / Januar 1941, 31 Januar.1941.

In the same period, District A reported from Saint-Germain that numerous arms were surrendered mostly by wealthy people who were fearful of the penalties.[62] District B at Angers noted sentences for anti-German demonstrations, weapons possession, theft, excessive prices, guerrilla activities, transfer of army goods, and resistance.[63] An eighteen-year-old shoemaker was sentenced to death for finding a revolver and procuring ammunition.[64] Hunting guns and revolvers were still in the hands of the population, and military courts intervened in fifteen cases. Roger Jeunet, an electrician working in the marine arsenal of Brest, was shot to death as he was aiming a pistol at two soldiers.[65]

MBF Stülpnagel issued a situation report for February praising the French police, who were supervised closely by the Germans, for their reliability and good work. The police prefect for District Paris reported several cases in which French police officers misappropriated weapons or kept them illegally, turning them over to the German authorities for prosecution.[66]

The MBF identified the main crimes committed as the cutting of communication cables, illegal crossing of the demarcation line, weapons possession, and giving aid and comfort to the enemy. Of eighteen death sentences, one was for illegal weapons possession and negligent bodily injury, and another for anti-German propaganda, illegal weapons possession, and failure to surrender anti-German flyers. Others were sentenced to prison terms for similar acts. Instances of illegal weapons possession for January 13 to February 12 were reduced to 176 from the previous month of 358. Thousands of firearms and tens of thousands of rounds of ammunition were confiscated.

Notices of the sentences of transgressors, often including several on one poster, were posted to deter future offenses. The following example would not have had much dissuasive force compared to the possible death penalty:

---

62. BA/MA, RW 35/1201, Lagebericht für den Zeitraum vom 15. November 1940 bis 15. Januar 1941, Chef der Militärverwaltung A, 16. Januar 1941.

63. BA/MA, RW 35/1260, Chef des Militärverwaltungsbezirks B, Südwestfrankreich, Gericht, 16. Januar 1941.

64. BA/MA, RW 35/1261, Chef des Militärverwaltungsbezirks B, Südwestfrankreich, Gericht, 19. Januar 1941.

65. BA/MA, RW 35/1261, Chef des Militärverwaltungsbezirks B, Südwestfrankreich, 22. Februar 1941.

66. BA/MA, RW 35/5, Lagebericht, Februar 1941.

farmer Jean Nolle was sentenced on March 17 to three weeks in jail for grenade and munition possession.[67]

Others got four years in prison for arms possession. In one case, the defendant possessed three rifles and over 100 rounds of ammunition that he stole from a captured property depot.[68]

More Confiscations of Hunting Guns

Meanwhile, hunting guns continued to be appropriated for use by the occupation forces. Brigadier General Adolph, head of District B at Angers, issued an order on March 19 reciting orders from 1940 about the surrender of arms and purchase thereof for use by the occupation authorities.[69] The hunting guns were not captured property but were private property belonging to those who surrendered them. Compensation for guns taken for the German forces would be determined by the MBF. The Reich Hunting Office (*Reichsjagdamt*) was taking 25,000 hunting guns from the depots at District A, while the commander in chief of the Luftwaffe (*Ob.d.L.*, or *Oberbefehlshaber der Luftwaffe*) was taking 20,500 from District Bordeaux. The latter suggests that this was a power grab by Hermann Göring, Germany's hunt master and Luftwaffe chief, to take over the above total of 45,500 hunting guns as loot. Göring was notorious for looting art, and looting firearms would have satisfied his artistic and hunting lusts as well as provided booty for Luftwaffe fighters.

The German brass did enjoy the delicacies of French game, courtesy of special officers assigned to hunting. Reinhard Kops, an officer in the *Abwehr* (German military intelligence), was quartered in a beautiful room in the palatial building in the rue de Paris, where the other personnel of the *Komandantur* (commander's headquarters) lived. In his memoirs, he recalled a hunt officer, a first lieutenant, who acted as a forest ranger in the forest of

67. Musée de l'Ordre de la Libération in Paris, exhibit #408 (on display April 2006).

68. BA/MA, RW 35/1203, Lagebericht für den Zeitraum vom 16. Februar bis 15. März 1941, Chef der Militärverwaltung A, 18. März 1941.

69. BA/MA, RW 35/1256, Der Chef des Militärverwaltungsbezirks B, 19. März 1941.

Compiègne, located sixty kilometers north of Paris, who provided game for the *Kommandantur*.[70]

Roast of wild boar was served at Kops's first lunch at the headquarters. Kops wrote, "All arms had been taken from the French. In the *Kommandantur*, there was a huge room full of hunting arms, all carefully numbered and provided with the names and addresses of the owners." The hunt officer and his minions had now replaced French hunters in controlling the stock of game.[71] These must have been some of the finest confiscated hunting guns to be stored in such a place.

The issue of compensation for confiscated arms was being pursued at the highest levels. On March 24, the French minister, state secretary of national economy and finances, sent a memorandum to the MVF on the confiscation of arms belonging to private citizens. It stated:

> Since the armistice came into effect, German authorities have confiscated, either directly or through the French police, all weapons and ammunition held by dealers for sale or by private citizens.
>
> This confiscation was apparently conducted pursuant to art. 53, paragraph 2, of the Hague Convention of October 18, 1907. That treaty provides that weapons and ammunition belonging to private citizens may be confiscated by the occupying forces, but that they may not be considered captured property. This means that when peace is reestablished, they must be returned and their owners reimbursed for any damage suffered. In reality it appears, however, that the German authorities did not limit their actions to the safeguarding of objects confiscated in this manner. Rather, they used them and often in a way that will make their return impossible.[72]

---

70. Juan Maler [Reinhard Kops], *Frieden, Krieg und "Frieden"* (Buenos Aires: J. Maler, 1987), 88. After the war, Kops escaped to Argentina and lived under the pseudonym "Juan Maler."

71. Maler [Kops], *Frieden, Krieg und "Frienden,"* 89.

72. BA/MA, RW 35/624, Der Minister, Staatssekretär der nationalen Wirtschaft und Finanzen ; Betr.: Beschlagnahme der Privatpersonen gehörenden Waffen und Munitionen, Paris, 24. März 1941.

The above-cited provision of the Hague Convention provided that "all kinds of munitions of war, may be seized, even if they belong to private individuals, but must be restored and compensation fixed when peace is made."[73] Hunting, competition, and other civilian firearms were not "munitions of war," which meant military weapons. Needless to say, no firearms were ever restored or compensation made.

The above French memorandum went on to say that weapons dealers should be indemnified immediately for the arms confiscated from then since their businesses were destroyed. Confiscations from private citizens such as hunters and marksmen need not be compensated until later. It suggested that the confiscation of weapons from dealers be treated the same way as all other confiscations and that the dealers be paid the same way. Incredibly, it ended that the Germans would be responsible for these payments, but they could be deducted from the amounts due from France to Germany under the armistice.

A response concerning payment for confiscated firearms was issued by the MBF, apparently authored by Dr. Rudolf Thierfelder of the military administrative office (*Kriegsverwaltungsrat*, or KVR).[74] Noting that in the beginning the plan was to secure about three million confiscated firearms, most could not be returned for the following reasons: (1) contrary to repeated orders of the MBF, ordnance staff treated many firearms as captured property and transferred them to collection centers without identification; (2) the Army High Command ordered 125,000 firearms to be transferred to Germany; (3) firearms loaned to German soldiers to hunt were no longer available; and (4) the safeguarding of firearms in collection centers was poor and many became useless.

A plan existed to negotiate compensation with the French government, but the criteria was unclear because the French government had ordered the surrender of some firearms even before the German invasion; some of the weapons collections at mayors' offices were then taken over by the Germans, while others were destroyed in battle. It was thus impossible to determine the number of firearms appropriated from French collection centers and their

---

73. Hague Convention, Article 53 (October 18, 1907).

74. BA/MA, RW 35/624, Militärbefehlshaber in Frankreich; Betreffend Entschädigung für sichergestellte Schusswaffen, Paris, 17. April 1941.

owners. Moreover, in many cases, the Germans did not issue receipts for firearms surrendered at their request. German compensation to the French for confiscated firearms, like compensation for untold other items, was a hypothetical exercise that would go nowhere.

The MBF issued a situation report for March noting that, of eighteen French citizens sentenced to death, one was for guerrilla activity—shooting at a German airman who made an emergency landing—and two others were for illegal weapons possession and assault on a German soldier. There were 193 weapons offenses for the previous four weeks, the highest number being 76 cases from District A. District A also had the largest number of hunting guns confiscated, numbering 2,760. Not many firearms were surrendered in the other districts for this period.[75] Not surprisingly, District A would brag about the good cooperation between German authorities and French police and gendarmes in a later report.[76]

Collaboration Against Resistance

As an example of the ongoing collaboration, what was described as an assassination attempt against Wehrmacht soldiers in Paris resulted in the apprehension of the terrorists with French cooperation. Fernand de Brinon, secretary of state and third-in-command for the Vichy government,[77] declared to the press:

> Two French construction site workers in a Paris suburb ran after a terrorist immediately after he had shot a German army soldier, and contributed to handing him over to the French authorities.
>
> You know what Marshal Pétain thinks of these cowardly and vain attacks; he stigmatized them himself, by saying that they were committed against men who do their duty. Therefore, I have decided to congratulate, tonight, on behalf of the Marshal, the two workers who

75. BA/MA, RW 35/5, Lagebericht März 1941.

76. BA/MA, RW 35/1205, Lage- und Tätigkeitsbericht für die Zeit vom 13. April bis 12. Mai 1941, Militärverwaltungsbezirk A, Tgb. Nr. 1131/41, 20. Mai 1941.

77. "1947: Fernand de Brinon, Vichy minister with a Jewish wife," April 15, 2008, www.executedtoday.com/2008/04/15/1947-fernand-de-brinon-vichy-minister-with-a-jewish-wife/; "NBC Tells France," *Time*, May, 26, 1941, www.time.com/time/magazine/article/0,9171,765661,00.html.

reacted with such determination and with courage, for their instinct worthy of good French citizens.[78]

This expressed Vichy's collaborationist policy that sought to ingratiate itself to the Germans. As de Brinon told AP correspondent Roy Porter in an interview, "France has only one way to look and that is toward Berlin."[79]

In this period, there was no organized armed French resistance. The Resistance instead was publishing underground newspapers and organizing for armed actions against the occupation when the appropriate time came. The *Réseau du Musée de l'Homme* (Network of the Museum of Man), a student group that used the museum's duplicating machine, began publishing the newspaper *Résistance* the previous fall.[80]

The group did not have any weapons, related Noël Créau, a member of the group who responded to my questionnaire in 2002.[81] Born in 1922, he was a college student living in a Paris suburb when the war came. He was supposed to go to the air force flight training school in June 1940, but the German occupation obviously changed that.

In prewar France, Créau explained, "[a]side from hunting guns, the law made it difficult to keep other types of arms." When the Germans came, "I think most French people were reticent to hand over their hunting guns to the gendarmerie, and delayed doing so. But my father, as well as my father-in-law, veterans of 1914–18, buried their weapons in their gardens. They had to replace the shoulder stocks once they retrieved them." They risked death: "It was common practice for the German police to execute firearm owners."

That last comment requires qualification. Execution for mere gun possession would have been less common in 1940–41 but more ordinary after the SS assumed police duties in 1942 and also as armed resistance grew, particularly

---

78. "Après l'arrestation à Paris d'auteurs d'attentats contre l'armée d'occupation," *Le Temps,* April 25/26, 1941, 1. Also in "Apres l'arrestation des terroristes a Paris," *Le Figaro,* April 25/26, 1941, 1.

79. Porter, *Uncensored France,* 67.

80. Humbert, *Résistance,* 23, 36.

81. Noël Créau, ancien président national, Amicales des Anciens Parachutistes S.A.S. et des Anciens Commandos de la France Libre, Neuilly-sur-Seine, France, letter to author, February 4, 2002. For more details on Noël Créau, see www.francaislibres.net/liste/fiche .php?index=62760.

in 1944. Moreover, there were only about 3,000 German police in France. Most of the killing would be done by the French police and particularly by the *Milice*, Vichy's paramilitary organization formed with German aid to fight the Resistance.

As Henri Frenay detailed in his memoirs, Resistance leaders changed their appearances and addresses often, and carried guns to defend themselves.[82] Yet Communist operative Charles Tillon opined about his organization, "The Paris region did not contain fifty combatants capable of using any weapons at all in the spring of 1941."[83]

Hunting-Gun Depots

The MBF issued a directive on May 20 regarding the management of hunting-gun depots. Noting insufficient adherence to previous orders, it mandated that each district must immediately establish a central depot large enough to store all confiscated hunting guns on shelves where they would be dry and secure from unauthorized access. Existing arms depots at district headquarters, mayors' offices, offices of the ordnance staffs, or in other locations were required to be transferred forthwith to the central hunting-gun depot.[84]

Smokeless powder hunting guns that needed little or no repair were required to be separated from those that needed repair or were old or unusable. They were to be categorized by those whose owners were known and those whose owners were unknown. Usable guns would be sorted by type, that is, shotgun, rifle, three-barrel or similar combination, and small bore rifle. Each district would stock up to 1,000 hunting guns to be issued to soldiers.

All of the usable hunting guns would be immediately confiscated from private French ownership and placed in the depots for use by the occupying forces. The unusable and old hunting guns would be safeguarded and administered as confiscated private French property. Weapons that could be traced back to their owners would be listed with the name and address of the owner and the weapon number.

---

82. Frenay, *Night Will End*, 73.

83. Pryce-Jones, *Paris in the Third Reich*, 118.

84. BA/MA, RW 35/624, Verwaltung der Jagdwaffenlager, Militärbefehlshaber in Frankreich, Paris, 20. Mai 1941.

The hunting-gun depots would be set up by the war administrative inspector (*Kriegsverwaltungsinspektor*) assigned to forest services at each district. The staff person for forests and woods would supervise all hunting-gun depots of a district, and hunting officers would be in charge of the local administration of the depots. French assistance for care of weapons was subject to restrictions.

Finally, depots for hunting ammunition would be secured separately from hunting-gun depots. All hunting and small caliber ammunition from existing depots or other stocks were required to be stored in those depots. All other ammunition, including pistol ammunition, had to be surrendered.

Soldiers were not getting the guns free. Purchasers of hunting guns were given a receipt with the buyer's rank and name, a recitation that the gun was purchased from captured property pursuant to AHM 1941, item 462, the price, the type of gun, manufacturer (if known), serial number, place and date, and disbursing officer. Payment for hunting guns was due by June 5.[85]

Meanwhile, the Vichy government was tightening the screws on Jews. The commissioner-general for Jewish affairs (*Commissaire-général aux questions juives,* or CGQJ), headed by Xavier Vallat, had been created in March. On June 1, Vichy issued a law prohibiting the possession, purchase, and sale of arms and ammunition by Jews.[86]

An internal debate within the Wehrmacht ensued about whether to declare an amnesty for new arms surrenders. The district military administrative counselor (*Feldkriegsgerichtsrat*) of the military court at Angoulême wrote on June 24 to Mr. Schmeichler, the MBF's senior military administrative counselor (*Oberkriegsgerichtsrat*).[87] He noted that the surrender decree of June 20, 1940, stated: "This order shall not apply to unusable weapons with sentimental value. [*Für Erinnerungswaffen ohne Gebrauchswert gilt diese Verordnung nicht.*]" However, the French translation of this sentence stated: "This order shall not apply to weapons with sentimental value that are *not in use.* [*Ce décret ne s'applique pas à des armes souvenirs hors d'usage.*]" Because of the mistranslation, many prosecutions had to be dismissed since the defendants believed

---

85. BA/MA, RW 35/1275, Tagesbefehl Nr. 60 des Militärverwaltungsbezirks C, Nordostfrankreich, 21. Mai 1941.

86. Loi N°2181 du 1er juin 1941, J.O., 6 juin 1941.

87. BA/MA, RW 35/544, Gericht der Feldkommandantur 540, Aussenstelle Angoulême, Vorschläge hinsichtlich der Verordnung über Waffenbesitz im besetzten Gebiet, 24. Juni 1941.

that the decree did not apply to weapons of sentimental value if they were not being used.

Many people, the counselor continued, missed the original deadline but feared to surrender their arms later because of the penalties. Because of that, the courts in several districts proclaimed a new deadline for the surrender of weapons and granted an amnesty. Out of fairness, prior offenders had to be resentenced. Such a proclamation issued in October 1940 had no effect because the prefect delayed its publication and the new deadline expired in just twenty-four hours. The counselor concluded that the victorious Wehrmacht could afford to issue a new decree and grant amnesty, which would result in the surrender of numerous weapons and a reduction in prosecutions.

Dr. Grohmann, military administrative counselor (*Kriegsverwaltungsrat*) to the MBF, soundly rejected the proposal in a memorandum dated July 5.[88] He doubted that the courts had authority to set surrender deadlines with the promise of amnesty. The twenty-four-hour surrender deadline in the decree of May 10, 1940, was absolutely necessary to protect the advancing troops. Some violators received death sentences that were carried out. Given the death sentences imposed so far, it would be inadvisable a year later to set a new deadline with the promise of an amnesty.

All hell was about to break loose with events that would dramatically increase activities of the Resistance. The German firing squads were about to shoot more French citizens than ever before, above all Jews and alleged Communists. People caught with anti-German propaganda or firearms, or who took steps to oppose the occupation, would be increasingly subject to execution.

88. BA/MA, RW 35/544, Militärbefehlshaber in Frankreich, Verwaltungsstab, Abteilung Verwaltung, Verordung über den Waffenbesitz im besetzten Gebiet vom 10. Mai 1940, 5. Juli 1941.

5

Weapons Possession
The Core of Criminal Activities of the French

ON JUNE 22, 1941, Hitler launched Operation Barbarossa, the blitzkrieg against his former ally—Soviet Russia. "The French experienced great happiness," observed Jean Guéhenno, "at least this time Hitler would be busy for a while. . . . For the first time Hitlerlian fanaticism is going to come up against another fanaticism."[1]

After the Hitler-Stalin pact of 1939, the French Communist Party had been friendly to Nazi Germany and was banned by the French government. When Germany occupied France in 1940, the party appealed to the Germans to legalize it, but the French police arrested its delegates. Now that the Soviet Union was being attacked, Stalin ordered the European Communist parties to oppose the Nazis.[2] French Communists demonstrated in Paris in July and August, but as Pierre Daix wrote, "We had no arms and no training. . . . We were obliged to improvise lodgings, arms, everything."[3]

At a meeting at the Führer Headquarters on July 16, recorded by Martin Bormann, Hitler alluded to "an assertion made in an impudent Vichy newspaper that the war against the Soviet Union was Europe's war," implying that "all European states ought to benefit from it." While the German motives would not be made public, they would pretend that they were "forced to occupy, administer and secure" a certain area, while still taking "all necessary

---

1. Guéhenno, *Diary of the Dark Years*, 95 (entry dated June 22, 1941).
2. Laub, *After the Fall*, 112.
3. Pryce-Jones, *Paris in the Third Reich*, 229.

measures—shooting, resettling, etc." In reality, their occupation of each area was "first, to dominate it; second, to administer it; and third, to exploit it."[4]

"Exterminate Everyone Who Opposes Us"

Hitler welcomed the Russian order for partisan warfare, Bormann's notes continued, as "it enables us to exterminate everyone who opposes us." He added, "Our iron principle must be and must remain: We must never permit anybody but the Germans to carry arms!" He reiterated that they would not "enlist the armed support of foreign, subjugated nations. . . . Only the German may carry arms . . . !" Field Marshal Wilhelm Keitel added, "The inhabitants had to understand that anybody who did not perform his duties properly would be shot, and that they would be held responsible for every offense." Although most of his tirade focused on the East, the same policies, albeit less harsh, were applied in France.

Jean Guéhenno saw evidence of that when he made a Sunday visit with friends at the Vallée-aux-Loups (Valley of the Wolves), a beautiful park outside Paris: "I learn today that in the depths of this very peaceful park, the Germans shoot people who have been sentenced by their courts martial—most recently a young Frenchman accused of Gaullism and a young German aviator who had lingered three days too long with his mistress."[5]

Simone de Beauvoir noted that "the yellow-and-red 'Warning' notices succeeded each other ever more rapidly on the tiled walls of the Métro." In July, a proclamation warned that reprisals would now include the 'terrorists' families: their closest male relations would be shot, their wives deported, and their children interned." Yet the killings on both sides and acts of sabotage did not slow.[6]

That may have been true at the time, but reprisal executions against violent attacks directed at Germans would have a dissuasive effect. As time went on,

---

4. Nuremberg Document 221-L, in U.S. Department of State, *Documents on German Foreign Policy, 1918–1945. Series D (1937–1945): The War Years* (Washington, D.C.: U.S. Government Printing Office, 1964), 13:149–56.

5. Guéhenno, *Diary of the Dark Years*, 99 (entry dated July 11, 1941).

6. de Beauvoir, *Prime of Life*, 618.

resistance groups stopped attacking members of the Wehrmacht and turned their attention to French collaborators.

District A at Saint-Germain reported numerous cases of illegal weapons possession, mostly hunting guns, many of which were useless. Prison sentences of over five years would be served in Germany. An armed poacher was shot to death. Hunting offenses had grown, probably due to minimal meat rations.[7]

"We have no problems with the French gendarmes. They do their best to meet our requirements," noted a report from District B at Angers. Cooperation with the police had improved, but they are not tough enough on traffic offenders. There were sixty-seven cases of illegal weapons possession in the two months ending on July 11.[8] A Monsieur Martin was sentenced to two years' imprisonment, and six others were imprisoned for concealing the crime. And a Madam Renaudeau got four months for telling a soldier to drop his waist belt and making the move of cutting his throat while declaring "Hitler is kaputt."[9]

Obviously, liberal sentences could be imposed for having a gun or insulting the Führer. Some occupation authorities understood that extreme sentences would only increase resistance. But more vicious repression would increase later when Germany experienced losses in the war.

It seems that gun dealers were remiss in surrendering their inventories. The search of a weapons dealer in Paris yielded pistols, barrels for hunting rifles, handgun parts, magazines, and hunting and pistol ammunition. It was assumed that other dealers did not surrender all of their weapons either, necessitating that the military police, with support from the French police, conduct a search of gun dealers.[10] A French police raid on illegal gun dealers netted thirty-six arrests.[11]

---

7. BA/MA, RW 35/1207, Lagebericht für den Zeitraum vom 15. Mai bis 15. Juli 1941, Chef der Militärverwaltung A, 20. Juli 1941.

8. BA/MA, RW 35/1263, Lage- und Tätigkeitsbericht für die Zeit vom 12. Mai bis 11. Juli 1941, Militärverwaltungsbezirk B, Tgb. Nr. 2508/41, 17. Juli 1941.

9. BA/MA, RW 35/1263, Lagebericht des Militärverwaltungsbezirks B für die Zeit vom 11. Juni bis 10. Juli 1941. 19. Juli 1941.

10. BA/MA, RW 35/1262, Chef des Militärverwaltungsbezirks B, 2. August 1941, Besondere Anordnung Nr. 406.

11. Mitchell, *Nazi Paris*, 59.

Communists Awake

Operation Barbarossa awoke French Communists from their slumber. An anti-German demonstration on August 13 led to arrests and to the banning of the French Communist Party by the Germans (the French government had banned it in 1939). Some 4,000 Jews were detained at a protest on August 20, and in August and September, 3,477 Jews were arrested for possession of firearms, leaflets, and other contraband.[12]

Charles Tillon, head of the Communist *Francs-Tireurs et Partisans* (Snipers and Partisans), published the first issue of *France d'Abord* in August, calling for armed struggle, no matter how unprepared. He quoted his lieutenant, Gilbert Brustlein, as saying, "It's one thing to derail a train or leave a bomb somewhere, but it's quite something else to attack a Nazi in the middle of Paris with old firearms that jam."[13]

On August 21, the young Communist Pierre Georges (aka Colonel Fabien) waited at the Barbès-Rochechouart Métro station in Paris with a lady's revolver in his pocket. When Germans in uniform appeared, he shot Naval Cadet Alfons Moser twice and killed him. Georges avoided capture by feigning that the assailant was escaping and shouting, "Stop him!"[14]

In retaliation for the shooting of Cadet Moser, Hitler demanded the shooting of hostages. If the culprits were not caught, French officials would propose a list of hostages to General Otto von Stülpnagel, the military commander in France (*Militärbefehlshaber*, or MBF), who would choose whom to execute. The reprisal policy was announced to the public in newspapers and posters and by radio.

The next day, the Vichy regime sent its condolences and urged that innocent French citizens not be punished for the act of Communists. Vichy Minister Jean-Pierre Ingrand, the representative of the French ministry of the

12. Laub, *After the Fall*, 217.

13. Pryce-Jones, *Paris in the Third Reich*, 118.

14. On the attack and its aftermath, see Jean-Marc Berlière and Franck Liaigre, *Le Sang des communistes: Les Bataillons de la jeunesse dans la lutte armée, automne 1941* (Paris: Fayard, 2004), 97–99; Laub, *After the Fall*, 114–15; Russell Miller, *The Resistance: World War II* (Chicago: Time-Life Books Inc., 1985), 76, 227–30; Matthew Cobb, *The Resistance: The French Fight Against the Nazis* (London: Simon & Schuster, 2009), 77.

interior to the German military administration, instructed the French police to collaborate fully with and provide all known intelligence to the German authorities. Wehrmacht Major Walter Beumelburg conferred with Ingrand and Vichy Ambassador Fernand de Brinon (whose Jewish wife had been named an "honorary Aryan"), threatening that the Wehrmacht would execute fifty hostages unless Vichy executed six. Ingrand agreed that the French would convene a special court set up by the French minister of justice to condemn six public enemies to be executed. After a number of French magistrates refused to participate, lackeys were found who adjudicated the formalities by sentencing two Communists and a Jewish merchant, who were guillotined the next day. After three weeks passed without further executions, Stülpnagel demanded action, and three more Communists were guillotined.[15]

Criminal and political prisoners sentenced to death by French courts were executed by guillotine. Military executions, carried out by the occupation forces for offenses such as aiding the enemy or possession of firearms, were carried out by German firing squads. The soldiers did not know whose rifle had an actual bullet. If the shot did not kill the condemned person instantly, the officer in charge shot him in the head.[16]

"In some neighborhoods the police are closing off the streets," wrote Jean Guéhenno on the day Moser was shot. "A whole arrondissement (the 11th) has been searched. Jews have been arrested, Communists shot. Every morning, new posters invite us to become informers and threaten us with death." That day he returned to the Vallée-aux-Loups to view the evidence of the executions that had been taking place:

We follow a path along the vegetable garden, jump over a little wall, and cross a path. It is there. The occupying authority "used the terrain," a rather deep hollow in a sparsely wooded area. Bullets have slashed into the slope. . . . The tree has been sawed off, ripped apart by bullets at the level of a man's heart. It was used all last winter, four or five

15. Porter, *Uncensored France*, 238–39; Eric Conan, "Jean-Pierre Ingrand: Les regrets d'un serviteur de Vichy," *L'Express*, August 8, 1991, www.lexpress.fr/actualite/politique/les-regrets-d-un-serviteur-de-vichy_492450.html (accessed October 25, 2017); Laub, *After the Fall*, 115–18.

16. Porter, *Uncensored France*, 72–74.

times every week. The earth is all trampled down at the foot of the tree. It has lost its bark. It is black from the blood that drenched it.[17]

That tree had been shot too many times for further use. "A few meters away, here's the tree that's in use today. It's a beech tree. It is hardly wounded yet. Its bark has burst, however, and we can already see its white flesh with blood stains still at the same height, the height of a man's heart. No trace of a bullet underneath. The firing squad has good aim."[18]

Assassination Attempt Against Laval

Meanwhile, with the German invasion of Russia, Vichy agreed to the formation of the Legion of French Volunteers Against Bolshevism (*Légion des Volontaires Français contre le Bolchevisme*) to serve on the eastern front. On August 27, Pierre Laval, de Brinon, and others were reviewing the volunteers who were about to depart when Paul Collette shot and wounded Laval and four others with a revolver. Collette had enlisted for the very purpose of getting close enough to collaborationist leaders for such an attack.[19]

Guéhenno wrote in his diary that "in Versailles, they were presenting its flag to the Anti-Bolshevik Legion recently formed by [Eugène] Deloncle, [Marcel] Déat, and [Pierre] Constantini, when shots rang out. From the very ranks of the Legion a man shot at the officials present at the ceremony. Laval and Déat, the colonel commanding the Legion, were wounded, along with a Legionnaire." Not surprisingly, "the whole people of Paris had difficulty concealing its joy when it read the news. . . . The people think only of taking revenge on its masters, the masters of taking revenge on the people, and the same impatience reigns on both sides."[20] Agnès Humbert, who had been a member of the network of *Musée de l'Homme*, wrote from prison, "I learned of the assassination attempt on Laval, who, alas, survived!"[21]

---

17. Guéhenno, *Diary of the Dark Years*, 108–09 (entry dated August 21, 1941).

18. Guéhenno, *Diary of the Dark Years*, 108–09 (entry dated August 21, 1941). It is unclear why quotation marks were used in the above passage.

19. Warner, *Pierre Laval*, 280–81.

20. Guéhenno, *Diary of the Dark Years*, 111 (entry dated August 26, 1941).

21. Humbert, *Résistance*, 87.

It was speculated that Collette was Jewish and Communist, but he had actually belonged to the *Croix de Feu*, the rightist veteran's organization. His death sentence would be commuted to life imprisonment, Laval thinking that had he been guillotined, he would have become a martyr like Jeanne d'Arc. AP journalist Roy Porter wrote that "this young Frenchman had actually done what a lot of others had been talking about. He had fired one of the first shots in a series which, as it developed, was to spread into violence against the Germans and start the active sequel to what hitherto been passive resistance." Surviving the war, he was presented with the Legion of Honor.[22]

Escalation of Gun Seizures and Executions

Executions continued to escalate. "The tree in the Vallée-aux-Loups will soon be cut down," observed Guéhenno. "At the doors of the newspaper vendors, in the cafés, and in the Métro, no one dares to talk anymore."[23]

Then, on September 3, Wehrmacht Sergeant Ernst Hoffmann was fatally shot by two men at the Terminus Hotel in Paris. Of the ten French men selected to be shot in reprisal, four had been found guilty of firearm possession and six of Communist subversion. In retaliation for the killing of Captain Scheben on the Boulevard de Strasbourg in Paris on September 15, twelve hostages were shot. Hitler demanded that many more be executed for the death of each German soldier.[24]

The MBF (*Militärbefehlshaber in Frankreich*, military commander in France) reported 716 cases of illegal weapons possession for July 13 to September 13. Besides 32 light machine guns, weapons seized included over 1,000 each of rifles and pistols, almost 2,000 hunting guns, and roughly 200,000 rounds of ammunition.[25] "Cooperation between military police and French gendarmes and police was excellent. The French police complain that it lacks trained officers because many of them are German prisoners of war."[26]

22. Porter, *Uncensored France*, 240–41; Guéhenno, *Diary of the Dark Years*, 111, n. 164.
23. Guéhenno, *Diary of the Dark Years*, 111.
24. Laub, *After the Fall*, 118–21; Berlière and Liaigre, *Le Sang*, 62.
25. BA/MA, RW 35/9, Militärbefehlshaber in Frankreich, Anlagen zum Lagebericht für die Monate August/September 1941.
26. BA/MA, RW 35/8, Militärbefehlshaber in Frankreich, Lagebericht für die Monate August/September 1941.

The MBF reported that the activity of the military police was limited to weapons searches, supervision of French police regarding surrender of weapons, search for and arrest of British citizens, searches for German emigrants, night watch, price control, and putting up of flyers against sabotage.[27] A memorandum entitled "Fight Against Communism. Here: Prohibition of Firearms Possession" *(Bekämpfung des Kommunismus. Hier: Verbot des Schusswaffenbesitzes)* identified Dr. Grohmann as the official in charge. As it stated, the MBF requested a draft proclamation informing the population that, in the future, the possession of firearms will be punishable only by death. It was published in the press on September 13.[28]

More specifically, General von Stülpnagel issued a public announcement from Paris on September 12 that was published in newspapers the next day:

> Pursuant to the order concerning weapons possession, the possession of firearms and war materials of any kind is prohibited and subject to the death penalty or imprisonment. As of today, anyone who possesses weapons or war materials contrary to this order will be subject solely to the death penalty.[29]

Announcements of such policies as well as the identities of people apprehended and sentenced to death thereunder would be increasingly publicized under the title *"Avis"* (notice) in posters and publications.

"As the tree in the Vallée-aux-Loups had become a shrine, the occupying authorities blew it up with dynamite," wrote Guéhenno. "The firing squads have worked elsewhere ever since." Noting the imposition of a three-day curfew of 9:00 p.m., he added, "They punish us like children, 'for our own good,' declares General von Stülpnagel. We are guilty of not denouncing the

---

27. BA/MA, RW 35/4, Lagebericht des Chefs der Militärverwaltung in Frankreich, Kommandostab, für den Monat August 1940 [*sic* 1941]. Notiz betreffend Ia/Stabs-Offiziere der Feldgendarmerie, S. 10.

28. BA/MA, RW 35/544, Militärbefehlshaber in Frankreich, Verwaltungsstab, Abteilung Verwaltung, Bekämpfung des Kommunismus. Hier: Verbot des Schusswaffenbesitzes, 15. September 1941.

29. BA/MA, RW 35/1, Abdruck aus *Pariser Zeitung* vom 13. September 1941, Bekanntmachung; BA/MA, RW 35/544, *Avis*, *Le Matin*, 13. September 1941. See "La détention des armes dans la zone occupée," *Le Temps*, September 14, 1941, 4.

authors of attacks on German soldiers. The occupying authorities have not been able to arrest a single one of them."[30]

The non-Communist Resistance and General de Gaulle himself opposed the assassination of random, unimportant German soldiers as ineffective and leading to unacceptable reprisals. French collaborationists, however, were fair game—the organization Combat killed several in the southern zone. Armed actions were also used to obtain supplies, ration cards, and documents.[31]

Working with the Allies

Long-term struggle involved sabotage and cooperation with the Allies. Switzerland proved a fertile venue to maintain contact with London. Swiss banks assisted with the surreptitious transfer of funds to the Resistance. Resistance leader Guillain de Bénouville noted, "I also foresaw the possibility of using our Swiss credits for the purchase of small arms, which could be freely bought in that fortunate country."[32]

De Bénouville described how firearms were essential for the personal security of members of the Resistance as they carried out their functions: "In France we were in sore need of pistols. A man of the underground who was carrying secret documents, or whose life was at the mercy of the courageous silence of a comrade being tortured by the Germans, should certainly be armed." But one never knew when he would be subjected to a pat-down search, which entailed raising one's hands for a quick check of the coat and pants pockets along with the chest and armpits. "The best way to conceal a revolver of medium caliber, it seemed to me, would be a pocket in the left sleeve where it would be handy for use and still out of reach of the searcher who made the suspect raise his hands." De Bénouville continued:

> The death penalty had just been decreed in France for anyone carrying arms without a special permit. Until we could get hold of a permit in order to make duplicates for our men, we had to take every precaution to conceal our arms. But whatever the risk, the arms were necessary.

---

30. Guéhenno, *Diary of the Dark Years*, 113.
31. Michel, *Shadow War*, 218–20.
32. de Bénouville, *Unknown Warriors*, 83.

At least we would have a chance of escape in case of arrest, and it was better to shoot it out than to face the awful torture that would certainly be in store for some of us if captured. Besides, it was good for our comrades to know that their chiefs did not intend to be taken alive.[33]

On one occasion de Bénouville and about twenty others were informed that a submarine from Britain would arrive at night with arms, messages, and three operatives. Before going to the beach to await its arrival, they were ordered, "You will load your revolvers. There's to be no needless shooting, of course, but in case something goes wrong, you must not allow the passengers or the mail to be taken under any circumstances." The operation was a success, especially the crates of Sten guns that would be taken to secret warehouses.[34]

Execution of Hostages

Stülpnagel announced on September 17 that ten hostages were shot following acts of violence in Paris against members of the German army a week before.[35] The executions of the hostages, identified as Jews and Communists, were announced in newspapers and on red posters on walls in Paris, along with the warning of such sanctions against a larger number if the violence continued.[36] Reporting the same, the *New York Times* added that French and German police together conducted house-to-house searches for arms in Paris.[37]

Stülpnagel issued an appeal asserting that most people were aware of their duty to assist the occupying authorities maintain calm and order, but that Communists sought to sow dissension. Since the cowardly murderers had not been apprehended, he said, harsh measures would be taken that would disrupt the population's everyday life, and the people and the police must be vigilant and assist in the apprehension of the guilty parties. He concluded, "French citizens, I hope you understand these measures I am taking in your interest."[38]

---

33. de Bénouville, *Unknown Warriors*, 83–84.
34. de Bénouville, *Unknown Warriors*, 91–93.
35. "Dix Otages Fusilles en zone occupée," *Le Figaro*, September 18, 1941, 1; "Dix otages fusillés à Paris par les troupes d'occupation," *Le Temps*, September 18, 1941, 2.
36. "Les otages fusillés à Paris," *Le Figaro*, September 19, 1941, 1.
37. "Nazis Threaten People of Paris," *New York Times*, September 18, 1941, 1, 8.
38. "Les Attentats contre les troupes d'occupation," *Le Temps*, September 20, 1941, 4.

Stülpnagel next published an *Avis* headlined in bold type that twelve hostages had been executed in retaliation for the killing of a German soldier on September 16, threatening many more if the murders continued. Besides six identified as Communists and two who attacked German soldiers, four were executed for possession of arms: Pierre Guignois (also for possession of Communist tracts), Georges Masset, Daniel Loubier, and Maurice Peureux.[39] Pétain delivered a radio address denouncing the "criminal" attacks on German soldiers, and exhorting the French people to contribute to the arrests of the guilty parties.[40]

Given that the death penalty was now automatic for possession of a firearm, it became necessary to ensure that people not be executed for items that were not serious weapons. Dr. Alexnat, military administrative counselor, on behalf of the MBF, sent a telegram to Heinrich Himmler, the Reichsführer SS and head of the German police.[41] He urgently requested copies of the German laws on slashing and thrusting weapons issued before the 1938 German firearms law,[42] particularly two laws decreed in 1931 by the Weimar Republic.[43]

Following a response from the Gestapo in Berlin,[44] Stülpnagel wrote to Ernst Schaumburg, the commander of Greater Paris, that people arrested for possession of unusable weapons with sentimental value, or slashing or thrusting weapons, must be released, unless there was another reason for their arrest.[45] He obviously realized that executing French citizens for antique guns or for knives would only create unnecessary resentment. Enough bitterness

39. *"Avis,"* *Le Matin*, September 22, 1941, 1.

40. "Le maréchal Pétain lance un appel radiodiffusé aux Français de la zone occupée," *Le Temps*, September 23, 1941, 1.

41. BA/MA, RW 35/544, Militärbefehlshaber in Frankreich, Verwaltungsstab, Abteilung Verwaltung, Erlass einer Verordnung über Hieb- und Stosswaffen, 19. September 1941.

42. Waffengesetz, *Reichsgesetzblatt* 1938, I, 265, § 3.

43. Gesetz gegen Waffenmißbrauch, *Reichsgesetzblatt* 1931, I, 77, § 3; Vierte Verordnung des Reichspräsidenten zur Sicherung von Wirtschaft und Finanzen und zum Schutze des inneren Friedens vom 8. Dezember 1931, Achter Teil, Kapitel I, *Reichsgesetzblatt*, I, S. 699, 742.

44. BA/MA, RW 35/544, Reichssicherheitshauptamt an den Chef des Verwaltungsstabes beim Militärbefehlshaber in Frankreich, Vorschriften über Hieb- und Stosswaffen, 29. September 1941.

45. BA/MA, RW 35/544, Militärbefehlshaber in Frankreich, Verwaltungsstab, Abteilung Verwaltung, an den Kommandanten von Gross-Paris betreffend Umfang der Waffenablieferungspflicht, 22. September 1941.

was already provoked by shooting subjects for possession of a hunting gun or a revolver.

Stülpnagel also wrote to Vichy representative Jean-Pierre Ingrand that unusable weapons with sentimental value—not including bayonets and swords—could be returned to their owners by asking the military police at the office of the commander for Greater Paris at Place de l'Opéra.[46] How trusting would a French man be to present himself to the German police and claim a weapon that he considered unusable, but that they might not?

Ingrand then met with Stülpnagel's representative, Lieutenant Dr. Rösch, who relayed Ingrand's opinion that the German police used inconsistent standards when searching houses for weapons. Arrests were made of people who only possessed firearms that had only historic value. There was also confusion concerning sports weapons such as swords and fencing foils. Clarification was needed on whether sabers, swords, fencing foils, and daggers as well as firearms with only historic value could be excluded from the definition of being a weapon.[47]

Ingrand further conceded that the French population still possessed large numbers of weapons. Since there was now great concern about the death penalty, he sought a final surrender deadline, which would take place at French police stations, perhaps under German supervision. Ingrand further reported that the special French court to pick hostages and impose death sentences had just imposed such judgments on four persons.

No Amnesty

Ingrand's proposal for a new amnesty was rejected. Noting numerous death sentences already imposed and carried out, Dr. Grohmann advised the MBF that any new deadline would have to be extended to the sentences already imposed. Yet it had been recently proclaimed that anyone found in posses-

---

46. BA/MA, RW 35/544, Militärbefehlshaber von Stülpnagel an den Generalbevollmächtigten der französischen Regierung beim Militärbefehlshaber in Frankreich, 22. September 1941.

47. BA/MA, RW 35/544, Militärbefehlshaber in Frankreich, Kdo.Stab Abt. V.O.V.F., Aufzeichnung über Besprechung Leutnant Dr. Rösch, Staatsrat Ingrand am 23.September 1941.

sion of firearms would receive the death sentence. Anyone still in possession of firearms could throw them away, surrender them to the French police (who would not likely inform the Germans), or turn them in to the German authorities—in which case proceedings would be terminated.[48]

All the while, death sentences for arms possession were being highly publicized. In bold type on the front page, an *Avis* (notice) in *Le Matin* reported that Eugène Devigne and Mohamed Moali, both from Paris, were sentenced to death on September 26 for arms possession and were executed the next day. It was prominently signed: "Der Militärbefehlshaber in Frankreich, VON STUELPNAGEL, General der Infanterie."[49]

Another announcement by Stülpnagel had more detail. Marcel Pilongery, from Orly-Saint-Loup, was sentenced to death and then executed for possession of a French infantry rifle, a German rifle, two hunting guns, two small caliber rifles, four revolvers, and ammunition, which were hidden in his attic.[50]

By this point, regular announcements by Stülpnagel were being made of executions of French citizens for possession of firearms. While each published *Avis* lacked details, such people would have been sentenced pursuant to the German decrees, not French criminal laws, which at this time had no death penalty for arms possession. The German military administration only had a few judges and could only prosecute a limited number of cases, which meant that French courts may have conducted many of the trials and the Germans approved the death sentences, or that in more significant cases German military tribunals tried the cases.

Meanwhile the members of a ten-person ring distributing alleged Communist tracts to factories in a west Paris suburb were arrested, and a printing machine, paper, and a firearm with ammunition were seized. A search of the home of Félix Pozzi, described as the leader and an anarchist, revealed a

48. BA/MA, RW 35/544, Militärbefehlshaber in Frankreich, Verwaltungsstab, Abteilung Verwaltung, Ablieferung der Schusswaffen und Tätigkeit des Staatsgerichtshofes, 27. September 1941.

49. "*Avis*," *Le Matin*, September 29, 1941, 1.

50. "Une exécution en zone occupée pour détention illégale d'armes," *Le Temps*, October 2, 1941.

revolver and ammunition, counterfeited food cards, and stolen blank registration cards for bicycles.[51]

A massive raid by hundreds of police took place in the 13th arrondissement of Paris on October 1. At 6:14 a.m., police surrounded several blocks of apartment buildings. No one was allowed to leave as police searched from house to house, netting a mere seven arrests. One had tracts hidden in the chimney pipe and some explosives; two women were arrested for complicity, and one of them—a mother of four—also had a duplication machine and a stack of tracts entitled "France Is Being Pillaged." Two suspects had revolvers, and another had three rifles and edged weapons.[52]

Misunderstood Duty to Surrender Arms?

The *Avis* columns signed by Stülpnagel announcing people executed for possession of firearms continued to appear regularly. Sylvain-André Tribouillois from Vaires (Seine-et-Marne) was executed for possession of a stolen German rifle and 196 rifle and pistol cartridges in the Vaires train station; another rifle was found in his home.[53] René Darreau from Vendôme was executed for possession of a revolver loaded with ten cartridges and for handing out anti-German tracts.[54]

Stülpnagel realized that the prospect of facing a firing squad did not entice many stubborn French to turn in their guns, and the policy demoralized collaboration. On October 9, he wrote to Vichy representative Jean-Pierre Ingrand that the populace must have misunderstood its duty to turn in their firearms, particularly hunting guns, usable parts of weapons, and damaged or destroyed weapons. He thus requested that the French authorities announce that all such arms should be surrendered to the French authorities by October

---

51. "Arrestation d'une bande de propagandistes," *Le Temps*, September 25, 1941, 2.

52. "Une descente de police à Paris," *Le Temps*, October 2, 1941, 3. An almost identical account was published in "Une vaste opération de police à Paris," *Le Figaro*, October 3, 1941, 2. It was also covered in "More Frenchmen Shot," *New York Times*, October 2, 1941, 6.

53. "*Avis*," *Le Matin*, October 3, 1941, 1. For another account, see "Une exécution en zone occupée pour détention d'armes prohibées," *Le Temps*, October 6, 1941, 2.

54. "*Avis*," *Le Matin*, October 6, 1941, 1.

25 without penalty. The French authorities were required then to turn them over to the Germans, who would transfer them to the weapon depots.[55]

Yet Stülpnagel announced two executions that same day for possession of firearms. Lucien Marcot from Vexaincourt (Vosges) was shot for having three guns, over a hundred rifle and revolver cartridges, and numerous cartridge cases, primers, and lead used for fabricating ammunition. Gaston Pinot from Courmelles (Aisne) was shot for possession of a French submachine gun, a Browning pistol, a revolver, three hand grenades, and over 600 cartridges.[56] An internal report called Pinot a Communist.[57]

Pinot's execution for arms possession was reported in the *New York Times*, which also noted the announcement of the seventy-fifth execution of a French citizen—Jean Labragere of Angoulême—for possession of firearms. It also reported the reissuance in Paris of the decree that all arms of any kind, including hunting arms, firearm parts, and inoperable guns, be surrendered to the police. October 25 was set as the deadline for compliance, after which people in possession of such items would be subject to the death penalty. On the same day as the above, four "youths" armed with revolvers attacked a munitions depot in a Paris suburb and carried away one hundred pounds of dynamite.[58]

The United States had not yet entered the war, and this was just a sampling of the regular coverage American reporters devoted to the German occupation of France.

• • •

"Those of the Liberation"

Maurice Daguier, president of *Ceux de la Libération* (Those of the Liberation)— a group of Resistance fighters who kept their organization alive after the war— responded to my questionnaire in 2002. During the occupation, he lived with

---

55. BA/MA, RH 36/435, Brief des Militärbefehlshabers in Frankreich, Paris, an Verteiler, betreffend Ablieferung der Waffen im besetzten Gebiet, 9. Oktober 1941.

56. *"Avis,"* *Le Matin*, Oct. 10, 1941, 1.

57. BA/MA, RW 35/1211, Lage- und Tätigkeitsbericht für die Zeit vom 7. September bis 6. November 1941, Militärverwaltungsbezirk A, Tgb. Nr. 2476/41, 17. November 1941.

58. *New York Times*, October 14, 1941, 12.

his parents in Paris. While some were afraid to possess a gun, he was not; he kept a 7.65 mm (32 cal.) automatic pistol as well as a 9 mm revolver from his service in 1939–40. "Moreover," he wrote, "I owned a small 6.35 mm [.25 cal.] pistol, a real jewel, which friends of mine had given me, afraid of keeping it themselves."[59]

He recalled that, despite the threatened death penalty, "many civilians continued to keep firearms, mostly revolvers and pistols. In our movement, called Ceux de la Libération, that was most important in 1940 and the beginning of 1941 as these arms were kept in order to be able to serve at the time of the battles for liberation."

Regarding those who hid their firearms despite the German decrees, Daguier remembered how he recovered his own guns in Vendée, located in west-central France, on the Atlantic Ocean:

> In the summer of 1941, I went to search for my hidden arms that were buried close to a tree in Vendée. I found them, a 7.65 mm automatic pistol and a 9 mm revolver, with ammunition. I then hid them under a marble plate over the chimney in the dining room in my domicile at my parents' house in Paris. Both of these arms served in the battle for the liberation of Paris. I also had a small 6.35 mm pistol, a little jewel that I kept during the whole campaign after the liberation, from the 2nd Shock Battalion. [J'avais aussi un petit pistolet 6,35 mm., petit bijou, que j'avais conservé pendant toute la campagne après la libération, au 2ème. Bataillon de Choc.] Fortunately, we had other, more serious weapons when the time came for combat.

Daguier recalled that arms used in the Resistance came from various sources. Some older people who were afraid gave their weapons to younger people. Abandoned or hidden French arms were found, but robbing a weapon from German soldiers was rare, because of the risk. However, during fighting in the liberation of Paris, he knew that some German soldiers sold their weapons, before disguising themselves as civilians to desert the routed German army.

---

59. Maurice Daguier, president, Ceux de la Libération, response to author's questionnaire, February 27, 2002.

Asked about use of arms by civilians, Daguier recounted how Roger Co-quoin (aka Lenormand)—chief of the movement Ceux de la Libération—fell into a trap set by the Germans. He drew his pistol and cut down one of the Germans before being shot down.

Daguier told the story of the Gallais group, called *La Toucheférond*, which was founded in July 1940 in Brittany by René Gallais and his family to-gether with Jules Frémont and three of his companions. Answering General de Gaulle's call, the group dedicated themselves to securing the passage of young people to the free zone and to England, to gathering intelligence on the German troops and their movements, and to the recovery of the aban-doned weapons of war. Numerous citizens from the commune of Fougères courageously came forward and swelled the ranks of the group.

Weapons and munitions were unearthed, cleaned, and repaired by the group and then transported to and hidden in nearby towns of the Ille-et-Vilaine department and the neighboring forests. The armaments of the group included thirty military rifles (twenty were German), a radio transmitter, nine French machine guns, four light machine guns, and a heavy machine gun with belts. They had plentiful ammunition, cheddite, and other explosives.

The group was organized in clandestine combat units that were decen-tralized into sectors. Small units operated with arms and explosives in the forests. The depots of German munitions were located, and the station and troop movements were carefully watched. A gendarme named Jagu kept the group informed of police checkpoints on the roads, allowing arms to be safely transported.

A denunciation led to tragedy on October 9, 1941. A number of German soldiers had been brought in during the night by the Gestapo. Extensive searches turned up two depots of arms, and fifty-eight persons were arrested, almost all members of the Gallais group. They were tortured by the Gestapo, but no one confessed. Seven were executed, in some cases by decapitation at the Stadelheim Prison in Germany, which was notorious for its use of the guillotine. Madame Gallais and her daughter Huguette Gallais were deported to death camps but survived.

The sixtieth anniversary of the mass arrests was commemorated in the city of Fougères on October 9, 2001. Maurice Daguier represented the Ceux de la

Libération, and various prefects, mayors, and former Resistance fighters from Brittany attended to pay homage to the group. The ever-valiant and animated Huguette Gallais, who had been part of the team to recover and render weapons serviceable during the Resistance and who survived her deportation, was there.

• • •

A Dire Need for Arms and Supplies

A true resistance movement required far more than the isolated acts of independent groups. Ties between the French and de Gaulle in London were sparse. Into the void stepped Jean Moulin, a former prefect who was very familiar with the groups operating in France. He made his way to London via Lisbon in October 1941. The Resistance, he reported to British intelligence and to de Gaulle, needed discipline, orders, financing, and especially arms. Isolated acts and disorganization was a recipe for failure.[60]

Independently of the above, in mid-October Henri Frenay met with two Americans, whose real names he was not told, in the dimly lit home of a Lyons businessman. He spoke at length about the Resistance and the secret army that was beginning to take shape, and which would attack when requested by the Allies. He noted that "the liberation of our country will be accomplished mostly by the Allied armies," but "our contribution to the struggle will save you valuable lives and equipment." He detailed the need for finances, radio sets, and weapons. Frenay later learned that the Americans were Colonel Barnwell Legge, the American military attaché in Bern, and Allen Dulles, Office of Strategic Services (OSS) operative in Switzerland.[61]

The Last Deadline?

While most announcements of executions for gun possession revealed not much more than the name, town of residence, and dates of sentence and execution, one Stülpnagel *Avis* gave more detail. Jean Labregère from An-

---

60. Cobb, *The Resistance*, 92–94.
61. Frenay, *Night Will End*, 100–2.

goulême (Charente) was sentenced to death on October 7 and executed on the 12th, rather than being shot on the day after sentencing, which was the usual timeline. Indeed, he had been apprehended in September. The delay of several weeks gave ample time to torture him in hopes that he would denounce comrades. He allegedly attempted to set fire to straw stored in the Angoulême train station, was caught by a German patrol, brandished a loaded pistol, and also had a revolver and over a hundred cartridges. *Le Matin* denounced his cowardly act that would make things worse for everyone.[62]

At this point, French authorities cooperated to inform the public of Stülpnagel's latest demand and threat to disobedient gun owners. On October 15, Paris newspapers published the following:

Last Deadline for Surrendering Arms

Communiqué from the Office of the General Secretary of Information:

In order to avoid any misunderstanding about the surrendering of firearms still possessed by private citizens, it is announced to the population that hunting guns, as well as usable parts of arms or deteriorated or inoperable arms, also must be turned in.

This turning in shall be risk- and sanction-free until October 25. These arms shall be surrendered in neighborhoods to the ward police stations, and in the suburbs to the district police stations. Upon request, a receipt shall be issued to the owner of hunting weapons, and the arm shall be tagged.

Anyone who does not take advantage of this last opportunity to get rid of the arms listed above risks the most serious punishment.[63]

As proof of the risks of punishment, newspapers went into a frenzy to publish notices of executions with admonitions to reject foreign propaganda and comply with the occupation authorities. Executions for possession of explosives

62. "*Avis,*" *Le Matin,* October 14, 1941, 1.
63. "Derniers Délais Pour La Remise Des Armes," *Le Matin,* October 15, 1941, 1; "La remise des armes en zone occupée," *Le Temps,* October 15, 1941, 2. For shorter versions, see BA/MA, RH 20-6/999, Veröffentlichung *Pariser Zeitung,* 15. Oktober 1941; BA/MA, RW 35/544, Militärbefehlshaber in Frankreich, Verwaltungsstab, Abteilung Verwaltung, Letzte Frist zur Ablieferung von Waffen, 1941.

and for complicity with the enemy were justified, given the air attack on Le Havre by the British, as a traitor must have guided the enemy strikes.[64]

Such seething propaganda extended to people whose only offense was the mere possession of firearms. Stülpnagel issued an *Avis* that René Baudet from Villejuif (Seine) was sentenced to death on October 17 and executed the next day for possession of a double-barreled shotgun with two spare barrels, a rifle, a revolver, and over 200 cartridges. *Le Matin* blamed this innocuous cache on the Gaullist and Communist criminals who would only bring bloodshed to France.[65]

Yet another *Avis* announced that Hubert Tuffery from Beaugency (Loiret) was executed for a hunting gun, a pistol, cartridges, and nine explosive charges. *Le Matin* asked whether France could rise from such chaos and ruin.[66]

"We're in a state of numbness," Jean Guéhenno confided to his diary. "Every morning the paper gives us the name of another man who has been shot. We grit our teeth as we read."[67] Yet the worst was yet to come.

Execution of 150 Hostages for the Shooting of Lt. Col. Hotz

On October 20, in Nantes, Communists Gilbert Brustlein and Guisco Spartaco were looking for Germans to shoot when two well-dressed officers suddenly appeared at the Place de la Cathédrale.[68] They quickly followed the officers until they reached the sidewalk of the rue du Roi-Albert. According to his account, Brustlein told Spartacos, "'You take the one on the right, I'll take that one.' I take my two 6.35s [mm, .25 cal. pistols] and Spartaco his 7.65 [mm, .32 cal. pistol]. We are on the sidewalk, a half meter right behind them. We fire. . . ." One collapsed, hit by Brustlein's pistol, the other looked back—he was not shot, as Spartaco's pistol had jammed. The shooters sprinted away and escaped on a tram.[69]

---

64. "*Avis,*" *Le Matin,* October 15, 1941, 1; "*Avis,*" *Le Matin,* October 16, 1941, 1.

65. "*Avis,*" *Le Matin,* October 20, 1941, 1.

66. "*Avis,*" *Le Matin,* October 21, 1941, 1.

67. Guéhenno, *Diary of the Dark Years,* 120.

68. See Berlière and Liaigre, *Le Sang,* 127–47.

69. Berlière and Liaigre, *Le Sang,* 130–31. See also Cobb, *The Resistance,* 78–79.

The dead officer turned out to be none other than the *Feldkommandant* of Nantes, Lieutenant Colonel Karl Friedrich Hotz. Hitler wanted as many as 150 prisoners executed in retaliation, but Stülpnagel urged delay to give the French police a chance to apprehend the perpetrators. Hitler relented, but ordered that 50 be executed immediately and another 50 be promptly executed if the killers were not quickly found.[70] Stülpnagel issued this *Avis* on October 21:[71]

> Cowardly criminals in the pay of England and Moscow shot the Nantes *Feldkommandant* in the back and killed him on the morning of October 20, 1941.
>
> As penalty for this crime, I ordered the execution of 50 hostages.
>
> Given the seriousness of the crime, 50 other hostages shall be executed, if the guilty parties are not arrested by midnight on October 23, 1941.
>
> I shall give a **FIFTEEN MILLION FRANC REWARD** to inhabitants of France who contribute to finding the guilty parties.
>
> Any helpful information can be given to any German or French police service.
>
> Upon request, this information shall be kept confidential.

Guéhenno quipped in his diary, "The newspapers, docile as they are, have printed the figure of 15 million francs in large capitals; it seems it's a new prize in the National Lottery."[72] The newspapers denounced the crime as an assassination directed by London and Moscow to disrupt French-German collaboration.[73]

The morning after the shooting, a list of one hundred names of hostages to execute was given to Dr. Franz Albrecht Medicus, chief military administrative officer (*Kriegsverwaltungschef*) of District B at Angers.[74] While the list was being considered, Medicus directed, "The military police are to report by November 10, 1941, the extent to which the population has followed the

---

70. Laub, *After the Fall*, 136–38. For a timeline of events following the assassination, see Umbreit, *Militärbefehlshaber in Frankreich*, 129–33.

71. *"Avis,"* *Le Matin*, October 22, 1941, 1.

72. Guéhenno, *Diary of the Dark Years*, 121.

73. "Après l'attentat criminel de Nantes," *Le Matin*, October 22, 1941, 1.

74. Laub, *After the Fall*, 138–39.

order to surrender [weapons]. This deadline must be observed at any cost."[75] Stülpnagel had ordered that a month earlier, but now it was ever more urgent either to scare gun owners to surrender their arms or to eradicate the gun owners who refused.

Stülpnagel issued the following further *Avis* the same day as the above, that the following people in eastern France were executed for possession of firearms: Henry Tirole from Saint-Hippolyte (Doubs), Georges Bourotte from Troyes (Aube), and Jules Steinmetz from Bayon (Meurthe-et-Moselle). *Le Matin* deplored the illusions propagated by the Communist-Gaullist radio that tricked such people to risk their lives and the lives of countless innocents.[76]

Yet another attack took place on the evening of October 21, this time in Bordeaux. A cyclist came upon Dr. Hans-Gottfried Reimers of the military administrative office (*Kriegsverwaltungsrat*) as he walked down Wilson Boulevard and fired five shots, killing him. Hitler again ordered the execution of as many as 150 hostages.[77]

Stülpnagel issued yet another *Avis* the next morning. He recounted that at dusk on October 21, a day after the Nantes murder, cowardly assassins in the pay of England or Moscow shot and killed a German in Bordeaux and were able to flee. As retaliation, he again ordered the execution of fifty hostages. If the murderers were not arrested by midnight on October 26, fifty more would be executed. He again offered a reward of fifteen million francs.[78]

A total of forty-eight hostages would be shot on October 22 in retaliation for the Nantes attack—two World War I veterans had been crossed off the list.[79] Most were Communists, but a few were Gaullists; a seventeen-year-old boy was included, as was a farmer with a death sentence for not turning in his hunting rifle.[80] Some of the hostages were shot at the firing range of Le Bêle, near Nantes, three or four at a time. The rest were taken to a quarry

---

75. BA/MA, RW 35/1262, Chef des Militärverwaltungsbezirks B, 21. Oktober 1941, Besondere Anordnung Nr. 472.

76. "*Avis*," *Le Matin*, October 22, 1941, 1.

77. Laub, *After the Fall*, 139.

78. "*Avis*," *Le Matin*, October 24, 1941, 1.

79. Laub, *After the Fall*, 139.

80. Robert Gildea, *Marianne in Chains* (New York: Henry Holt and Company, 2002), 235–36. For an account of the entire episode, see Lecornu, *Préfet sous l'Occupation allemande*, 48–100.

near Châteaubriant, where they were tied to stakes and shot nine at a time. A film entitled *La mer à l'aube* (*Calm at Sea*) that depicts the episode was released in 2011.[81]

The Germans never discovered who shot Hotz. Spartaco would be arrested and executed the following year because of other activities. Brustlein was never apprehended. After the end of the war, he revealed his role, but he was not seen by all as a heroic resister: Hotz was not a Nazi and followed a lenient occupation policy; Brustlein shot him in the back, and then allowed almost fifty hostages to be executed instead of turning himself in.[82]

De Gaulle: Random Shootings Premature

The evening of October 22, Pétain broadcast a speech deploring the deaths of the Germans and of the fifty hostages, to which would be added fifty more if the guilty parties were not found. He admonished, "Fellow French, your duty is clear: the killing must stop. As a result of the Armistice, we have handed over our arms. We may not take them back to strike the Germans in the back."[83]

Guéhenno summarized the speech thus: "At two o'clock, the Marshal spoke to us once more. He denounced foreign plots, hatched in England, and invited us to become informers."[84]

Admiral François Darlan, Vichy's prime minister, met with Stülpnagel after the Nantes attack to urge that collaboration counseled restraint.[85] In a radio address, Darlan condemned the attacks and implored the French people to abide by the armistice, adding that while the occupation was heavy, it was supposedly correct.[86]

Le Matin justified the executions of hostages under this premise: "It is the law of war."[87] Stülpnagel himself, while willing to carry out orders from Berlin, told General Eduard Wagner, a member of the Wehrmacht general

---

81. *La mer à l'aube* (*Calm at Sea*), directed by Volker Schlöndorff (Strasbourg: Arte Éditions, 2012), DVD.
82. Gildea, *Marianne in Chains*, 243, 375–76.
83. "Le Pathétique Discours Du Chef De L'État," *Le Matin*, October 23, 1941, 1.
84. Guéhenno, *Diary of the Dark Years*, 122.
85. Laub, *After the Fall*, 141.
86. "Le Message Due Vice-Président Du Conseil," *Le Matin*, October 23, 1941, 1.
87. "Le seul devoir des patriotes," *Le Matin*, October 23, 1941, 1.

staff, that "the attacks were carried out by small terror groups and English soldiers or spies who move from place to place; that the majority of Frenchmen do not support them. I clearly believe that shooting hostages only embitters the people and makes future rapprochement more difficult. . . . I personally have warned against Polish methods in France."[88] Wagner called back with Hitler's response, ordering that fifty hostages be executed for each attack.

The French leadership in London thought the random shooting of German soldiers to be premature. Charles de Gaulle broadcast from BBC on October 23 that, as the aggressors, "Germans should be killed by Frenchmen. . . . Those of them who now fall under the rifle, the revolver or the knife of patriots precede the others in death only a little." However, tactics must be followed in war, and thus "my orders to those in occupied territory are not to kill Germans there openly. This for one reason only: that it is, at present, too easy for the enemy to retaliate by massacring our fighters, now, for the time being, disarmed." The time for attack would come when the forces were ready.[89]

More Executions and Looting of Arms

Executions for possession of weapons continued on an almost daily basis. Stülpnagel issued an *Avis* on October 23 that Pierre Lerein from Floirac (Gironde) was executed that day for possession of arms and explosives. *Le Matin* could not resist condemning such people and finding their execution to be just.[90] The next day saw another Stülpnagel *Avis* announcing the execution of the following people for possession of arms and ammunition: Roger Jean Bonnand from Paris, Paul Grossin from Mitry-Mory (Seine-et-Marne), and Hubert Sibille from Cornimont (Vosges). *Le Matin* again had this tonguelashing: "They were keeping arms, why? There are people who foolishly or deliberately hide arsenals at home. . . . Anyone in possession of a pistol or a gun can only be looked at as a potential assassin. And expect the most serious sanctions."[91]

---

88. Laub, *After the Fall*, 139, citing T-77/1624/55-7.
89. Berlière and Franck Liaigre, *Le Sang*, 273–74 (full text in French); Charles de Gaulle, *The Complete War Memoirs of Charles de Gaulle*, trans. Richard Howard (New York: Carroll & Graf, 1998), 263–64.
90. "*Avis*," *Le Matin*, October 24, 1941, 1.
91. "*Avis*," *Le Matin*, October 25, 1941, 1.

The Vichy government negotiated three and four-day extensions of the next hostage execution dates for the attacks in Nantes and Bordeaux respectively. It was said to be doubling its efforts to apprehend the assassins and save the lives of hostages.[92] In Bordeaux, the mayor and town council issued calls to help search for the guilty parties.[93] After some French people provided information that narrowed the scope of the search for the Nantes and Bordeaux attackers, and refused the financial award, Stülpnagel decided that any of their parents held as prisoners of war in Germany could return to France, and would consider release of other family members.[94]

Stülpnagel then declared a grace period on the executions to allow the people to assist the investigations. He was pleased to inform Vichy that the Führer agreed, thus allowing the French to help apprehend the assassins.[95]

Meanwhile, the confiscation of usable arms continued unabated, with nuances. An order from the district headquarters (*Kreiskommandantur*) in Lunéville on October 28 required the surrender of all rifles, carbines, hunting firearms, pistols, revolvers, other firearms, and sidearms (bayonets and swords) produced in 1870 or later. It exempted arms produced before 1870, together with all other slashing and thrusting weapons, regardless of date of manufacture. The owner of each exempted weapon was required to have paperwork confirming that the item need not be surrendered.[96] The Germans did not want to fool with arms that would be useless for resistance.

However, looting the good stuff could continue. The head of the Armed Forces High Command (*Oberkommando der Wehrmacht*, or OKW) in Berlin issued an order on October 28 that no compensation would be paid for hunting guns confiscated from private citizens in France and Belgium. The excuse was that neither France nor Belgium reimbursed Germans for hunting guns confiscated during the occupation of the Rhineland after World

---

92. "Le sort des cent derniers otages," *Le Temps*, October 25–26, 1941, 1.

93. "Les suites des attentats contre les armées d'occupation," *Le Temps*, October 27, 1941, 2; "Les attentats de Nantes et de Bordeaux," *Le Temps*, October 29, 1941, 1.

94. "Après les attentats de Nantes et de Bordeaux," *Le Figaro*, October 28, 1941, 1; "Sur la piste des responsables des attentats de Nantes et de Bordeaux," *Le Temps*, October 28, 1941, 2.

95. "Les attentats de Nantes et de Bordeaux," *Le Temps*, October 29, 1941, 1; "Le Sort des Otages de Nantes et de Bordeaux," *Le Temps*, October 30, 1941, 1.

96. BA/MA, RH 36/526, Tagesbefehl Nr. 40/41 der Kreiskommandantur I/594 in Luneville, 28. Oktober 1941.

War I.[97] While it is difficult to believe that these post–World War I confiscations remotely compared to those in World War II, this was no more than a
justification for massive looting of firearms from private citizens in violation
of international law.

In the German perspective, plundering public and private property was
revenge for the reparations Germany had to pay France based on the Versailles
Treaty following the Great War. Requiring the French to pay occupation costs
and the confiscation of art, firearms, and everything of value that was not
nailed down (and much that was nailed down) seemed like just retribution.
Besides, in the Führer's view, the *deutsches Volk* (German people) were entitled
to the world's riches.

Among the great quantity of arms surrendered in Dijon, the seat of District C, as a result of the recent decree, was a cannon manufactured in 1864
in Saint-Étienne. Turned in by an anonymous collector, it weighed 187 kilos
and had a barrel 3.6 meters long nine centimeters in diameter.[98]

"Based on latest deadline imposed, large numbers of weapons were surrendered or thrown away everywhere," noted the MBF. Measures against Gaullist and Communist organizations as well as individuals possessing weapons
were successful, particularly because of effective participation by the French
authorities. Some sixty-four French were sentenced to death for resistance
activities, violent crime, and illegal weapons possession.[99]

Appended to the report was data for September 13–November 12 showing
870 instances of illegal weapons possession compared to 716 for the previous
period. Confiscated weapons included 55 machine guns, 7,313 rifles, 6,764
pistols, 6,532 hunting guns, 425,692 rounds of hunting ammunition, and
445,673 rounds of other ammunition.[100]

Incentives for denunciations paid off. Two prisoners of war were released
after their relatives acted as informants regarding the Nantes and Bordeaux

97. BA/MA, RW 35/544, Oberkommando der Wehrmacht, Jagdwaffen aus französischem
und belgischem Privatbesitz, 28. Oktober 1941.

98. "Une arme curieuse est remise à la police de Dijon," *Le Matin*, October 31, 1941, 1. See
also "A quoi pouvait servir ce fusil de 3 mètres 60 de long," *Le Figaro*, November 1, 1941, 2.

99. BA/MA, RW 35/10, Militärbefehlshaber in Frankreich, Lagebericht für die Monate
Oktober/November 1941.

100. BA/MA, RW 35/11, Militärbefehlshaber in Frankreich, Anlagen zum Lagebericht
für die Monate Oktober/November 1941.

attacks.[101] Three railroad workers were paid for preventing sabotage of the railroad by an explosion.[102]

In Vichy France, sentences were reported for distribution of tracts and for Communist cells. Police in Clermont-Ferrand conducted a vast operation resulting in thirty arrests and the seizure of duplicating equipment, typewriters, paper and ink, six automatic pistols, and alleged Communist and Masonic literature.[103]

In view of increased communist activity, MBF staff considered whether to ban slashing and thrusting weapons (*Hieb- und Stosswaffen*). A prohibition was considered unwarranted in that it was difficult to distinguish such a weapon and a simple pocket knife; there had been only one attack on a German soldier with a slashing weapon, and in raids, no one in the street was found to carry such a weapon.[104]

Hunting guns were another matter. A mid-November report from District B noted the surrender of large numbers as a result of the new deadline, although results varied from department to department, perhaps because the prefects did not all issue the same orders to the police. The success of the action proved that it was correct, as it enhanced the security of the occupying forces.[105] For the previous two months, over 1,500 hunting guns, around 300 rifles, 1,000 handguns, and 20 cane guns were turned in. House searches conducted in the investigation of the murder of a Captain Marquardt netted 17 persons found in possession of weapons, mostly hunting rifles, and they were handed over to the military courts for prosecution. French gendarmes discovered a weapons cache in Plessé, in the Nantes area.[106]

A District B court sentenced a Mr. Cautret to death for aiding the enemy and added a year of prison for not surrendering ammunition, and then executed him. Besides distributing anti-German flyers, he was apprehended in

101. "Après les attentats de Nantes et de Bordeaux," *Le Temps*, November 1–2, 1941, 4.

102. "Nouvelles diverses," *Le Temps*, November 3, 1941, 4.

103. "La Répression Des Menees Communistes," *Le Temps*, November 3, 1941, 4.

104. BA/MA, RW 35/544, Militärbefehlshaber in Frankreich, Verwaltungsstab, Abteilung Verwaltung, Erlass einer Verordnung über Hieb- und Stosswaffen, 10. November 1941.

105. BA/MA, RW 35/1264, Lagebericht des Militärverwaltungsbezirks B, Verwaltungsstab, Verwaltungsgruppe, für die Zeit vom 16. September bis 15. November 1941.

106. BA/MA, RW 35/1264, Lagebericht des Militärverwaltungsbezirks B, Abt. Ic für die Zeit vom 16. September bis 15. November 1941.

Saint-Nazaire with several small bags of lead, 65 finished hunting cartridges, and an additional 30 cartridges. The same court sentenced Fleurimond Royer to death for failing to surrender ammunition, firearms, and military gear. He too was executed.[107]

France was awash in arms being hidden, surrendered, and confiscated, but members of the emerging Resistance could never find enough. *Défense de la France*, an underground newspaper established by students in Paris, implored, "[O]btain firearms; someone will know how to find them. Each should know how to use a revolver, a rifle, a submachine-gun, a light machine gun, a machine gun. . . . The day will come."[108]

On November 18, Paris police announced the arrest of terrorists responsible for recent attacks. Numerous searches netted arms along with just one man (another was dead) and a woman, who admitted to having sabotaged railroads and factories and to the arson of farms. The police and the gendarmerie pursued a fugitive considered armed and dangerous who escaped.[109]

"A new armed attack on Boulevard Magenta," noted Jean Guéhenno in his diary on December 3. "A German officer killed. Now it's the turn of the 10th arrondissement to be punished. And all Paris is threatened with the most vigorous reprisals if we do not denounce the guilty parties before December 10."[110]

On November 27, MBF Stülpnagel ordered that all confiscated weapons, except hunting arms surrendered pursuant to the recent decree, had to be transferred immediately to the Wehrmacht's collection area in Versailles. That included all rifles and pistols, regardless of kind, caliber, or state of repair.[111] Two weeks later, he issued a report, signed by Dr. Werner Best, that large numbers of French civilians surrendered arms without the risk of punishment pursuant to the October 9 decree.[112] The results were as follows:

107. BA/MA, RW 35/1264, Lagebericht des Militärverwaltungsbezirks B, Kommandostab Abt. III, für die Zeit vom 15. November 1941 bis 15. Januar 1942, 17. Januar 1942.

108. "Ni Allemands, ni Russes, ni Anglais," *Défense de la France*, N° 3, 20 novembre 1941, reprinted in *Le Journal Défense de la France* (Paris: Presses Universitaires de France, 1961), 13–14.

109. "Arrestation de terroristes coupables de récents attentats," *Le Temps*, November 20, 1941, 1.

110. Guéhenno, *Diary of the Dark Years*, 123 (entry dated December 3, 1941).

111. BA/MA, RW 35/1276, Tagesbefehl Nr. 143 des Militärverwaltungsbezirks C, Nordostfrankreich, 5. Dezember 1941.

112. BA/MA, RW 35/544, Militärbefehlshaber in Frankreich, Verwaltungsstab, Abteilung Verwaltung, Ablieferung der Waffen im besetzten Gebiet, 10. Dezember 1941.

Kind of weapons and ammunition surrendered	District A	District B	District C	District of Bordeaux	Total	Comment
Machine guns	38	8	45	5	96	Plus 16,500 military and small-caliber rifles reported as total number by Bordeaux
Military rifles	4,191	1,163	5,940	see comment	11,294	
Hunting guns	10,189	3,250	9,152	see comment	22,591	
Small caliber rifles	1,814	–	1,185	see comment	2,999	
Rifle parts	243	91	see comment	–	334	District C reported large numbers of weapons parts, but no specific numbers
Pistols and revolvers	3,485	1,345	4,795	2,460	12,085	
Other weapons	–	–	1 grenade launcher 12 signal pistols	–	–	
Rifle ammunition	12,069	3,948 plus 4 cases	50,000	–	66,017 plus 4 cases	District Bordeaux reported large amounts of military and hunting ammunition, but no specific numbers
Pistol ammunition	–	2,321	6,000	–	8,321	
Hunting ammunition	77,422	13,505	281,503	–	372,430	
Hand grenades	–	6 plus 4 cases	188	–	194 plus 4 cases	
Explosives, etc.	–	6 cases plus 25 kg of powder	25 kg of powder	–	6 cases plus 50 kg of powder	
Bombs	–	11	8	–	19	
Ammunition parts	–	45 kg of pellets	620 kg of lead	–	–	
Sidearms	2,149	1,209	10,109	370	13,837	

The above did not include arms surrendered in Greater Paris because the numbers were too great, but they included: 12 trucks with guns of all kinds and calibers; 3 trucks with pistols; 2 trucks with ammunition, powder, and explosives; and 9 trucks with sidearms. While they were still being counted, the confiscated weapons from Greater Paris included: 4,100 hunting guns; 150,000 rounds of hunting ammunition; 3,000,000 cartridge cases; 350 kg of shot; 1,600 *Tesching* (parlor) rifles; 317 barrels for double-barreled shotguns; 162 shoulder stocks; and 170,000 rounds of parlor rifle ammunition. The French police had not yet finished their delivery of weapons surrendered in Paris. It was estimated that this represented only half of the surrendered weapons.

The civilian population left some previously unsurrendered military weapons and pistols in the vicinity of mayors' offices and police stations, the above report continued. Apparently the proclamation published in the press about the weapons surrender had indicated freedom from punishment only for hunting guns, weapons parts, and damaged or destroyed weapons, but not for usable weapons. District of Bordeaux therefore inquired whether people surrendering usable military weapons should be prosecuted by a military court. While this was seen as contrary to the intent of the measure to give people a last chance to surrender weapons of any kind, the report concluded that the command staff division would have to decide the issue.

The above amnesty to surrender arms theoretically began on October 9 when it was decreed, but it was apparently not published widely until October 15, and it closed on October 25. It is thus likely that most of the weapons were turned in during the final ten days of the period.

While actual figures will never be known, the *Saint-Hubert-Club de France* estimated that through the end of 1941, 700,000 civilian firearms had been surrendered, of which 100,000 had been sent to Germany.[113]

The Night and Fog Decree

Meanwhile, on December 7—the same day as the Japanese sneak attack on Pearl Harbor—Hitler issued the Night and Fog (*Nacht und Nebel*) Decree.

113. "Le recensement des armes de chasse," in *Le Saint-Hubert*, organe officiel du Saint-Hubert-Club de France, n° 6, 40e année, novembre–décembre 1941, 65.

OKW Chief of Staff and Field Marshal Wilhelm Keitel explained, "In the eyes of Hitler, punishing crimes with prison sentences . . . is a sign of weakness. An effective and enduring deterrence can only be had through death sentences and equally far-reaching measures, measures that leave the relatives and public uncertain over the fate of the perpetrator. Deportation to Germany also serves this purpose."[114]

To be sure, many of the condemned continued to be identified in the newspapers. Just a day after the above decree, the commander of Greater Paris announced that the following Parisians had been sentenced to death and executed for possession of arms and ammunition: Joseph Brunet, Albert Antoine, Louis Buchmann, and Marcel-Auguste de Priou.[115]

On December 10, the general secretary of the Vichy government announced that attacks against the occupation forces endangered France, and thus new edicts had been issued to repress the foreign paratroopers, Communists, and Jews who were responsible. Foreigners who committed crimes would be subject to court martial and execution. Jews would be placed in work camps or concentration camps. Communists would be arrested, as had some 13,000 in the last six weeks in the free zone.[116]

A plea to the people of Paris was issued to condemn recent attacks against the Wehrmacht. It was signed by Fernand de Brinon, the French ambassador to the Germans in the occupied territory; the prefect and general secretaries of the Seine department; and the bishop and archbishop of Paris.[117]

"The firing squads are in action again," wrote Guéhenno in his diary on December 12. "Eleven people in Brest the day before yesterday, five Parisians yesterday."[118] That was followed by the execution for arms possession of Henri Jahier from Drancy and Auguste Lemaire from Fontenay-aux-Roses,[119] and of Mohamed Bounaceur (also spelled ben Naceur) of Ivry.[120]

---

114. Laub, *After the Fall*, 157.

115. "Avis," *Le Matin*, December 13–14, 1941, 1.

116. "Les Mesures De Répression contre le Terrorisme," *Le Figaro*, December 11, 1941, 1.

117. "Un Appel à la population parisienne," *Le Figaro*, December 12, 1941, 1.

118. Guéhenno, *Diary of the Dark Years*, 134 (entry dated December 12, 1941).

119. "Avis," *Le Matin*, December 24–25, 1941, 1.

120. "Avis," *Le Matin*, December 30, 1941, 1; "Exécution capitale à Paris," *Le Temps*, December 31, 1941, 4.

A Crime not to Denounce?

Denunciations had always been grist for the execution mill, but now the time had come to make it a crime not to denounce. Informing on one's neighbors was the subject of a decree issued on December 27: "Whosoever may have knowledge that arms are in the possession or keeping of an unauthorized person or persons is obliged to declare that at the nearest police headquarters." In the post-war Nuremberg trials, French prosecutor Charles Dubost stated that "in their determination to impose their reign of terror the Germans resorted to means which revolt the conscience of decent people. Of these means one of the most repugnant is the call for informers."[121] While the penalty for failure to inform was unclear, in the coming year the death penalty was debated as the ultimate sanction.

Official reports for roughly the final two months of 1941 reveal a still disobedient element of the French population who refused to surrender arms and an ever more deadly, repressive occupation policy. Conditions were deteriorating, according to the Council of the Higher Military Court in northwestern France, which had good cooperation from the French judicial authorities. Offenses punished by death were on the rise, including aiding the enemy, weapons possession, dissemination of anti-German flyers, sabotage, and attacks against members of the Wehrmacht. A Gaullist student group whose members had arms and engaged in espionage had been broken up. Food shortages prompted hunting offenses by poachers.[122]

As the year drew to a close, despite all of the efforts to eradicate French gun ownership, the task appeared impossible. District B reported numerous incidents of weapons possession for the two-month period beginning November 16. To be sure, the October 9 amnesty had netted 426 hunting guns and rifles, 84 revolvers, and some 20,000 rounds of ammunition. But arrests, proceedings, and executions for weapons possession went on and on. For that offense, a municipal worker from the town of L'Huisserie was

121. *Trial of the Major War Criminals before the International Military Tribunal: Nuremberg January 22–February 4, 1946* (Buffalo, New York: William S. Hein & Co., 1995), 6:395 (January 31, 1946).

122. BA/MA, RW 35/1213, Lagebericht für die Zeit vom 16. November 1941 bis 15. Januar 1942, Chef der Militärverwaltung Nordwestfrankreich (not dated).

executed and a sixty-seven-year-old estate owner was sentenced to six months in prison, while in Chailland three were arrested for weapons possession and a municipal worker and a woman were arrested for aiding and abetting weapons possession. The military court at Le Mans sentenced six and dismissed charges against eleven. In Tours, eight were sentenced and one was awaiting sentencing for possession of a machine gun with 2 full magazines, 2 French rifles, 178 rounds of carbine ammunition, and 5 sidearms.[123]

Besides two arrests in the district of Pontivy, testimony of a poacher in a murder trial led to nine additional arrests for illegal arms. Four old rifles and two pistols were found there, probably thrown away by their owners. And in Nantes, a harness maker named Fleurimond Royer of Saint-Marie had been arrested on November 11, sentenced on December 2, and executed on December 17, 1941. This timeline may have reflected how long it took to try and extract information on other people who possessed firearms.

The above report ended ominously but tellingly: "Illegal weapons possession still represents the core of criminal activities of the French. It appears almost impossible to get rid of it."

123. BA/MA, RW 35/1264, Lagebericht des Militärverwaltungsbezirks B, Südwestfrankreich, für die Zeit vom 16. November 1941 bis 15. Januar 1942, 19. Januar 1942.

An anti-government demonstration in Paris on February 6, 1934, culminated in disorders at the Place de la Concord. Police and Mobile Guards opened fire on civilians, killing eighteen, while one policeman was killed. The resulting National Union government of rightists and Radical-Socialists reacted by restricting public assemblies and firearm possession. ERVL0016203 ©ROGER-VIOLLET / THE IMAGE WORKS

French Foreign Minister Pierre Laval signs accord with Italian Prime Minister Benito Mussolini (standing, right), January 7, 1935. By mid-year, Laval became Prime Minister, and on October 23, he issued the decree-law (décret-loi) requiring the registration of firearms. KEYSTONE, ULLSTEIN BILDERDIENST, 01022355

On May 10, 1940, Germany launched its blitzkrieg against France, Belgium, and Holland. In every town, as shown in this scene, posters were immediately nailed up ordering the surrender of firearms under the penalty of death. *Die Deutsche Wochenschau* (German Weekly News), May 15, 1940. BUNDESARCHIV, TRANSIT FILM GMBH

This decree concerning the surrender of firearms and radio transmitters in the occupied territories was posted throughout Nazi-occupied France. See translation in sidebar.
MUSÉE DE L'ORDRE DE LA LIBÉRATION, PARIS

Decree Concerning the Possession of Arms and Radio Transmitters in the Occupied Territories

1) All firearms and all sorts of munitions, hand grenades, explosives and other war materials must be surrendered immediately.

Delivery must take place within 24 hours to the closest "Kommandantur" [German commander's office] unless other arrangements have been made. Mayors will be held strictly responsible for the execution of this order. The [German] troop commanders may allow exceptions.

2) Anyone found in possession of firearms, munitions, hand grenades, or other war materials will be sentenced to death or forced labor or in lesser cases prison.

3) Anyone in possession of a radio or a radio transmitter must surrender it to the closest German military authority.

4) All those who would disobey this order or would commit any act of violence in the occupied lands against the German army or against any of its troops will be condemned to death.

The Commander in Chief of the Army

French troops of the 14th regiment of Zouaves, after an honorable defense against overwhelming German forces, surrender their arms at Lille on May 31, 1940.
BUNDESARCHIV, BILD 1011-126-0311-14 / HEINZ FREMKE

Citizens with hunting guns on their shoulders passing German soldiers to surrender their arms at the town hall. DOMINIQUE VENNER, LES ARMES DE LA RÉSISTANCE (PARIS: PENSÉE MODERNE, 1976), 146

Wehrmacht troops march into Paris, June 14, 1940. The French army was ordered not to defend the city. BUNDESARCHIV, BILD 146-1994-036-09A / HORST STURM

The carriage at Compiègne, June 22, 1940, Germans on the left, French on the right. The French government signed an armistice agreeing to enforce German occupation policy, which included the ban on possession of firearms. BUNDESARCHIV, BILD 146-1982-089-18 / HORST STURM

Collaborators: Fernand de Brinon and General Otto von Stülpnagel, the German Commander (Militärbefehlshaber), in conversation on the left, General Eugène Bridoux and Colonel Hans Speidel on the right, November 1941. Stülpnagel ordered numerous executions of firearm owners. ERVL0208506 ©LAPI/ROGER-VIOLLET/THE IMAGE WORKS

"Firearms, Munitions, and Explosives: Very Important Notice" from the Préfet of Ardennes, June 5, 1941, repeating that all arms— "including hunting arms" is bolded—must be surrendered under threat of the death penalty. The re-issuance of such orders reflected the refusal of countless French to comply. ARMES A FEU, 1919– 1946, 4MB, OCCUPATION ALLEMANDE. ARCHIVES DÉPARTEMENTALES, DÉPARTEMENT DES ARDENNES, CHARLEVILLE-MÉZIÈRES

Etat Français -- Préfecture des Ardennes

POLICE GÉNÉRALE
Armes à feu, Munitions et Explosifs

AVIS TRÈS IMPORTANT

En vertu d'une ordonnance des Autorités d'occupation du 10 Mai 1940, publiée au *Recueil des Actes Administratifs* n° 7 (page 233) tout détenteur d'armes à feu, munitions, grenades à main, explosifs et autre matériel de guerre, devait en faire la remise **sans délai** aux Autorités allemandes.

Il est rappelé que toute personne possédant des armes à feu, munitions, grenades à main, explosifs et autre matériel de guerre, à l'encontre de cette ordonnance, sera punie de la peine de mort ou de travaux forcés ; en cas plus léger de prison.

En outre, toute personne commettant des actes de violence soit contre l'armée allemande ou un de ses membres, sera punie de mort.

D'autre part M. le Généralmajor, Feldkommandant des Ardennes, en date du 30 Mai 1941, rappelle aux habitants du département des Ardennes qu'ils doivent se conformer expressément aux prescriptions de l'ordonnance du 10 Mai 1940.

En conséquence, les armes, **inclusivement les armes de chasse**, doivent être déposées dans les Mairies qui les remettront globalement aux Kreiskommanturen compétentes. Les armes de chasse seront, autant que possible, munies du nom de leur propriétaire.

M. le Commandant de Gendarmerie et MM. les Commissaires de police sont chargés de veiller à ce que les habitants se conforment à l'ordonnance précitée, et MM. les Maires sont tenus responsables de son exécution.

Fait à Mézières, le 5 Juin 1941.

Le Préfet,
Edmond PASCAL.

Imp. P. Anciaux et Cie — Charleville.

A German arms depot storing 60,000 hunting guns confiscated from French citizens.
"La restitution des armes de chasse déposées aux Autorités Allemandes,"
Le Saint-Hubert, Juillet-Août 1941, 37. LE SAINT HUBERT CLUB DE FRANCE

Vichy France meets with the Führer on the Eastern Front at Winniza, Ukraine,
December 18–20, 1942. Hitler demanded creation of supplemental French police to help
the Germans maintain order. Left to right, German Foreign Minister Ribbentrop, an
interpreter, Pierre Laval, Hitler, Italian Foreign Minister Ciano, and Hermann Göring.
BILDARCHIV PREUSSISCHER KULTURBESITZ, ART RESOURCE, NY, ART540476 /
HEINRICH HOFFMANN

Laval with Karl Oberg, chief of the SS in France, May 1, 1943. Assuming his duties a year before, Oberg gave orders to the French police and took charge of reprisals and anti-Jewish measures. BUNDESARCHIV, BILD 183-H25719 / HORST STURM

A Wehrmacht execution squad shoots members of the Manouchian resistance group at Fort Mont-Valérien on February 21, 1944. During the years of the occupation, many French were similarly executed for mere possession of firearms. LES AMIS DE FRANZ STOCK

Rifle instruction for members of the Maquis, who operated from rural, mountainous areas like the Vercors in southeastern France, to harass and attack German forces. TRAINING YOUNG RESISTANCE FIGHTERS, 1944 / BRIDGEMAN IMAGES

At the barricades with pistols and rifles in the liberation of Paris, August 25, 1944. NATIONAL MUSEUM OF THE U.S. NAVY, LOT 4568-4

The execution of Pierre Laval, found guilty of treason after the Liberation, October 15, 1945. Laval decreed firearm registration in 1935 and was the chief collaborator with Germany, 1940–44. ASSOCIATED PRESS, 451015062

6

Amnesty or Execution

THERE WERE NEVER more than 3,000 German policemen in France, but the gendarmerie numbered 47,000.[1] Just as they served the occupation agendas on other issues, the French police continued to consult the registration records to track down registrants who failed to surrender their firearms. As an example, the prefect of Lot, which is in southwestern France, wrote on January 5, 1942, to the prefect of police of Paris that one Gabriel Léon Antoine Gautier left the area and was now residing at 32, rue Delambre, in Paris (14th arrondissement). He had registered three handguns on November 13, 1935, but had not turned them in: an 8 mm revolver, a 7.65 automatic pistol, and a 6.35 automatic pistol.[2] This information was forwarded to the police commissioner of the quarter of Montparnasse in Paris.[3]

The police investigation revealed that Monsieur Gautier left his firearms in his small estate in Assier, Lot, but he had not been there since the armistice in 1940. His mother lived there but did not know where the handguns were, so he promised to give instructions to his mother in order to surrender them.[4] His fate thereafter is unknown.

But the fates of other gun owners were well publicized. The new year hardly began before the routine *Avis* from Ernst Schaumburg, the commander

---

1. Laub, *After the Fall*, 177.

2. Le Prefet du Lot à Monsieur le Prefet de Police Paris, 5 janvier 1942, Archives de la Préfecture de Police, Paris, BA 2259.

3. Note pour Monsieur le Commisaire de Police du Quarter du Montparnasse, 21 janvier 1942, Archives de la Préfecture de Police, Paris, Réf: 140. D. BA 2259.

4. Rapport le Commisaire de Police du Quartier au Montparnasse a Monsieur le Préfet de Police, 28 janvier 1942, Archives de la Préfecture de Police, Paris, Réf: 140. D. BA 2259.

of Greater Paris and second in command of occupied France, announced that Lucien Gourlot from Paris was sentenced to death for illegal possession of arms and ammunition and was executed on January 9.[5] Auguste Chaussin from Montreuil-sous-Bois (Seine) and Essaid Haddad from Paris were executed for arms possession a few days later.[6]

Death sentences were typically carried out a few hours after sentence was pronounced. Firing squads were composed of ten members of the order police (*Ordnungspolizei*, or Orpo), standing in two rows at five paces. Prisoners were tied onto posts, blindfolded, and shot. The killing was stressful for the executioners, who needed schnapps and cigarettes, and who sometimes refused to untie the corpses from the stakes and place them in coffins.[7]

Otto von Stülpnagel, military commander of France (*Militärbefehlshaber*, or MBF), had no hesitation to approve the execution of gun owners, but opposed the large numbers of hostages Hitler ordered to be executed in the wake of attacks on Wehrmacht soldiers. On January 15, he reported to Berlin that German and French police solved twenty-two of the sixty-eight attacks since the Nantes shooting on August 21. He was thus only willing to order "a *limited* number of executions" for the attacks, but "I can no longer arrange *mass shootings* and answer to history with a clear conscience. . . ."[8] A few days later, he resigned from his position as MBF.

Before doing so, he issued yet another admonition to the French to surrender their guns: "All of those who still possess weapons that are not authorized are urged to turn them in. The turning in of weapons shall be done without formal procedure and with complete impunity."[9] That sounded like an amnesty, but the authorities who collected the arms must have asked a few questions. The directive was dated January 18, but that night a soldier was shot near Luna Park in Paris. A young woman seen standing near him was urged to come to the police préfecture, who guaranteed extreme discretion.[10] It is unclear whether anyone was apprehended, but it was equally clear that things would only get worse.

---

5. "*Avis*," *Le Matin*, Janurary 13, 1942, 1.

6. "*Avis*," *Le Matin*, January 15, 1942, 1.

7. Mitchell, *Nazi Paris*, 61–62.

8. Laub, *After the Fall*, 160–61.

9. BA/MA, RW 35/544, Etat Francais, 18. Januar 1942.

10. "*Avis*," *Le Matin*, January 20, 1942.

Jean Moulin Returns

The Resistance took a step forward when, before daybreak on January 2, Jean Moulin parachuted out of an RAF airplane with two other men and radio equipment near Avignon in southern France. Fresh from meetings with de Gaulle in London, Moulin's mission was to organize the disparate resistance movements.[11] On January 23, alerted by code words heard on BBC, members of Combat received the first cache of arms to be parachuted from British airplanes. The containers were trucked to a nearby farm and temporarily hidden in a haystack.[12]

Patriotic French police tried to divert and hide arms that were turned in, for future use against the Germans. Combat reported, "In Paris, a police chief of the rue Bois-le-Vent (16th arrondissement) has just been shot, along with the owner of a small café. They buried arms in the café courtyard that people had brought to the police station."[13]

The commander of Greater Paris made sure that executions were prominently published. Some January executions for arms possession were Lucien Michard from Livry (Seine-et-Oise);[14] Louis Blaise from Paris;[15] and Henri Bourbon from Paris, which was also reported in the *New York Times* and who German data indicated to be the two hundredth French citizen executed.[16] The *Times* further reported the execution of four more Parisians: Amar Zebbouddi was shot for illegal possession of arms, two others for Gaullist activities, and the last for "activities in favor of the enemy." Reprisal executions were on the increase after a lull following the executions of 198 people at Bordeaux and Nantes during the fall of 1941.[17]

The above reports combine executions of specific people for arms possession and other crimes with executions of hostages for crimes committed by

11. Cobb, *The Resistance*, 94.

12. de Bénouville, *Unknown Warriors*, 106–8.

13. "Ceux qui se refusent à la honte," *Combat, organe du mouvement de libération française*, n° 2, février 1942. Bibliothèque Nationale de France.

14. "*Avis*," *Le Matin*, January 23, 1942, 1.

15. "*Avis*," *Le Matin*, January 24–25, 1942, 3.

16. "*Avis*," *Le Matin*, January 26, 1942, 3; "2 More Executed in Paris," *New York Times*, January 26, 1942, 3.

17. "Germans Execute 20 in Paris and Belgium," *New York Times*, January 29, 1942, 9.

others. Executions announced by an *Avis* from the MBF were presumably carried out by the Germans, but Vichy may have executed more French than the Wehrmacht in this period. As discussed below, who got shot or guillotined for what became even more blurred after the SS took charge of German security on June 1, 1942.

Daily Searches for Arms

American intelligence operatives were watching closely. Royall Tyler, a League of Nations appointee who now worked with the American Office of Strategic Services (OSS), reported after a three-day visit at Lyons with Paul Squire, the American consul in Geneva, that the recent entry of the United States into the war encouraged anti-Axis sentiment. A bank manager in Dijon in the occupied zone observed that German troop morale was very low—many had been sent from the Russian front to recuperate and became mutinous when about to be sent back, resulting in numerous German enlisted men being executed by firing squad. The report continued:

> There are daily searches for arms, and those in whose houses arms are found are shot—an average of about one a day in this particular town. The banker exhibited several issues of the local newspaper announcing executions to substantiate his assertion. Only a very small percentage of the arms concealed, he stated, are ever discovered. There are huge quantities ready for use when the opportunity comes. Hatred of the Germans is becoming fiercer as time passes and executions continue. Arms concealment is no longer just a matter of individual initiative, but there is a very efficient organization directing it.[18]

Indeed, the MBF in France reported that in January, eighty-eight French citizens were sentenced to death, fifty-two for illegal arms possession. To be sure,

---

18. Notes of Paul C. Squire, American Consulate, Geneva, Switzerland, reporting to Washington (January 29, 1942), in Luzi Stamm, Johannes Hofmann, Stefanie Frey, and Lotti Wanner, eds., *Liberty, Independence, Neutrality* (Lenzburg, Switzerland: Verlag Merker im Effingerhof, 2006), 171–72.

not all death sentences were carried out. Of seventy-eight prison sentences of over five years, seventy-three were for the same offense.[19]

Numerous incidents were reported. From Béthune, it was reported that extensive house searches for arms and Communist or Gaullist propaganda, often based on anonymous tips, were successful, with active cooperation from the French police.[20] Cooperation between the military police and the French gendarmes and police elsewhere was reported as good. At Rouen, the capital of Normandy, someone shot a soldier with a pistol and escaped. A Frenchman named Denoyelle was shot to death for weapons possession at the Rouen shooting range. In February, at Amiens, three French citizens on bicycles threw a homemade bomb into the window of the French Legion recruiting office—the bomb failed to explode. A German guard and two French policemen apprehended one of the perpetrators.[21]

A specific gun became of special interest. District B in Angers inquired as to which hunting-gun depot was the storage place of a Drilling 16 x 16 x 9.3 three-barreled Teschner Collath-Söhne rifle no. 19207. It was delivered to the French police by the wife of a German citizen named Vormbaum on September 6, 1939, just days after Hitler attacked Poland and France declared war on Germany. After the German occupation, it was transferred to a German hunting-gun depot. If the gun was loaned to a holder of an army hunting permit, it was ordered that he must be tracked down and reported.[22] Perhaps the gun was claimed by someone influential.

Death Penalty for Failure to Denounce?

In this period, drafts were circulated of a new weapon surrender order by Dr. Grohmann, military administrative counselor to the MBF. Section 3 required

---

19. BA/MA, RW 35/12, Militärbefehlshaber in Frankreich, Lagebericht Dezember 1941–Januar 1942, 31. Januar 1942.

20. BA/MA, RH 36/420: Lagebericht, 19. Monatsbericht der Kreiskommandantur 635, Berichtszeit: 1. bis 28. Februar 1942, Béthune, 7. März 1942.

21. BA/MA, RW 35/1215, Lage- und Tätigkeitsbericht für die Zeit vom 7. Januar bis 6. März 1942, Militärverwaltungsbezirk A, Tgb. Nr. 476/42, 17. März 1942.

22. BA/MA, RW 35/1262, Chef des Militärverwaltungsbezirks B, 3. Februar 1942.

a person with knowledge that another possessed a firearm to denounce such person to German or French authorities, with the death penalty for failure to comply. An exception was made for spouses, children, the elderly, and siblings.[23] Vichy Minister Jean-Pierre Ingrand met with the Germans in Paris on the matter on February 2.

Werner Best, the chief military administrative officer (*Kriegsverwaltungschef*), recommended that the MBF not issue a new order with yet another deadline to surrender weapons. That was despite the fact that Vichy officials had just been asked to meet with the MBF to discuss a new deadline. Yet issuance of an order without an amnesty deadline, Best noted, would make people unable to turn in arms without punishment. That would make it more difficult for the French officials who were collaborating and who were willing—at the suggestion of the MBF—to request a new surrender deadline. Further, the denunciation provision in section 3 would only increase criminal proceedings. Best concluded that further discussions with Vichy officials would take place about whether the French government planned to issue an order, after which the Germans could weigh the pros and cons further.[24]

Best's arguments were buttressed by the French minister of state, who endorsed Best's memorandum, noting that since the decree of May 10, 1940, the population had been ordered enough times to surrender their arms. Repeatedly setting new deadlines for the surrender of arms without punishment, even though hundreds had been executed, would cause the populace to lose all respect for the authorities. Moreover, the extension of penalties to people who had knowledge of the weapons possession of others would lead to a great increase of denunciations. Housekeepers, maids, and spouses would report arms possession when they argued with the owner and sought revenge, which had happened enough already. The French representative continued:

> A new proclamation that weapons are prohibited, subject to a grace period, may result in the surrender or dumping into the Seine of thou-

---

23. BA/MA, RW 35/544, Militärbefehlshaber in Frankreich, Verwaltungsstab, Abteilung Verwaltung, Ablieferung von Waffen, 5. März 1942.

24. BA/MA, RW 35/544, Kriegsverwaltungschef, Staatsminister, an Militärbefehlshaber in Frankreich, 13. Februar 1942.

sands of pistols and rifles and tens of thousands of rounds of ammunition. But weapons and explosives kept in hiding or newly procured for the purpose of attacking the occupying forces will not be surrendered. Neither will large numbers of weapons (including machine guns, grenade launchers, etc.) that we did not surrender to Germany back then, but rather moved them from one place to the next, sometimes under the eyes or with the help of the police, and in that fashion saved all of the items.

Thus, a new order would result in an increased number of denunciations. We would have to sentence to death harmless little people. In the meantime, terrorists and organized nationalists would ignore the new order the way they ignored the old one and the urgent requests to surrender weapons which each time were made under the threat of severe penalties.

As if to illustrate the above points, the commander of Greater Paris announced that Lucien-Louis Selve of Ivry-sur-Seine, who was sentenced to death for illegal possession of arms, was executed that day.[25] Roger-Georges Laus of Paris met the same fate days later.[26]

Sensitive to the attacks on the occupiers, Dr. Best directed that Reich Germans may be issued weapons permits that would be valid for the entire occupied territory without regard to their profession.[27]

On February 16, Carl-Heinrich von Stülpnagel—the cousin of Otto von Stülpnagel—assumed command as MBF. Unlike Otto, Carl-Heinrich would follow orders from Berlin without protest, but he would also join the anti-Hitler conspiracy that was brewing within the Wehrmacht. A week after taking office, Communists threw a grenade at Wehrmacht soldiers at Le Havre. Hitler ordered that thirty hostages be executed. Some of those selected had been convicted of firearm possession and anti-German activity.[28]

25. *"Avis,"* *Le Matin*, February 17, 1942, 2.

26. *"Avis,"* *Le Matin*, February 23, 1942, 3.

27. BA/MA, RW 35/544, Militärbefehlshaber in Frankreich, Verwaltungsstab, Abteilung Verwaltung, Erteilung von Waffenscheinen an Zivilpersonen, 26. Februar 1942.

28. Laub, *After the Fall*, 168, 172–73.

Trial of Resistants of the *Musée de l'Homme*

In this period, a major show trial took place. It involved the group associated with the *Musée de l'Homme* (Museum of Man) that published the underground paper *Résistance*. The nineteen conspirators were betrayed by a Vichy infiltrator. Agnès Humbert, one of the defendants, wrote a vivid account of the ordeal.[29] A Wehrmacht judge named Ernst Roskothen presided, and the defendants were represented by French lawyers. After several weeks, the verdict was rendered. Roskothen later wrote, "Because these tracts [*Résistance*] were clearly an incitement to armed revolt against the occupation . . . they may be considered as aiding and abetting the enemy . . . Under martial law, the death sentence is mandatory." And yet the judge openly stated his admiration for these French patriots.[30]

Jean Guéhenno wrote in his diary that "the plea for clemency sent to Berlin last week was useless, and they were shot yesterday afternoon [February 23]. Seven men and three women, almost all of them from academia. . . . For one of them, I can imagine what his last look was like, in front of the firing squad."[31]

The firing squads were operating at Fort Mont-Valérien, to the west of Paris, where around a thousand people would be executed during the war.[32] The shots of the execution squads could be heard at the suburb of Suresnes. As Guéhenno learned, the three women were actually not executed but were pardoned and sent to prison. "They shot the seven men . . . , one after the other, every five minutes. . . . No notice appeared in the newspapers. Thus, when they tell us almost every morning that one or two men have been shot, it's only to keep us in suspense." Guéhenno was further informed about the condemned men and the group's leader, Boris Vildé:

> The first thing Monday morning they told them they were going to be shot that day. Vildé saw his wife that morning and had the strength

29. Humbert, *Résistance*, 93–105 (entries dated January 8 through February 17, 1942). See also Laub, *After the Fall*, 297–98.

30. Humbert, *Résistance*, 318–19.

31. Guéhenno, *Diary of the Dark Years*, 147 (entry dated February 24, 1942).

32. Humbert, *Résistance*, 350.

to tell her nothing. In the afternoon, they drove them from the prison in Fresnes to Mont Valérien. They went through all of Paris piled in a truck with their guards. They were singing. Each of them had a white paper square pinned over his heart and they were killed at nearly point-blank range. Vildé, as he had asked, was executed last.[33]

Agnès Humbert, one of the imprisoned women, would record her deportation to Germany to work as a slave laborer for Hitler's war machine. Her diary records the horrendous conditions suffered by countless French and other nationalities who were deported for crimes against the occupation. When liberated by the Americans in April 1945, she helped protect the liberated prisoners from the German diehards called Werewolves. An American soldier gave her two revolvers to do so.[34]

Noël Créau was a member of the group who escaped. Responding to my questionnaire in 2002, he explained that prewar French law made it difficult to own weapons other than hunting guns, and that the group had no arms.[35] He next joined "the Réseau CND – Castille—tracking, counting the different types of enemy airplanes at airports I and F in Normandy." That referred to the network CND (*Confrérie Notre-Dame,* Brotherhood of Our Lady) – Castille, which was a Free French intelligence network.[36] In that role, he noted that "[i]n the event of a control point, it would have been dangerous to carry a weapon." He next joined the Special Air Service (SAS) parachutists of Free France in Great Britain. He was "[d]ropped by parachute over Brittany in early June 1944—to perform acts of sabotage and establish contacts with the Résistance network, parachute drops of arms, instruction, supervision, and combat."

---

33. Guéhenno, *Diary of the Dark Years,* 147–48 (entry dated February 26, 1942).

34. Humbert, *Résistance,* 234–37 (entry dated April 7, 1945).

35. Noël Créau, ancien président national, Amicales des Anciens Parachutistes S.A.S. et des Anciens Commandos de la France Libre, Neuilly-sur-Seine, France, letter to author, February 4, 2002. For more details on Noël Créau, see www.francaislibres.net/liste/fiche.php?index=62760.

36. Cobb, *The Resistance,* 294.

A New Surrender Order for Hunting Guns?

Most of France suffered quietly under the occupation. Not long after the occupation began, the *Saint-Hubert-Club de France*, an association of hunters, had organized the sending of questionnaires throughout France to solicit information on the identities of gun owners who had surrendered their firearms but left no identification for their return. Tens of thousands of trusting gun owners, four-fifths of them farmers, had returned the questionnaires, prompting Club President Maxime Ducrocq to visit Marshal Pétain at Vichy to seek a protocol for the eventual return of the firearms. On February 20, Fernand de Brinon, Vichy ambassador for the occupied territory, congratulated Ducrocq on his efforts to identify the owners of the hundreds of thousands of guns owned by unknown civilians.[37] Vichy, of course, was powerless to do anything.

The MBF's Dr. Grohmann met with Ingrand on February 26 so that the Germans could receive the French govenment's attitude of a possible change in the gun surrender policy. Ingrand expressed the following points from the French side:

1. *Hunting Guns*

   It is to be expected that the French population, in particular out in the countryside, still possesses "thousands of hunting guns." These people will only surrender their weapons if they are given assurances that they will receive the weapons back once the occupation ends. Thus, the success of a new surrender action for hunting guns will depend on the issuance of a receipt.

2. *Other Weapons, in Particular Military Arms*

   The French government thinks that a new order to surrender would not be successful. Anybody who still owns weapons of that kind will keep them even if promised a new amnesty. Contrary to the owners of hunting guns, owners of such arms tend to be opposed to the occupying forces.

---

37. "Le recensement des armes de chasse," *Le Saint-Hubert*, n°2, 41e année, mars 1942, 13.

3. The French government is concerned about the provision contained in the order of the Military Commander in Belgium and Northern France regarding the duty to report third persons who are known to possess weapons. The French government thinks that such a provision would result in denunciations and greatly expand the circle of persons who might be subject to the death penalty.[38]

The Germans listened without comment, particularly regarding whether the MBF intended to issue a denunciation order. In the internal German report after the meeting, Lieutenant Rösch, a liaison officer to the French who is mentioned above, was skeptical about issuing receipts for surrendered hunting guns. The German Armistice Commission opined that private citizens should not be compensated for firearms they surrendered for the reason that, at the beginning of the war, the French government had equipped its units with hunting guns to fight parachutists. Since the French thus used hunting guns in France to wage war on the German Reich, the Germans could seize or destroy them under Article 23 of the Hague Convention Respecting the Laws and Customs of War on Land of 1907. However, the MBF's economic office (called *Wirtschaft IV*) opposed that opinion.

The referenced Article 23 made it forbidden "[t]o destroy or seize the enemy's property, unless such destruction or seizure be imperatively demanded by the necessities of war." Since the war with France ended a year and a half before, it is unclear how the necessities of war demanded the seizure of the arms of private citizens which had *not* been issued to French soldiers.

The Decree of March 5, 1942

In a March 5 meeting, Dr. Grohmann presented a revised version of the decree on the surrender of weapons to be issued by the MBF.[39] Its preamble began with these words: "Frequent reports of illegal firearms possession show that the

---

38. BA/MA, RW 35/544, Militärbefehlshaber in Frankreich, Verwaltungsstab, Abteilung Verwaltung, Verordnung über Ablieferung von Waffen, 27. Februar 1942.

39. BA/MA, RW 35/544, Militärbefehlshaber in Frankreich, Verwaltungsstab, Abteilung Verwaltung, Ablieferung von Waffen, 5. März 1942.

French population still owns numerous weapons. In the interest of the security of the occupying forces, we must obtain as many of these weapons as possible." Then followed the Decree Concerning Possession of Weapons of March 5, 1942. The date was misleading, as it would not be given to the French and published until March 18. Reciting the power bestowed on him by the Führer and commander-in-chief of the armed forces, the MBF decreed as follows:

Section 1.1 provided that "[t]he possession of firearms of any kind, including hunting guns, ammunition, hand grenades, explosives and other war materials and any parts of such items is prohibited." Section 1.2 exempted people who carried weapons in an official capacity approved by a German office or who had a German-issued weapons permit. Excluded were unusable weapons with sentimental value and 4.5 mm air rifles.

Whoever possessed items listed in section 1.1, unless an exemption applied according to section 1.2, "will be subject to the death penalty." In petty cases, punishment could be jail or prison.

Section 3 originally included the denunciation provision, but it was deleted from the final draft. It would have provided that whoever knew that another was in illegal possession of items listed in section 1, or knew where such items were hidden with the owner unknown, must immediately report that to the nearest German or French office. Whoever failed to do so would be sentenced to death or prison, or in petty cases, to jail. However, the duty to denounce such people did not apply to spouses, parents, children, or siblings of such people. By rejecting this draconian provision, MBF Carl-Heinrich von Stülpnagel sought to moderate what was already a deeply resented policy against gun owners that interfered with collaboration.

What was now the new section 3 provided that whoever possessed arms would not be punished if they were delivered by April 1, 1942, to the closest German headquarters, the mayor, or French police or gendarme office. A provision was deleted that also granted amnesty for failure to denounce others in possession of arms within that time period, since the denunciation provision had been deleted. Finally, whoever discovered arms in his or her possession after the surrender deadline was promised amnesty if the arms were surrendered immediately to the nearest surrendering location.

Finally, section 4 provided that the decree was effective on its publication date, and that it repealed the provisions of the decree of May 10, 1940, requiring surrender of arms within twenty-four hours and imposing the death penalty for failure to do so. But no one already arrested would get off the hook, as the amnesty did not apply to them.

The March 5 decree was quite a testament to the tenuous success of almost two years of German gun control in France. Since the decree of May 10, 1940, the French had been threatened with the death penalty for possession of a gun, but countless people ignored the order. More recent amnesties had netted enormous quantities of firearms, but so many irascible French citizens just would not turn in their hunting guns, and members of the Resistance were focused on acquiring more guns with military utility.

The next day the French delegation to the occupied territory delivered a lengthy missive through Lieutenant Rösch to the Germans. It touted the unity of interest of the German and French authorities to protect the occupiers and the occupied: "If the German authorities want to make sure that the French civilians in occupied territories are without arms to ensure total protection of the German army, the French authorities want to avoid, legitimately so, that public order be disturbed, and want to ensure the protection of administration and civilian population. . . . In fact, it is about ensuring the protection of the German army, as well as that of the French civilian population, from criminal acts aimed only at creating chaos."[40]

The letter noted that until September 12, 1941, the German authorities punished arms possession with the death penalty only in particularly serious cases. (That was a reference to the MBF's announcement that date, following shootings of German soldiers, that arms possession would be punished only by execution.[41]) By the end of 1941, sixty-seven death sentences had occurred in the occupied territories for possession of arms, but in the two months from the beginning of 1942 to the present, thirty-six executions occurred for that offense. Contrary to what the Germans said about the death penalty being applied only in the most serious cases, the ultimate sanction was being applied against people not involved in political activity and with no harmful intent.

40. BA/MA, RW 35/544, Délegation Générale du Gouvernement Français, Note Officieuse Pour Monsieur Le Lieutenant Roesch, 3. Mars 1942.

41. BA/MA, RW 35/1, Abdruck aus *Pariser Zeitung* vom 13. September 1941, Bekanntmachung. BA/MA, RW 35/544, *Avis, Le Matin*, 13. September 1941.

In rural areas reached irregularly by newspapers, the letter continued, farmers ignored both the German decrees and the severe sanctions they would receive if they disobeyed them. In some places, such as Côte d'Or, agreements signed between the prefect and the German authorities counseled a flexible interpretation of the decrees. In others, people in possession of hunting guns were sentenced to light jail terms, as the German authorities did not deem that leniency would compromise the security of their troops. Finally, statistics disproved any direct relationship between severe punishment for arms possession and a reduction of attacks against the German army.

The French letter next focused on hunting guns, which it said were not offensive or defensive weapons. Owners of hunting guns—it exaggerated somewhat—had no intention of aggression against the German army. The guns had sentimental value to families, and German recognition of the French psychology thereon would demonstrate that the Germans only wished to intervene as necessary to promote security for their troops.

But a new decree to surrender hunting guns by a fixed deadline, the French missive naively continued, would not be obeyed unless the owners received guarantees that they would be returned at the end of hostilities. Thus, the letter recommended that any new surrender measures be widely advertised in villages through communiques and posters with the announcement that hunting guns would be turned over to a Franco-German agency or cantonal commission, a receipt describing the weapon would be signed by both a French and German member, and the gun would be stored in a safe place.

The pleas of the French to safeguard surrendered guns and return them when hostilities ended would be nothing but illusions. While the French were not even aware that the Germans had already decided on a decree without these conditions, the MBF's justice group still had no word on whether the Armistice Commission had decided whether privately owned hunting guns should be considered captured property and therefore confiscated without remuneration.[42]

It was not until March 18 that Werner Best at the MBF's office noted that the decree, which he had approved, was relayed by Jean-Pierre Ingrand

---

42. BA/MA, RW 35/544, Verwaltungsstab, Abteilung Verwaltung, Gruppe Justiz, Ablieferung von Waffen, 9. März 1942.

to the French government with the order to publish it immediately.[43] Specialist (*Sonderführer*) Vogt of the propaganda division was told to make certain that it was published without delay.[44] It was published that day in the MBF's official journal[45] and reprinted in the French newspapers.[46] The Decree Concerning the Possession of Arms was dated March 5, 1942:

> By virtue of the powers given to me by the Führer und Oberster Befehlshaber der Wehrmacht, I order the following:
>
> § 1.
>
> 1. The possession of any kind of firearms, including hunting arms, ammunition, hand grenades, explosives and any other war equipment, as well as any parts of these items is forbidden.
> 2. This interdiction does not apply to:
>   a. weapons and ammunition for which a permit has been delivered to the owner by German authority;
>   b. weapons and ammunition which have been authorized by German authority by reason of their profession;
>   c. any weapons and any other war equipment whose owner was issued a written document certifying that the weapons were left in his possession by the German authority;
>   d. inoperable souvenir arms;
>   e. 4.5 mm air rifles.
>
> § 2.
>
> 1. Anyone in possession of any objects listed in section 1, paragraph 1, who does not meet the conditions listed on paragraph 2 of said section, shall be sentenced to death.

43. BA/MA, RW 35/544, Militärbefehlshaber in Frankreich, Verwaltungsstab, Abteilung Verwaltung, Bekanntgabe der neuen Waffenverordnung durch die französischen Behörden im besetzten Gebiet, 18. März 1942.

44. BA/MA, RW 35/544, Militärbefehlshaber in Frankreich, Verwaltungsstab, Abteilung Verwaltung, Verordnung über den Besitz von Waffen, 19. März 1942.

45. BA/MA, RW 35/544, Verordnungsblatt des Militärbefehlshabers in Frankreich, Journal Officiel contenant les ordonnances du Militärbefehlshaber in Frankreich, Nr. 56, 18. März 1942.

46. For example, "Une Ordonnance Concernant La Détention Des Arms," *Le Matin*, March 18, 1942, 3.

2. In less serious cases the sentence may be forced labor or imprisonment.
3. The arms shall be confiscated.

§ 3.
1. Individuals in possession of arms listed in section 1, paragraph 1, who turn them in to the authorities before April 1, 1942, shall not be brought to court. The said turning in must be done to the local German commander, or to French city halls, police, or gendarme stations.
2. Individuals who, having discovered he or she possessed arms listed in section 1, paragraph 1, after April 1, 1942 shall not be brought to court if he or she turns them in without any delay to the nearest above named authority.

§ 4.
1. This decree shall be enforced as soon as it is posted. On that same date, paragraphs 1 and 2 of the May 10, 1940, decree concerning the possession of arms in occupied territories shall be repealed (VOBIF page 4).
2. The stipulations contained in this decree do not apply to pending offenses before the police or legal authorities at the date of its posting.

Under that last provision, while the decree was dated March 5, it was not effective as to pending cases until posted on March 18. Any poor fool who surrendered arms between those dates was subject to the death penalty. The referenced provisions of the decree of May 10, 1940, ordered that all arms be surrendered within twenty-four hours, and that violation was subject to the death penalty or imprisonment. By its terms, that decree expired on May 11, 1940, or twenty-four hours from whenever it was posted!

The new decree was far more detailed in allowing an effective amnesty from March 18 to April 1, and even allowance to surrender arms at any time if a person discovers that he or she possesses arms. Two years of the iron-fisted approach obviously had not worked, despite the threat and use of the death penalty.

Acknowledging the collaboration of the French police, the MBF directed that from then on, city halls, police, and small-town police stations were authorized to receive the weapons. And to assure the reluctant that the arms would be returned when peace returned, a receipt would be issued to anyone who requested one.[47]

The news that the military authorities in Paris published a new decree threatening the immediate execution of any person found in possession of any kind of arms quickly spread across the Atlantic and was published in the *New York Times*.[48]

The French press went to work admonishing resistance to the latest decree. *Le Matin* pleaded about the latest gun ban, "What does this mean, other than there are still offenders who resist, and whose ideas, if they ever are even partially carried out, would mean bloody retaliations? When will these mad people understand that we are all in solidarity . . . ?"[49]

Executions No Longer to Be Published

That was according to script. The justice group had directed the propaganda group to arrange for the French press to educate the French population about the importance of the order. There would be repeated references to it on French radio. It was to be emphasized that this was the last opportunity to surrender arms, including hunting guns, without punishment. "In the future, anybody found to possess weapons illegally will be sentenced to death." Moreover, until now, the public was informed about death sentences for possession of weapons to remind them of the duty to surrender them. "In the future, there will be no more reminders. Executions will no longer be published."[50]

Without publication of death sentences, the population would be kept wondering about the extent to which violators were being ferreted out and

---

47. BA/MA, RW 35/544, Der Militärbefehlshaber in Frankreich, Bekanntgabe der neuen Waffen-Verordnung durch die französischen Behörden im besetzten Gebiet, 19. März 1942.

48. "Paris Extends Arms Ban," *New York Times*, March 19, 1942, 8.

49. "La détention des armes à feu," *Le Matin*, March 21–22, 1942.

50. BA/MA, RW 35/544, Gruppe Justiz an Gruppe Propaganda, Verordnung über den Besitz von Waffen, 23.März 1942.

shot. This was a further implementation of the Night and Fog (*Nacht und Nebel*) policy announced at the end of 1941, under which the disappearance of people with no explanation would terrorize the population into submission.

This marks a turning point in the history of the disarming of the French citizenry. Press announcements of executions for firearm possession would no longer be routinely reported. After multiple decrees to surrender arms under penalty of death, starting with the May 10, 1940, decree with its twenty-four-hour deadline, and ending with the March 5, 1942, decree—which was not even announced until March 18—with its effective two-week deadline, further decrees were deemed useless. While internal Wehrmacht documents would continue reporting statistics on weapons confiscated and would occasionally report specific cases, the Germans were out of patience with the failure of many French civilians to surrender their firearms. It was time just to shoot those who failed to comply without further notice or fanfare.

As the end of March neared, the newspapers continued to publicize the order, which the Germans carefully monitored.[51] *Le Matin* warned a week in advance that April 1 was the deadline, noting that the French minister of the interior had just instructed all French services (courthouses, police offices, and gendarmeries) to receive the arms, and warned gun owners to avoid the extreme risks of not surrendering their arms.[52]

Some apparently thought little of enforcing the arms prohibition. The Vichy delegation mentioned that the prefect of the department of Côte d'Or and local occupation authorities struck a deal to interpret the decree mildly to implement it in a just manner. The MBF sternly demanded to be informed who entered into such an agreement in violation of orders.[53]

Major General Eduard Freiherr von Rotberg of District C in Dijon shot back that neither his office nor the military police made any agreement with the prefect of Côte d'Or for a lenient interpretation of the arms decree. The military police had inspected weapons that had been surrendered, eliminated any misunderstanding about the meaning of "unusable weapons," and con-

---

51. BA/MA, RW 35/544, Gruppe V 9 Prop. an Gruppe V 8, 25. März 1942, Verordnung über den Besitz von Waffen vom 25. März 1942.

52. "1ᵉʳ Avril, Dernier Delai Pour La Remise Des Armes, *Le Matin*, March 25, 1942, 1.

53. BA/MA, RW 35/544, Militärbefehlshaber in Frankreich, Verwaltungsstab, Abteilung Verwaltung, Ablieferung von Waffen, 13. März 1942.

fiscated those that were usable. Rotberg claimed that he told the prefect that the amnesty was a generous gesture, but that anyone who failed to comply would be punished severely.[54]

The Vichy plea to the Germans to issue yet another amnesty ignored that no amount of leniency or threats of death would induce many French to surrender their hidden arms. Resistance member Jacques Demange wrote to me relating how in 1940 he surrendered the least desirable of his father's hunting guns, but buried his father's good shotgun, a revolver, and some daggers, greased and oiled in a wooden box, in a cow pasture.[55] In 1942, he dug them up only to find that they had rusted, although the shotgun still worked. He continued the story:

> In those days, my parents and I were farmers. So of course we had to provide the Germans with food, and they enforced the controls with their interpreters. They would come at different times of the day without warning. Those controls were very serious. Foreseeing the danger, I dug a second cellar in a remote place, under a mound of straw. I placed our food reserves for the year there. From that point on, the Germans could come whenever they wanted; the food was safely guarded by the gun that I had put at the same place.
>
> Then years passed, little by little "les Boches" lost their control and the liberation arrived. And the shotgun is still with me, hanging on the wall. It does not work, yet what memories does it bring me!

For February and March 1942, the MBF reported 113 French citizens sentenced to death. Of these, 40 gave aid and comfort to the enemy, 39 possessed weapons, 18 committed espionage, and the handful of the rest committed acts of violence, guerrilla activity, hid a British citizen, committed murder or robbery, and demoralized the troops.[56] In a report of other sentences, the judge acknowledged the difficult task of the French lawyers, and thanked

---

54. BA/MA, RW 35/544, Chef des Militärverwaltungsbezirkes C, Ablieferung von Waffen, 27. März 1942.

55. Jacques Demange, vice-président de l'association d'anciens combatants du village, Mont-sur-Meurthe, France, letter to author, June 3, 2003.

56. BA/MA, RW 35/14, Militärbefehlshaber in Frankreich, Lagebericht für die Monate Februar 1942 bis März 1942.

the French police for their collaboration with the German police, making the arrest of the terrorists possible.[57]

French Police Trace a Registered Pistol

When a member of the Resistance shot a German and dropped his handgun at the scene, the commissioner of police of Rouen ordered the issuance of an alert to every prefect in France, in both the occupied and unoccupied zones, to check the registration records to determine the owner of the firearm.[58] René Bouffet, the prefect of the department of Seine-Inférieure, urgently wrote to every other prefect in France under the subject heading "Identification of a firearm owner":

> On April 24, 1942, around 10:10 p.m., in Rouen, at Crevier Street, a German sailor was attacked and seriously wounded by a revolver bullet, shot point-blank in the back, when he was walking down this street with a woman.
>
> The two assailants, on bicycles at the time of the attack, fell down; one of them fled on his bicycle and probably abandoned his glasses with a neutral lens, while the other man ran away and abandoned his bicycle, his Basque beret, and notably his firearm.
>
> This firearm is a 6.35 mm automatic pistol marked Oméga, serial number 1901, in new condition.
>
> *It is extremely urgent* to check the firearm registration records in your department carefully, to determine if the pistol found in Rouen was registered in your department, in order to submit all information about the owner to me immediately.[59]

---

57. "Vingt-cinq communistes condamnés à mort," *Le Figaro*, April 16, 1942, 1.

58. Procès verbal n° 234/1, commissariat de police du service de sûreté de la ville de Rouen. 4 M 262, Cab 4/15 cote provisoire. Port et détention d'armes. Archives départementales de la Marne, Châlons-en-Champagne.

59. Le Préfet de la Seine-Inférieure à Messieurs les Préfets de la Zone Occupée et à Messieurs les Préfets de la Zone non Occupée. Rouen, le 30 avril 1942. 1 W (M 5381), Port et détention d'armes. Archives départementales de la Marne, Châlons-en-Champagne.

The Omega was a small .25 caliber pistol made by Armero Especialistas in Spain. It was not normally marked "Oméga," indicating that the above acute accent on the "e" may have been a mistake or that "Oméga" was stamped on a pistol by another manufacturer to avoid a trademark violation. The results of the attempt to trace the pistol to its owner are unknown, as further records could not be found.

German occupation policy in all countries reflected Hitler's premise: "The most foolish mistake we could possibly make would be to allow the subject races to possess arms. History shows that all conquerors who have allowed their subject races to carry arms have prepared their own downfall by so doing." However, while the occupation model in France depended on the use of the French police, in the East the Führer rejected use of "any native militia or police," insisting that "German troops alone will bear the sole responsibility for the maintenance of law and order throughout the occupied Russian territories. . . ."[60] He added, "The iron law must be: None but the Germans shall be permitted to bear arms . . . only a German has the right to carry a weapon; no Slav, no Czech, no Cossack, no Ukrainian."[61]

Pierre Laval Returns

Since the beginning of the occupation, Germany made ever-increasing demands on France to exploit its resources and labor force and to cooperate with its brutal reprisal policies. Vichy was deemed insufficiently cooperative, prompting the Germans to seek the reinstatement of Pierre Laval to head the government. Jean Guéhenno wrote in his diary on April 11, 1942, "In

---

60. *Hitler's Secret Conversations*, trans. Norman Cameron and R. H. Stevens (New York: Signet Books, 1961), 403. The first two sentences in the original German were:

Der größte Unsinn, den man in den besetzen Ostgebieten machen könnte, sei der, den unterworfenen Völkern Waffen zu gegen. Die Geschicte lehre, daß alle Herrenvölker untergegangen seien, nachdem sie den von ihnen unterworfenen Völkern Waffen bewilligt hätten.

From *Hitlers Tischgespräche im Führerhauptquartier 1941–1942* (Stuttgart: Seewald Verlag, 1963), 272.

61. *Trial of the Major War Criminals before the International Military Tribunal*, 7:167 (February 8, 1946).

Vichy, Laval is having mysterious conversations with the Marshal. No doubt we have some more progress to make in shame and degradation." On April 20, he added:

> It's done. Hitler wanted Laval to be the head of the French government and he is. The old man is giving him his full power and has now become a ghost even before he has died. He spoke last night without much energy. We can guess that he yielded to an ultimatum. Two weeks of intrigues ended in a strange combination. There are, when all is said and done, two governments: military power in the hands of Darlan, and civil power in the hands of Laval.[62]

De Gaulle reacted to Laval's appointment as prime minister with this broadcast from the BBC: "It is the duty of every Frenchman and Frenchwoman to fight actively, by all means in their power, against the enemy itself and against the agents of Vichy who are the accomplices of the enemy."[63] That meant carefully organizing the Resistance, not using arms without strategic goals.

At this stage, firearms were more for protection than attack. Combat leader Claude Bourdet related that, until his arrest, his role in organizing and writing resembled that "of an ordinary bureaucrat except its precarious state, a habit of looking both ways when leaving a building, and the frequent presence of an automatic pistol under my left arm."[64] Among Jewish resisters, weapons were few—some were obtained from dealers who hid their stocks—and novices had to be trained in firearm use.[65]

On May Day, Resistance groups organized an enormous demonstration in the unoccupied zone, in Lyon at the Place Carnot under the statute of the Republic. Between 50,000 to 100,000 demonstrators cried "Death to Laval!" and sang the *Marseillaise*, with its line *"Aux armes, citoyens* (To arms, citizens)."[66]

---

62. Guéhenno, *Diary of the Dark Years*, 152 (entry dated April 20, 1942).
63. Cobb, *The Resistance*, 118.
64. Cobb, *The Resistance*, 126.
65. Latour, *Jewish Resistance*, 106–7, 178.
66. Frenay, *Night Will End*, 164–65.

The SS Takes Over

At this time, Berlin was changing the leadership role for repressive policies from the military to the SS. Karl Oberg, SS and police head in Radom, Poland, was appointed as senior SS and police leader (*Höherer SS- und Polizeiführer*, or HSSuPF), who Hitler authorized to "supervise and issue instructions to French authorities and police forces." Reinhard Heydrich, *SS-Obergruppenführer* and chief of the Reich Main Security Office (which included the Gestapo and SD), flew to Paris on May 5 to present Oberg to French functionaries, including Fernand de Brinon, the Vichy ambassador, and Douis Darquier de Pellepoix, commissioner-general for Jewish affairs (*Commissaire-général aux questions juives*, or CGQJ). Heydrich and Oberg met with René Bousquet, secretary-general of the police (*Secrétariat-général à la Police*), about closer German-French police collaboration.[67]

Earlier that year, Heydrich had orchestrated the Wannsee conference, which outlined the "final solution" of the Jewish question—a euphemism for what became the Holocaust. Now in Paris, he laid the groundwork for the mass deportation of the French Jews to the death camps in the East. Just a month later, on June 4, Heydrich would be assassinated by a Czech hit team in Prague.[68]

While an amnesty to surrender weapons existed under the March 5 decree, the issue arose of arms retained as evidence in French court cases.[69] Dr. Grohmann discussed the matter with Dr. Gilsdorf of the justice group, and pointed out that the situation should not arise. That was because the French prosecutorial and judicial authorities were required to turn over all proceedings concerning weapons possession to the German authorities without delay. If a person committed a homicide using a firearm, then the German authorities would first conduct proceedings for illegal weapons possession. Usually, these cases ended with a death sentence and the French proceedings became moot when the defendant was executed. If the defendant was not sentenced

67. Laub, *After the Fall*, 184; Umbreit, *Militärbefehlshaber in Frankreich*, 111.
68. Herbert, *Best*, 320–21.
69. BA/MA, RW 35/544, Chef der Militärverwaltung Bezirk C (Nordostfrankreich), Ablieferung von Waffen, usw, die als Beweisstücke in französischen Strafverfahren dienen, Verordnung über Waffenbesitz vom 5. März 1942, 2. Mai 1942.

to death, the French prosecution would proceed and the German court would make the weapon available to the French court as evidence.[70]

In practice, the Germans lacked the resources to prosecute all firearm possession cases, but could review all cases and select those of particular interest for prosecution, such as possession of military firearms and use of firearms in crimes like sabotage and attacks on Germans. This work focuses on gun control under the occupation authorities based on the German military archives. It should not be forgotten in context that the Vichy authorities had their own priorities and practices as to enforcement of gun control, executions, and such matters.

District A at Saint-Germain reported 130 cases of illegal weapons possession in the period March 16 to May 12.[71] But the good news was the success of the decree for amnesty for turning in weapons, which netted 1,404 hunting guns, 657 military weapons, 507 other weapons, and 823 pistols and revolvers.[72]

However, the MBF had more grisly statistics for April and May—142 sentenced to death, compared to 113 for the past period, of which 60 were for giving aid and comfort to the enemy, 47 for weapons possession, and 25 for guerrilla activity. Sentences for espionage dropped considerably to just 5.[73]

On June 1, SS General Karl Oberg officially assumed his duties in France. This gave the SS far more power over the German and French police to enforce Hitler's reprisal measures, anti-Jewish policies, and other Nazi agendas in lieu of the military's more cautious approach. Answering directly to Heinrich Himmler, Oberg assumed direction of the French police and took over major security policies from the Wehrmacht.[74]

In just a week, Nazi authorities ordered that Jews wear the Star of David. When diarist Hélène Berr's father was arrested for not wearing the badge in

70. BA/MA, RW 35/544, Militärbefehlshaber in Frankreich, Verwaltungsstab, Abteilung Verwaltung, Ablieferung von Waffen, 14. Mai 1942.

71. BA/MA, RW 35/1217, Lagebericht für die Zeit vom 16. März einschliesslich 12. Mai 1942, Sachgebiet Gerichtswesen, Chef des Militärverwaltungsbezirks A, 15. Mai 1942.

72. BA/MA, RW 35/1217, Lagebericht vom 16. März 1942 bis 12. Mai 1942, Chef des Militärverwaltungsbezirks A, Verwaltungsstab, 21. Mai 1942.

73. BA/MA, RW 35/16, Militärbefehlshaber in Frankreich, Lagebericht für die Monate April/Mai 1942.

74. Laub, *After the Fall*, 168–69, 177–78, 181–83.

the correct manner, the French police who took him prisoner expressed so much sympathy that she commented, "You might have wondered what we were all doing there. But that was because there were no Germans present. The full meaning, the sinister meaning, of it all was not apparent because we were among French people."[75] The sad truth was that the French police, at the behest of the SS, would brutally round up and supervise the deportation of the Jews.

The Yellow Star

Imposing the yellow star on Jews illustrated the cleavage between the new SS commanders and the more restrained military authorities. "I suddenly felt embarrassed to be in uniform," Captain Ernst Jünger confided to his diary after first seeing three Jewish girls with the yellow star.[76] A literary figure before and after the war, Jünger was now on the command staff at the MBF as a censor of French newspapers and as a cultural attaché. He collaborated and socialized with the likes of Werner Best, who made Wehrmacht policy to repress firearm possession by the French. Jünger had no affinity for Hitler, who he codenamed Kniébolo in his diary.[77]

Oberg's appointment and resultant staff changes pushed Werner Best out of his duties. Best was then appointed German Reich plenipotentiary in Denmark, where he again implemented a decree threatening execution for anyone not turning in their firearms in twenty-four hours.[78]

Raiding a Gun Depot

Since the occupation began, many surrendered arms had been stored by French mayors or local German forces. Resistance groups were eyeballing these depots to see what they could take back. The experience of one group was related to me in response to my questionnaire.

75. Hélène Berr, *The Journal of Hélène Berr* (New York: Weinstein Books, 2008), 71, 75 (entry dated June 24, 1942).

76. Allan Mitchell, *The Devil's Captain: Ernst Jünger in Nazi Paris, 1941–1944* (New York: Berghahn Books, 2011), 27.

77. Mitchell, *Devil's Captain,* 40, 70.

78. Flender, *Rescue in Denmark,* 40–41; Best, *Dänemark in Hitlers Hand,* 52–53.

Guy Faisant was born in 1925 in Rennes, a city in the east of Brittany, and was a fourteen-year-old student in a private school when the Germans invaded. Recalling the order to surrender arms published in newspapers and public notices, he stated, "Upon the arrival of occupation troops, those in possession of firearms were invited to turn them in to their local police stations. In Rennes, the weapons were stored in an 'unguarded' warehouse."[79]

French gun owners, in Faisant's experience, had firearms mostly for hunting and shooting matches, and not so many had handguns. Many complied with the decrees for fear of reprisals. Arrests occurred after denunciations to the police, and those who possessed arms were deported.

The young Faisant joined a resistance group at the end of 1941, and his duty was to distribute anti-German leaflets. But a more dangerous mission was in store—the unguarded arms at the warehouse mentioned above did not go unnoticed. He remembered:

> I was in a professional school, *l'École pratique d'industrie*, and with a few of my classmates, we carried out our mission. We had learned that the requisitioned arms were stored at the depot, as indicated above. So, we went to retrieve those arms—revolvers and pistols. Three of us went together; two entering the depot after having scaled the wall, the third person keeping watch—giving the order to retreat.

The heist was successful. More counterseizures of arms were to come: "Some members from our group stole revolvers from the Germans when they took their belts off in a restaurant or at the barbershop." When engaged in operations, Resistance members would hide their firearms "in varied caches; personally, I used a rabbit cage with a false bottom."

Unfortunately, a medical student who had been arrested for gold trafficking began working for the Germans and infiltrated the group. Faisant explained:

> We were denounced by a French informer of the Nazis, and ten of my coworkers were arrested. Searches were performed in our homes by the SD. We were incarcerated in the Jacques Cartier Prison in Rennes. Those in whose houses the Germans found arms were deported on

79. Guy Faisant (born August 23, 1925), Rennes, France, (circa 2000).

June 4, 1942, to concentration camps in Germany in accord with the
"Nacht und Nebel" German decree of December 7, 1941.

The SD was the *Sicherheitsdienst* (Nazi security service); the Jacques Cartier
Prison was a maximum security prison taken over by the Nazis; and *Nacht und
Nebel* (Night and Fog) was the program under which enemies of the occupation would be arrested and transported to concentration camps in Germany
without any trace so that no one would know their fate.

One member of the group, Jean Renault, tried to flee and fired at the
Germans, who shot him dead. The others were deported. Faisant himself was
arrested on March 5, and deported with the rest on June 4. He was imprisoned
at the Gross-Rosen concentration camp in lower Silesia in Hirschberg, where
he was freed on May 8, 1945, by the Soviet army.

The above experiences are revealing in that execution for firearm possession was by no means automatic, even for members of a subversive group.
Deportation to a concentration camp could lead to death, but not always.
Methods of enforcement of Nazi gun control varied, depending to some
degree on who made the decisions in specific cases.

Denunciations Based on Ulterior Motives

A legal system based on denunciations can have detestable results, even from
the perspective of those in power. On June 5, the MBF ordered an amendment to the March 5 decree concerning weapons possession stemming from
the increase of cases where Wehrmacht courts sentenced defendants to death
after their own relatives turned them in. While it was necessary to prosecute
gun possession cases without leniency to confiscate as many arms as possible,
"the death penalty is odious in cases where the French person makes the report
based on ulterior motives (revenge, jealousy, etc.) and uses the German legal
system to get rid of an unwanted family member."[80]

---

80. BA/MA, RW 35/544, Militärbefehlshaber in Frankreich, Verwaltungsstab, Abteilung
Verwaltung, Änderung der Verordung über den Besitz von Waffen vom 5. März 1941, Anzeige
des Täters durch Angehörige, 5. Juni 1942. See also Ordonnance du 5 Juni 1942 modifiant
l'ordonnance du 10 Mai 1940, concernant la détention des armes en territoire occupé de la
France, Verordnungsblatt des Militärbefehlshabers in Frankreich (VOBIF), No. 64, 5 Juni
1942, 385.

In such cases, the MBF continued, the guilty person should be sentenced to jail or prison rather than death, except for severe cases involving possession of numerous weapons or where family members had a valid motive for their report. Section 2 of the decree as written provided for the death penalty in paragraph 1, but paragraph 2 provided that "[i]n less serious cases the sentence may be forced labor or imprisonment." The amendment added the following to paragraph 2: "The same will happen to any offender who shall be taken to court following a report against him or her by his or her spouse, parents, children, or brothers and sisters."[81]

The issue continued to be debated by German authorities in Berlin. In response to a German decree, or draft of a decree, requiring that a person with knowledge that another possesses a firearm report it to the nearest police headquarters, French authorities protested that if the French occupied Germany, a person who denounced others to the occupying power would be considered as having no honor.[82] In the post-war Nuremberg trials, a French prosecutor stated that the policy was "so obviously contrary to international law that the Foreign Ministry of the Reich itself took cognizance of it." In a note signed by a Herr Strack, the ministry in Berlin opined on June 29:

> The Foreign Office considers it questionable whether punishment should be inflicted on whomsoever fails to denounce a person possessing or known to possess arms. Such a prescription of penalty under this general form is, in the opinion of the Foreign Office, the more impracticable in that it would offer the French the possibility of calling attention to the fact that the German Army is demanding of them acts which would be considered criminal if committed by German citizens.

The French prosecutor commented, "There is no more severe condemnation of the German Army than that expressed by the Reich Ministry of Foreign Affairs itself." But in a response dated December 8, the High Command of the Wehrmacht said to the Ministry that "since it does not seem desirable to enter

---

81. BA/MA, RW 35/544, Verordnungsblatt des Militärbefehlshabers in Frankreich, Journal Officiel contenant les ordonnances du Militärbefehlshaber in Frankerich, Nr. 64, 5. Juni 1942.
82. *Trial of the Major War Criminals before the International Military Tribunal*, 6:395 (January 31, 1946).

into discussion with the French Government on the questions of law evoked by them, we too consider it appropriate not to reply to the French note." Any relaxing of orders, it added, would be considered a sign of weakness.[83]

Examples of arms that were confiscated without criminal charges are contained in reports of the district military unit at Bar le Duc. Heinrich Dargent, aged sixty-two, who resided in Chardogne, found a pistol in his house's ash container, which was built into the kitchen wall. The family had been evacuated during the German invasion, when it was assumed that a soldier threw the pistol into the container. Dargent turned the pistol in at the mayor's office immediately when he found it, and the military police believed his account. He thus complied with the March 5 decree.[84]

In a second incident, the mayor of Noyers-le-Val emptied a pond in a park and found a French infantry rifle model 1874 and two live, egg-shaped hand grenades. The military police assumed that the weapons dated back to the time when there had been combat in the park.[85]

In a third incident, Louis Mercier found a pistol in his attic at his house in Ligny and turned it in to the French police, who turned it over to the Germans. He had been evacuated in June 1940 and returned in June 1942. When he cleaned up his apartment, he found the pistol and ammunition in the clutter. The messy apartment had been occupied by German soldiers for a year, and it was concluded that the items were left by German or French soldiers.[86]

The SS Terror

For those who chose to resist in any manner, it was a different story. "For some time now our guests have been committing their crimes in silence," wrote Jean Guéhenno in his diary on July 10. "They have been executing people every day in the prisons, but no notice was published." But that afternoon, in the

83. *Trial of the Major War Criminals,* 6:396.
84. BA/MA, RH 36/231, Bericht der Feldkommandantur 590, Feldgendarmerietrupp 590, in der Strafsache gegen Dargent Heinrich, Bar-le-Duc, 16. Juni 1942.
85. BA/MA, RH 36/231, Bericht der Feldkommandantur 590, Feldgendarmerietrupp 590 betreffend Waffenfund in Noyers le Val, Bar-le-Duc, 25. Juni 1942.
86. BA/MA, 36/231, Bericht eines Oberfeldwebels der Feldgendarmerie, betreffend Auffinden einer Pistole in Ligny, Bar-le-Duc, 7. Juli 1942.

corridors of the République Métro station, he saw crowds, with horror written on their faces, gathered around yellow posters with an announcement by the SS:

1. All male relatives of the runaways over eighteen (cousins and brothers-in-law included) will be shot;
2. The women will be sentenced to hard labor;
3. Children under eighteen will be sent to reform school.[87]

The above was SS General Karl Oberg's new policy that applied to relatives of resistance fighters who did not turn them in within ten days of the crime.[88]

"It appears that the SS have taken command in France and that terror must follow," wrote Hélène Berr in her diary. The word was going around that a massive roundup of Jews was coming, and it took place on July 16–17. "In Montmartre there were so many arrests that the streets were jammed. . . . Mothers have been separated from their children." Not all French police officers were accomplices: "Apparently several policemen have been shot for warning people so they could escape."[89]

The Jews were thrown into the Vélodrome d'Hiver, a cycling stadium. Hélène Berr noted, "Twelve thousand people are incarcerated, it's hell. Many deaths already, sanitary facilities blocked up, etc." They were then taken to the rail center at Drancy and forced into trains, "stacked like cattle, without even any straw, for deportation."[90] Concentration camps and death camps awaited them in the East.[91]

Resistance to the Terror

Members of the Resistance operated in countless ways to save lives. Louis Charmeau, whose recollections on German disarming policies was reported to me in 2003, lived in the region of Bourgogne in eastern France. Charmeau saved a number of people by diverting mail being sent to the German com-

---

87. Guéhenno, *Diary of the Dark Years*, 164 (entry dated July 10, 1942).

88. Laub, *After the Fall*, 188.

89. Berr, *Journal*, 97–99 (entries dated July 15 and 18, 1942).

90. Berr, *Journal*, 103, 105 (entries dated July 18 and 21, 1942).

91. Gildea, *Marianne in Chains*, 259.

mand: "As a mail carrier, every morning I took letters addressed to the *Kommandantur*, transported them in my countryside route the distance of 49 kilometers, and opened them in the evening. From July 1942 through the date of my arrest on May 22, 1944, I was able to save two Jewish families and twenty-five persons denounced for possession of arms or other offenses that would have led them straight to deportation or execution." The Jews he helped included a doctor and a tailor. He also smuggled people across the demarcation line near Charolles, transported arms, and sabotaged the SNCF (*Société nationale des chemins de fer français*) railroad central hub depot in Paray-le-Monial. He was captured, and when he was liberated on May 5, 1945, he weighed 116 pounds.[92]

Charmeau commented, "The underground resistance became really organized and armed only after the reunification of the different resistance 'branches' by Jean Moulin in May 1943 as the *Mouvements Unis de la Résistance* (United Movements of the Resistance, MUR). Arms from civilians were only used, from the end of 1940 to the end of 1941, by scattered groups, who often were adventurers, or even for settling political scores." Where did arms used in the Resistance come from? "Maybe 15 percent came from civilians who had left for the Maquis [rural resistance fighters] with their old arms, often without ammunition. Eighty-five percent came from airdrops. Yes, some were taken from German soldiers, but only after 1944, when they were prisoners."

During this period, weapons were literally falling from the sky, including items parachuted by the Allies to resistance groups and Allied airplanes crashing. The MBF declared the death penalty for anyone who discovered any object dropped from an airplane or taken from a downed airplane without informing the nearest German military post.[93]

As reported by the Resistance newspaper *Combat*, on July 25 the German military tribunal at Lille imposed twenty-eight death sentences against miners for sabotage, possession of prohibited arms, and anti-German activities. The sentences were carried out.[94]

92. Louis Maurice Charmeau, président de l'Union Départementale des Combattants Volontaires de la Résistance, Bordeaux, France, letter to author, June 10, 2003.

93. "*Avis*," *Le Matin*, July 8, 1942, 3.

94. "Morts pour la France," *Combat*, août 1942 (citing *La Revue*, Lausanne, Switzerland, 29 juillet 1942).

The Vichy cabinet convened on July 31 and imposed the death sentence for possession of explosives and stocks of arms. Any demonstration likely to disturb public order was also prohibited.[95] The London *Times* commented that this reaffirmed existing preparations to resist the opening of a second front in France by American and British forces.[96]

Issued by Marshal Pétain, Pierre Laval, and Justice Minister Joseph Barthélemy, the decree-law amended the prewar law of April 18, 1939, to provide in part: "Anyone who shall be in possession of an arm or ammunition cache of category 1, 4, 5, or 6 shall be handed over to the special court created by the law of April 24, 1941, and sentenced to death."[97] These prohibited categories included military arms, firearms for self-defense and ammunition therefor, hunting arms and ammunition, and edged weapons.[98]

This was the first time the Vichy government decreed the death sentence for unauthorized possession of firearms. Since it applied in the unoccupied, "free" zone, it reflected great distrust by the French authorities of the French people themselves. It also applied in the occupied zone, as French criminal law applied there as long as it did not conflict with German decrees. In the occupied zone, the Vichy government arrested, tried, and punished people for arms possession, subject to the power of the German authorities to review, investigate, and take over cases of interest for their perceived security.

An exemption existed for authorized manufacturers or dealers, or people who registered the items with the police within five days.[99] This obviously applied only in the unoccupied zone.

In more welcome news, the Vichy government announced that hunting season in the nonoccupied zone would begin on Sunday, September 6, at 7:00 a.m. However, pheasant hunting would open on October 11, and certain spe-

95. "Au conseil des ministres," *Le Matin*, August 1-2, 1942, 3; "Les manifestations de nature à nuire à l'ordre public sont interdites," *Le Figaro*, August 3, 1942, 1; *The Times* (London), August 5, 1942, 3e.

96. *The Times* (London), August 5, 1942, 3e.

97. Art. 2, Loi N° 773 du 7 août 1942 punissant de la peine de mort la détention d'explosifs et les dépôts d'armes, *Journal Officiel*, N° 189, 8 août 1942.

98. Art. 1 & 2, Décret-loi du 18 avril 1939 fixant le régime des matériels de guerre, armes et munitions, *Journal Officiel*, 13 juin 1939, 7463–7466.

99. Art. 4., Décret-loi du 18 avril 1939 fixant le régime des matériels de guerre, armes et munitions, *Journal Officiel*, 13 juin 1939, 7463–7466.

cies would close as early as November 2—white hare, grouse, hazel grouse, rock partridge, and male "tetras" (a sort of grouse). It was prohibited to hunt chamois, ibex, marmot, or female tetras.[100]

As reported by *Combat*, among a list of people shot by the Germans on August 29 at Montceau-les-Mines was a First World War veteran. They found a rifle in his house.[101] Nor could university students be trusted—a revolver was found at the Lycée Charlemagne, prompting an urgent Gestapo investigation.[102]

While the quantities of arms surrendered or confiscated suggested that France was awash in arms, the Resistance was in desperate need of effective weapons. Henri Frenay of the organization Combat made a secret visit to London to meet with General de Gaulle in September, stressing that "we in France are expecting a lot, especially in the way of arms. We must have arms!" De Gaulle answered, "I know. Try and explain that to the English. *A bientôt* [goodbye]." Frenay estimated the need for 1,000 tons of weapons to be parachuted into France each month, but for many months they received "nothing but a dribble in the way of arms."[103]

District A reported on October 5 some 380 cases of illegal weapons possession, an increase partly due to smuggling, along with 12 cases of espionage and 58 cases of sabotage. Cases of illegal weapons possession were frequently associated with anti-German demonstrations. While the high number of cases of arms possession was due in part to the population's submission to German orders to denounce others, many reports were made anonymously and were based on personal revenge or hatred. Many proceedings were terminated because they were baseless. The report praised the French gendarmes and judicial authorities for their cooperation.[104]

The MBF reported for June through September a total of 276 French citizens sentenced to death by the courts for the following charges:[105]

100. "L'ouverture de la chasse aura lieu le 6 septembre," *Le Figaro*, August 19, 1942, 1.

101. "Morts au Champ d'Honneur. France," *Combat*, n° 36, novembre 1942.

102. Mitchell, *Nazi Paris*, 77–78.

103. Frenay, *Night Will End*, 202, 205.

104. BA/MA, RW 35/1221, Lagebericht für den Zeitraum vom 16. Mai 1942 bis 30. September 1942, Chef der Militärverwaltung A, 5. Oktober 1942.

105. BA/MA, RW 35/289, Militärbefehlshaber in Frankreich, Monatsbericht für September 1942, 12. Dezember.1942.

126 giving aid and comfort to the enemy

103 illegal weapons possession

 24 espionage

  8 guerrilla activity

  5 violent acts

  2 murder

  1 robbery, helping British soldiers, and failure to report planned crimes

The Vichy regime was certainly cooperating. At the meeting of the cabinet of ministers on October 19, the chief of state insisted that disturbance of public order and of work would not be tolerated. Economic ministers declared that the commitments by French workers to labor in Germany were improving greatly. Laval's instructions to reinforce the prefects' authority were approved. The cabinet also approved measures proposed by Minister of Justice Joseph Barthélemy against Allied airdrops of arms and explosives.[106]

An Eyewitness

Gilles Lévy, who was then seventeen years old, became active in the Resistance in 1942 in the region of Auvergne, which is located in central France near Vichy. He was a member of Combat, *Franc-Tireur, Mouvements Unis de la Résistance* (MUR), and *l'Armée Secrète* (AS). He fought with the Maquis against the Germans in several battles in 1944.[107] After the war, Lévy would become a general, rendering military service to France for sixty-eight years. He wrote several works on the Resistance in Auvergne.[108] As vice-president delegate of the Association of the Friends of the Resistance (*Association des Amitiés de la Résistance*), he responded to my questionnaire.[109]

---

106. "Le Conseil des Ministres s'est réuni à Vichy," *Le Figaro*, October 19, 1942, 1.

107. He described some of the conflicts in Général Gilles Lévy, "Les Maquis d'Auvergne dans la Résistance: Pourquoi le Mont-Mouchet?" at lesamitiesdelaresistance.fr/lien1-maquis.php. See also http://www.memoresist.org/?s=Gilles+L%C3%A9vy.

108. For example, see Gilles Lévy, *Drames et secrets de la Résistance* (Paris: Presses de la Cité, 1984) and *Guide des Maquis et hauts-lieux de la Résistance d'Auvergne* (Paris: Presses de la Cité, 1986).

109. Gilles Lévy, Saint Maur des Fossés, France, response to author's questionnaire, October 4, 1999.

General Lévy brought to my attention discoveries of firearms mentioned in the monthly reports made by the Vichy prefects in the department of Haute-Saône, which was partially in the occupied zone and partially reserved for German settlement. In one example, in Velleclaire a crate of 1,370 cartridges together with a carbine and an automatic weapon were confiscated from a house. In another, after being denounced, a man was arrested after the Feldgendarmerie of Lure found four war weapons and 1,000 cartridges in his house. In another case, a stock of 127 hunting guns and 3 rifles were discovered in Plaux at the house of the father of a gunsmith, and was apparently kept for commercial purposes.[110]

Lévy's perceptions would have reflected his experiences in the region of Auvergne, which was in the free zone until occupied by the Wehrmacht on November 11, 1942. He responded to my questionnaire as follows:

The possession of firearms by civilians before the war was common, including hunting guns, sporting firearms, and collections of arms from the First World War. Some civilians had a permit to carry an arm such as a revolver for self-defense. Gunsmiths also sold arms if an authorization from the police was provided.

For the most part, people complied with the decrees and turned in their arms, others kept them in hopes of using them some day to fight the occupying forces. Others got rid of them by burying them. Hunting firearms were brought to the gendarmeries or police stations.

People were searched during identity controls in the streets, and those who were carrying an arm were immediately arrested, brought to court, and sentenced to be deported or shot.

As to how people who were executed for possession of firearms were discovered, Lévy stated that it was usually by an anonymous denunciation. In his experience, most of the arms used by the Resistance were airdropped by the Allies—the British Special Operations Executive (SOE) and the American Office of Strategic Services (OSS)—or were recovered from hidden storage depots of the French army.

---

110. Archives Nationales F1cIII 1183, monthly report of the Haute-Saône prefect, 1940–1944 (first two cases); Archives Nationales F1cIII 1199, monthly report of the Puy de Dôme prefect, December 1, 1942 to January 1, 1943 (third case).

Lévy's observation was consistent with France's prewar ban on civilian possession of "war weapons," such as bolt-action rifles in calibers used by the military. The populace had been primarily limited to possession only of shotguns and small caliber rifles and handguns. Such arms could be used by members of the Resistance in individual self-defense, but far better arms were needed for organized confrontation with Wehrmacht forces. That day would come.

7

Arms for the Resistance

OPERATION TORCH, THE American-British invasion of French North Africa, was launched on November 8, 1942. After initial resistance from French forces, an agreement was made on the 10th with Admiral François Darlan, the highest-ranking French officer there, to lay down their arms. Many would join the Allies with the Free French Forces. Hitler immediately ordered the occupation of the free zone of France. "The German army is panicked, runs to the Mediterranean, occupies all of France, and the whole French Empire is entering the war," as Jean Guéhenno put it in his diary.[1]

Pierre Laval was awakened at 4 a.m. on November 11 to be informed that the Axis would now occupy Vichy France. Vichy authorities let Pétain continue to sleep as they ordered that the military and police not resist. French police could remain armed, but the French military would be disbanded and disarmed, other than certain exceptions for officers explained below. Days later, power was conferred on Laval to issue laws and decrees without Pétain's approval.[2]

Seeking to justify his actions after the war while awaiting trial, Laval wrote, "The most lurid violation of the Armistice Convention was the crossing of the demarcation line by the German army" in 1942, adding that "the Armistice lasted four long years, and we had no means, no weapons, other than negotiations described to-day as 'intelligence with the enemy,' to serve as a barrier to German cruelty and rapacity." The lack of weapons could be traced in part to Laval's own 1935 decree that firearms be registered with

---

1. Guéhenno, *Diary of the Dark Years*, 181.
2. Warner, *Pierre Laval*, 336, 350.

the police and his subsequent collaboration with the Germans. Laval justified his continued collaboration with the Nazis who now occupied all of France as follows:

> Had I abandoned my post in November 1942 the whole of the country would have become one vast *Maquis*. The cost would have been thousands and thousands of dead. It is understandable that brave men and true patriots did not hesitate to expose themselves to the consequences of Article 10, which outlawed them as guerillas or *francs-tireurs*. But how could the head of Government be justified in taking a decision which would expose the entire French population to this terrible risk?[3]

The whole of France as "one vast *Maquis*," as rural resistance fighters were called, would have meant a popular armed struggle against Nazi occupation. The liability of guerillas, also known as *francs-tireurs*, not to be treated as prisoners of war under Article 10 of the armistice was a brutal but expected consequence of being in the Resistance. Laval's continued collaboration only delayed the defeat of Nazi occupation. It goes without saying that the conjured disaster would not have occurred had Laval, to use his words, abandoned his post.

The handwriting was on the wall for gun owners in the newly occupied free zone. Maxime Ducrocq, president of the *Saint-Hubert-Club de France*, wrote to the interior minister in Vichy—that was Pierre Laval—on November 13 expressing the dread of hunters that decrees would be issued requiring all hunting arms to be turned in to town halls or to *Kommandanturen* and banning hunting, either along the coast or in the entire free zone. If arms were required to be surrendered, Ducrocq urged that labels with the name and address of owners be firmly attached, noting that this was not done in 1940 in three-fourths of the cases, which would have made return of the guns much more difficult.[4] His hope that surrendered firearms would be returned to their owners after the war was an illusion.

3. Laval, *Diary*, 63, 65.
4. "La guerre et la chasse en zone non occupée," *Le Saint-Hubert*, n°6, 41e année, novembre–décembre 1942, 65.

The Gestapo Confronts the Resistance

Members of the Resistance had far broader issues in mind. Reflecting that many were in the previously unoccupied zone, Resistance leader Henri Frenay noted, "For Combat, for my comrades and for myself, the battle was to change radically. We were now confronted by the Gestapo itself." The Gestapo aggressively repressed the Resistance in Lyon, a center of anti-German activity. Frenay recalled, "Soon I was packing a loaded pistol whenever I went out. That way, if the enemy were to appear, he and I would be a little more evenly matched."[5]

When defeated in 1940, the French army had not turned in all of the arms required by the armistice. Vichy had an arms-concealment program for hiding large numbers of firearms, ammunition, and artillery throughout the unoccupied zone. Frenay had actually met with the member of the general staff in charge of the program, and later wrote him, "The army's weapons belong to the nation and not to you alone. It is your duty to give them to those who will use them for the liberation of our homeland." He warned against them falling into the enemy's hands. Frenay would bitterly recall, "Soon afterward, Laval ordered that all existing arms caches be turned over to the Germans, which, with a few exceptions, they were."[6]

Vichy planned to make good use of the firearms it was confiscating from its August 1942 decree-law that imposed the death penalty. The ministry of the interior categorized confiscated weapons as follows: *Group 1*, weapons that can be used by the police—6.35 mm and 7.65 mm pistols; 8 mm revolvers; 1892 models or similar light machine guns; military rifles; hunting rifles in good condition and well taken care of; *Group 2*, weapons that can be used by other entities that maintain law and order—pistols, revolvers, rifles in good condition and well taken care of that are not listed in the first group; and *Group 3*, weapons that do not qualify for either.[7]

---

5. Frenay, *Night Will End*, 215, 227–28.

6. Frenay, *Night Will End*, 225–26.

7. BA/MA, RH 31/29, Weisungen des Innenministeriums betreffend Verwendung der eingesammelten Waffen, 30. November 1942.

Weapons of groups 1 and 2 would be retained permanently. Regional prefects would consult with the Central Armament Service and requisition weapons necessary to equip police forces in their respective regions. The remaining inventory was to be sent to the Service to distribute them to occupied or unoccupied territories.

Of group 3, weapons from collections would be returned to the private citizens who surrendered them or to local authorities if the owner could not be established. Hunting guns not confiscated by the Central Armament Service would be given to holders of hunting permits for the years 1942 to 1943. Unusable or obsolete weapons would be scrapped and paid for by weight.

No compensation would be paid for several categories, including the types of revolvers or self-loading pistols used by foreign armies, described as Parabellum, Mauser, Walther, Colt, Smith & Wesson, Erfurt, Webley & Scott, Eagan, FN Herstal, Beretta, Star, Eibar, etc. Browning five-shot self-loading hunting shotguns would also be kept without compensation if the owners were unable to prove that they acquired them before the law of 1934 entered into force.

Up to now, civilians in the free zone were subject to the decree-law on war matériel, arms, and munitions of April 18, 1939. It banned "war weapons," defined to include any firearm chambered for the same cartridge used by the military, such as handguns using the 7.65 mm long or greater caliber rounds. Other handguns were "defensive arms" requiring authorization from the police station or the gendarmerie, and were limited to only one weapon per home. Prefects of the free zone issued decrees that progressively forbade firearm possession, and required them to be surrendered to gendarmeries or to town halls.[8]

Vichy Decrees the Death Penalty for Gun Possession

At this point, as ordered by Field Marshal Gerd von Rundstedt, commander-in-chief–West,[9] the Vichy regime decreed a further ban on firearms other than those belonging to the military and police. Following consultation with the Council of Ministers, Pierre Laval decreed a law on December 3 modifying

<hr>

8. Venner, *Armes de la Résistance*, 147–48.
9. BA/MA, RH 31/29, Brief des Oberbefehlshabers West, Oberkommando Heeresgruppe D, Arbeitsstab Frankreich, Nr. 319/43, an die französische Regierung, 17. April 1943.

the 1939 law, and amended it two days later to make it more draconian.[10] It began with a general prohibition on firearms: "Sale, possession, transportation and carrying of firearms of any kind, including hunting guns, ammunition of any kind, explosives and individual parts of these items are prohibited."[11] In the first version, violation was punishable by imprisonment, or by death if an arms cache was possessed.[12] In the version decreed two days later, that was amended to apply to any firearm, not just a cache: "Any violation of the provisions of this decree shall be punished by imprisonment or the death sentence."

The prohibition did not apply to French military personnel who remained in service after December 1, 1942, or to government employees whose jobs put them at risk of aggression, such as police officers and penitentiary guards. It also excluded inoperable arms with only collector's or sentimental value.[13] Prior permits to carry or possess arms were revoked, and any new ones would be issued by the ministry of the interior.[14]

Anyone in possession of arms was required to surrender them within ten days of the posting of the decree to the places designated by the prefects.[15] Anyone aware that arms or ammunition were not turned in was required to report them to the police or the city hall.[16] In the first version of the decree, failure to inform was punishable by two to five years' imprisonment. In the revised version two days later, an exemption was made to the duty to inform for direct relatives of the person possessing the arms or ammunition. It also deleted the special penalties for failure to inform and subjected violators to the general sentences of imprisonment or death.

In short, within a two-day period, the decree was changed so that one could get the death sentence not only for possessing a gun, but also for not

---

10. Loi N° 1061 du 3 décembre 1942 modifiant le décret du 18 avril 1939 fixant le régime des matériels de guerre, armes et munitions, *Journal Officiel*, N° 290, 4 décembre 1942; Loi N° 1065 du 5 décembre 1942 modifiant la loi N° 1061 du 3 décembre 1942 fixant le régime des matériels de guerre, armes et munitions, *Journal Officiel*, N° 292, 6 décembre 1942. See also BA/MA, RH 31/29, Auszug aus dem Gesetz vom 3. und 5. Dezember 1942, Artikel 1 und 2.

11. BA/MA, RH 31/29, Auszug aus dem Gesetz vom 3. und 5. Dezember 1942, Artikel 1.

12. BA/MA, RH 31/29, Auszug aus dem Gesetz vom 3. und 5. Dezember 1942, Artikel 7.

13. BA/MA, RH 31/29, Auszug aus dem Gesetz vom 3. und 5. Dezember 1942, Artikel 2.

14. BA/MA, RH 31/29, Auszug aus dem Gesetz vom 3. und 5. Dezember 1942, Artikel 3.

15. BA/MA, RH 31/29, Auszug aus dem Gesetz vom 3. und 5. Dezember 1942, Artikel 4.

16. BA/MA, RH 31/29, Auszug aus dem Gesetz vom 3. und 5. Dezember 1942, Artikel 5.

informing the police that someone else possessed a gun. Perhaps the German occupiers did not like the first decree and ordered Laval to make it harsher. A final amendment to the decree clarified that violators would be under summary procedures for trial,[17] usually meaning a quick finding of guilt with little due process.

The day the decree was announced on the radio in Paris, the *Saint-Hubert-Club de France* sent a letter to the *Sociétés Départementales de Chasseurs* (Departmental Societies of Hunters) detailing its efforts to alleviate the burdens and secure the firearms that must be turned in, including giving a receipt to the owner, the keeping of a registry, and securely fixing labels with the owner's name and address. Hunters were urged to contact their prefect and admonish that protective measures be taken to safeguard the arms. Vermin that destroyed the crops could still be hunted, but not with guns (the letter did not say how, but archery and trapping were likely intended).[18]

The hunters were assured that Saint-Hubert President Maxime Ducrocq would be received by Marshal Pétain to express their concerns.[19] If the senile Pétain stayed awake in the meeting, he was powerless to do much.

As an example of how the law was administered, the prefect of Gard in southern France informed the mayors that all weapons must be deposited in town halls with a strong cardboard label attached to the trigger guard and bearing the following information: name, address, type of weapon, caliber, and number if applicable. Each commune would transport the weapons to the gendarmerie and the lists would be sent to the prefect by December 26.[20]

The weapons, which included 1,124 long guns and 51 pistols, would later be transported to a warehouse in Nîmes. One family surrendered 12 long guns, 3 carbines, 4 pistols, 1 child's carbine, 198 cartridges, and quantities of bullets and gunpowder for reloading. The author of this account noted, "And

---

17. Loi N° 1005 du 31 décembre 1942 modifiant la loi du 3 décembre 1942 fixant le régime des matériels de guerre, armes et munitions, *Journal Officiel*, N° 21, 24 janvier 1943.

18. "Le dépôt des armes de chasse en zone non occupée," *Le Saint-Hubert*, N°1, 42e année, janvier– février 1943, 65.

19. *Le Saint-Hubert*, n°1, 42e année, janvier-février 1943, 1.

20. "Les armes de chasse," *SSH 1992 Bulletin* N°2, 22 mai 2006. http://sommieresetson histoire.org/SSH/spip.php?article75.

we know perfectly well that every self-respecting hunter hid his best gun and cartridges in a country cottage or chicken coop."[21]

As for the exemption in the new decree for French military personnel, the Germans had other ideas. Carl-Heinrich von Stülpnagel issued a directive on December 18 stating that, in connection with the dissolution and disarmament of the French armed forces, the military commander-in-chief–West announced that French officers could keep, but not carry, sidearms and pistols that were their personal property.[22]

An *Avis* (notice) with the details was published in the press. French military officers demobilized after November 10, 1942, were required to register their firearms by make, serial number, and caliber and their ammunition between January 4 and January 20, 1943, to the security police and SD (*Sicherheitspolizei und Sicherheitsdienst*), which would issue them a certificate. Weapons could be kept only in their residences. All other firearms were required to be surrendered. Any officer who failed to register would be subject to the death penalty under the decree of March 5, 1942.[23]

The year 1942 ended with a discussion of Stülpnagel's Summary Order for the Protection of the Occupying Forces, which may have been the order to the French to issue the above decree requiring denunciation of gun possession. Dr. Rudolf Thierfelder of the dubiously named "Justiz" group, the German legal authority, noted the previous loophole, allowing that no duty existed to report illegal weapons possession or unknown weapons caches: "In practice, this lack of a provision turned out to be an important gap in the fight against illegal weapons possession and the endeavors to collect all weapons in the occupied territory." The gap was now closed with the duty to denounce others who possessed firearms, excluding close relatives.[24] The death penalty awaited those who failed to inform on gun possessors.

---

21. "Et nous savons parfaitement que tout chasseur qui se respecte, a caché, qui dans un mazet, qui dans un poulailler, son meilleur fusil et des cartouches."

22. BA/MA, RW 35/544, Militärbefehlshaber in Frankreich, Waffenbesitz französischer Offiziere und Wehrmachtsbeamter im Offiziersrang, ohne Datum, 18. Dezember 1942.

23. "Avis concernant la déclaration d'armes et de munitions détenues par les officiers français démobilisés de l'armée de transition française," *Le Matin*, December 23, 1942, 1.

24. BA/MA, RW 35/312, Militärbefehlshaber in Frankreich, Verwaltungsstab, Abteilung Justiz, Sammelverordnung zum Schutz der Besatzungsmacht, 18. Dezember 1942.

Execution Without Trial

As the screws tightened, the danger increased that the Germans would dispense with the formality even of a secret trial and shoot anyone who possessed a firearm on the spot. As provided by the January 12, 1943, order signed by Belgium Military Governor Alexander von Falkenhausen, "Persons who are found, without valid authorization, in possession of explosives and military firearms, pistols of all kinds, sub-machine guns, rifles, *et cetera*, with ammunition, are liable in future to be shot immediately without trial." At the Nuremberg Trials in 1946, French prosecutor Charles Dubost characterized the order as showing that the Nazis saw all citizens of France and the rest of Europe as engaged in resistance, thereby calling for "arbitrary measures of repression" and "extermination."[25]

In January 1943, Vichy transformed the *Service d'Ordre Légionnaire* (SOL), supposedly a patriotic organization established in 1941, into the *Milice* to repress anti-Nazi forces.[26] The *Milice* became Vichy's primary force, in the words of Simone de Beauvoir, that "suppress[ed] all 'disaffections on the home front,' and which hunted down members of the Resistance even more ruthlessly than the S.S. did."[27]

Meeting in Casablanca, Allied heads Franklin Roosevelt and Winston Churchill together with Generals Charles de Gaulle and Henri Giraud representing the Free French Forces planned the next strategic moves against the Axis. Roosevelt famously announced the "unconditional surrender" doctrine, precluding any negotiated terms, much to Churchill's surprise. The Allies would thereafter rely on bombing to obliterate the Axis war machine, although the British Special Operations Executive (SOE) favored sabotage. The Resistance also favored sabotage over bombing, which could not be pinpointed and would kill innocent civilians and destroy cities.[28]

---

25. *Trial of the Major War Criminals Before the International Military Tribunal*, 6:380, available at avalon.law.yale.edu/imt/01-31-46.asp.

26. Pryce-Jones, *Paris in the Third Reich*, 179–81.

27. de Beauvoir, *Prime of Life*, 633.

28. Michel, *Shadow War*, 212.

Unifying the Resistance

On January 26, the groups Libération, Combat, and Franc-Tireur united under the *Mouvements Unis de la Résistance* (MUR, or United Movement of the Resistance).[29] The Resistance was becoming increasingly active, although its members were always short of arms. They started with a few civilian arms from before the war and military arms left from the battles of 1940. The Allies began dropping arms by parachute, allowing the Resistance to escalate its activities involving sabotage and even direct combat.[30]

In February, Combat chief Henri Frenay sent an envoy to report on the secret army, the Groupes Francs, and the Maquis to the American Office of Strategic Services (OSS) chief Allen Dulles in Bern, Switzerland. Dulles promised funds, weapons, and radio communications to support the French Resistance. Twice a week, de Bénouville sent intelligence and requests for arms to the Resistance delegation in Geneva for their Allied contacts. Over the mountains, the delegation would send arms and munitions purchased in Switzerland back to the Resistance.[31]

On February 16, Laval signed the law creating the *Service du travail obligatoire* (STO, or Obligatory Labor Conscription), which subjected all males aged eighteen to twenty to being sent to Germany as forced laborers.[32] Large numbers of young men fled to the mountains of Haute-Savoie. As Frenay related, those who could "procured sidearms and were ready to defend themselves against arrest." As an associate said, "They've taken to the Maquis." *Maquis* literally means a scrub-wooded upland, and the term came to be used to describe the rural armed Resistance in the mountains. Individual members were known as *Maquisards*. Groups of Maquis composed of a dozen fighters

---

29. Cobb, *The Resistance*, 153.

30. See, for example, Frenay, *Night Will End*, 202–4, 231–32, 237–38, 311, 332; Ian Ousby, *Occupation: The Ordeal of France, 1940–44* (New York: Cooper Square Press, 2000), 241–42, 261.

31. Frenay, *Night Will End*, 250–53; de Bénouville, *Unknown Warriors*, vii–viii, 183–84.

32. Loi du 4 septembre 1942 relative à l'utilisation et à l'orientation de la main-d'œuvre (law of 4 September 1942 on the use and guidance of the workforce).

each would grow—the organization *Combat* gave them instructions and supplied them with food, arms, and ammunition.[33]

But they also seized arms from the police, some members of which collaborated with the Resistance. Maquis policy was that "each weapon should bring in at least one other weapon each week." The Maquis grew quickly, but they were ever lacking in arms and money. A recruitment leaflet read: "Men needed in the Maquis to fight. . . . Equipment to bring: . . . firearm if possible. . . ." A unit in the Ain region just had two hunting rifles and two revolvers. Historian Matthew Cobb wrote, "Food and safety were vital concerns, but the key problem for the Maquis—and for the Resistance as a whole—was how to get weapons."[34]

In the search for arms, one never knew who to trust. The German security police (*Sicherheitspolizei*, or SiPo) and security service (*Sicherheitsdienst*, or SD) recruited French citizens to infiltrate the Maquis and Resistance groups. An infiltrator helped to break up one Maquis group and then claimed to another group that he had a stock of weapons that the Germans had not found belonging to the first group. Members of the second group fell for the ploy and were arrested.[35]

Over time, arms and sabotage equipment were parachuted to the Maquis, who in turn supplied the American OSS with intelligence. Distrustful of American influence, de Gaulle's people in London sought to sever communication between the OSS in Bern and the Resistance in France.[36] Conflict between the French in exile in London and the Resistance in France had been brewing for some time.

Simone de Beauvoir wrote in her diary that "a strange news item appeared in some Swiss and British papers: 'Armed rebellion in Haute-Savoie,' it ran. This was something of an exaggeration. But it is true that such armies were in the process of formation, both in Savoie and Central France; that they were obtaining arms and equipment, and training for guerilla warfare."[37]

33. Frenay, *Night Will End*, 231, 237–38.
34. Michel, *Shadow War*, 276–77; de Bénouville, *Unknown Warriors*, 201–02; Cobb, *The Resistance*, 175.
35. Lecler, "Les auxiliares français, 77.
36. Frenay, *Night Will End*, 263.
37. de Beauvoir, *Prime of Life*, 645.

In his memoirs, de Gaulle would pay tribute: "By more or less important groups, the Maquis multiplied and began the guerrilla warfare that was to play a role of the first importance in the attrition of the enemy and, later, in the evolution of the Battle of France." The Maquis—consisting of "few men and fewer weapons"—ambushed supply conveys, derailed trains, attacked patrols, and sabotaged tanks. Triumph meant dead Wehrmacht soldiers and captured weapons; defeat meant being executed on the spot or after a mock trial.[38]

Reflecting Vichy's December 3 and 5, 1942, decrees, the media warned: "The crime of possession of arms shall be tried by the Special Court *which shall sentence to death or imprisonment.*"[39] The words in italics were meant to emphasize the deadly serious consequences.

René Bousquet, the minister of the interior and the secretary of state for the maintenance of order (*le ministère de l'intérieur et le secrétaire d'Etat au maintien de l'ordre*), ordered the prefects to compare gun registrations with licensed hunters, obviously to uncover hunters who had not registered their firearms and who still possessed them. Panic abounded in the ex-free zone, and prefectures were overwhelmed by denunciations. Archives in the department of Isère, in the Auvergne-Rhône-Alpes region in the east of France, indicate sixty-three police searches for one pistol, one revolver, three magazines, and twenty-four cartridges. Raids in Haute-Loire uncovered virtually nothing. The prefect of Saône and Loire instructed all mayors to respond that to their knowledge no undeclared weapons were any longer present in their jurisdiction.[40]

Separating Barrels from Guns: A Clever Strategy

As to the countless firearms surrendered to French authorities in the former free zone under the December 1942 decree, nothing was being done to preserve them from rust and deterioration, and the threat loomed that the Germans would consolidate them into depots and ship them to Germany. It was

---

38. de Gaulle, *War Memoirs*, 586–87.

39. "Le délit de détention d'armes sera jugé par le tribunal spécial *qui condamnera à mort on à la réclusion,*" *Le Matin*, January 25, 1943, 1. Emphasis in original.

40. Phillibert de Loisey, "Le déclarations d'armes de 1942–43," *Gazette des armes*, mai 2004, 26, 29.

then that Dr. Arnaud, the president of Savoie hunters (*des chasseurs de Savoie*), with the support of Maxime Ducrocq, president of the *Saint-Hubert-Club de France*, proposed that the barrels and forends (*longuesses*)—now rusting away in storage—be returned to their owners for maintenance. In March and April, they proposed it to Laval, who supposedly exclaimed: "[T]hat is the egg of Columbus [*c'est l'œuf de Colomb*]."[41] That meant a problem whose solution is simple, yet clever. Gun owners would be mollified, and the absence of operable firearms that might be stolen from official custody by the Resistance would give Vichy and the Germans less to worry about.

Ducrocq met with Pierre Laval and the Secretary of State for the Interior Fernand de Brinon with a proposal allowing a twenty-day grace period in which hunting guns could be turned in but the barrels retained by the owners, and returning the barrels of guns already surrendered to their owners.[42] This would permit the owners at least to maintain the barrels, which were rusting in storage. Laval wrote Ducrocq promising his support.[43] The plan only applied to hunting guns, not to pistols, revolvers, or military arms.[44]

The proposal was mentioned by Gruppe We/Ia (Defense Operations Group) in occupied Vichy, expressing grave concerns about the French gaining access to firearms. Pursuant to the Vichy decree of December 3, 1942, civilians in the area controlled by this office had so far surrendered about 300,000 hunting guns and more than 67,000 pistols. The military command ordered that the arms be stored by department and controlled by the French police, subject to German supervision. However, leaving this many weapons in French hands created a grave danger. If the British and the Americans invaded France, the growing number of French opposing the Axis could, with police assistance, seize the weapons and start a guerrilla war. That would gravely endanger the security of the Wehrmacht and limit their freedom of movement. Informers reported a secret Gaullist fighting troop with 200,000 followers.[45]

---

41. de Loisey, "Le déclarations d'armes," 26, 29.
42. *Le Saint-Hubert*, n°2, 42e année, mars–avril 1943, 13.
43. *Le Saint-Hubert*, n°3, 42e année, mai–juin 1943, 25.
44. *Le Saint-Hubert*, n°4, 42e année, juillet–août 1943, 45.
45. BA/MA, RW 34/61, Anlage 1 zu D.W.St.K. Gruppe We/Ia Nr. 213/43 geh., Waffen-ablieferung seitens der Zivilbevölkerung.

Not only were the population and the police hostile to the Germans, but also it was reported that policemen advised citizens intending to surrender their weapons pursuant to the decree not to do so. The solution? Transfer the arms to depots in places where the Wehrmacht was stationed. The civilians could retain their ownership rights. Moreover, the prefect of the department Drôme in southeastern France reported to the Germans that Vichy was considering whether barrels could be returned to their owners for maintenance, leaving only the frames and shoulder stocks in the depots. The Germans would not oppose that.

The same document by Gruppe We/Ia noted that the Army Control Delegation for the Alps Section (*Heereskontrolldelegation für den Alpen-Abschnitt*, DECSA) reported that arms dealers were still selling weapons to civilians. The weapons included centerfire long guns with both rifled and smooth-bore barrels, repeating centerfire carbines of 6 mm or smaller caliber, and semi-automatic centerfire pistols of 6 mm or smaller caliber. The dealers justified these sales with the exclusion from the Vichy decree of weapons of the seventh category, but that only included shooting gallery and salon arms. Since the weapons being sold could shoot at considerable distances, the document argued, they should be banned. The prefects claimed to be powerless without orders from Vichy.

As noted, Gruppe We/Ia perceived the French population and police as hostile to the Germans. While few French supported resistance before the roundups of the Jews at the Vélodrome d'Hiver in July 1942 and the creation of the *Service du travail obligatoire* in February 1943, those events greatly increased support for the resistance groups. While some collaborators and members of the *Milice* would support Germany to the end, the German assessment at this point was that neither the people at large nor the police could be trusted, particularly if they could seize confiscated firearms being held by the Wehrmacht or by French authorities.

District Headquarters 635 in Béthune reported several instances in which French civilians found unusable weapons of war, such as rifles and revolvers, in open fields or empty lots, and surrendered them.[46] More seriously, on January

---

46. BA/MA, RH 36/421, Tätigkeitsbericht - 4, Zweimonatsbericht der Kreiskommandantur 635, Berichtszeit 1. Januar bis 28. Februar 1943, Béthune, 5. März 1943.

28, 1943, unknown perpetrators killed Robert Zacrzewski, the head of the German Cultural Community in Hulluch, with two shots from a pistol while he was on his way from his apartment to the bus stop. On February 24, three soldiers at the restaurant "Oskar" in Lens were threatened by two "bandits" with pistols. The bandits took an 08 Lugar pistol from one of the soldiers and pay booklets and money from the other two, fired two shots, and escaped.[47]

While there was no wave of organized armed resistance at this time, there was much to do. The resistance publication *Notre Parole* (*Our Word*) advised Jews to hide their children with others and join the partisans. "Arm yourselves and fight for the destruction of the brown-shirted barbarians, if you do not want to be destroyed yourselves!"[48]

Admiral Jean Platon, secretary of state at the Office of the Head of Government, wrote from Vichy on March 9, 1943, to General Alexander Freiherr von Neubronn, liaison officer of Field Marshal Gerd von Rundstedt, the commander-in-chief–West, regarding the surrender requested by certain German authorities of pistols and revolvers handed over to the French civilian authorities by civilians. He related that General Hans Schuberth ordered prefects to surrender all firearms turned in under the decree of December 3, 1942. Yet the prefects were not under any obligation to do so, as the decree, approved by the Germans, mandated that the French police secure weapons surrendered by civilians. He requested that, without further agreement, the local German authorities refrain from insisting on the surrender of hunting guns stored under the supervision of French gendarmes.[49]

The Control Authority of the German Armistice Commission at Bourges, the supervising office on such matters, directed an inquiry regarding privately owned French weapons to the German Armistice Commission at Wiesbaden, Germany. It noted that, after the invasion of the formerly unoccupied territory, the French government, at the request of Rundstedt, ordered the surrender of all weapons in private possession to the pertinent prefects. The

47. BA/MA, RH 36/421, Tätigkeitsbericht - 4, Zweimonatsbericht der Kreiskommandantur 635, Berichtszeit 1. Januar bis 28. Februar 1943, Béthune, 5. März 1943.

48. Cobb, *The Resistance*, 202.

49. BA/MA, RW 34/61, Regierungschef, Militärischer Verbindungsstab, Durch gewisse deutsche Dienststellen verlangte Auslieferung von Handwaffen, 9. März 1943.

French ministry of the interior ordered that the confiscated firearms be used as equipment for police officers and other purposes.[50]

Yet it needed to be decided, the Control Authority continued, whether to order the French to hand over the weapons. As previously ordered, weapons, ammunition, and war equipment of any kind had to be surrendered, requiring determination of which items in depots were included. If only weapons of military origin were required to be surrendered, the question arose whether weapons of private origin that could be used against the German army (for example, shotguns, small caliber rifles, revolvers, pistols) should be stored and administered with or separately from the hunting guns.

Transport All Hunting Guns to Germany for Safekeeping?

General von Neubronn responded to Admiral Platon that it was intended to transfer all of the hunting guns from the previously unoccupied territory to Germany. Hunting guns included not only actual guns used for hunting, but also all civilian arms such as pistols surrendered under the French decree of December 3, 1942. Reassuringly, he noted (joked?) that the French owners would keep their ownership. But the arms could not be safely secured in France.[51] Neubronn then telegraphed Rundstedt: "Laval called the note regarding the transfer of all hunting guns to Germany as having a great effect on the mood, in particular of inhabitants of the flat land. Since he considers the note as also disquieting for German interests, he plans to make counter-proposals."[52]

Next, the regional prefect's office in Clermont-Ferrand sent a note to the Armistice Commission in Royat. It first recited that the laws of December 3 and 5, 1942, exempted from the prohibition on possession of firearms officials and employees of the public administration who were subject to attack, such as gendarmes, police officers, and judges. Unusable weapons with only collector's or sentimental value were also exempt. Ministerial orders had also

---

50. BA/MA, RH 31/29, Brief der Kontrollinspektion der DWStK, Gruppe II Az.:D, Nr. 3110/43, an die Deutsche Waffenstillstandskommission Wiesbaden, 13. März 1943.

51. BA/MA, RH 31/29, Brief des deutschen Generals des Oberbefehlshabers West in Vichy an den Staatssekretär beim Regierungschef, Admiral Platon, 15. März 1943.

52. BA/MA, RH 31/29, Geheimes Telegramm Nr. 924 des Deutschen Generals in Vichy an Oberbefehlshaber West/Abt. Ic betreffend Jagdwaffenabtransport, 17. März 1943.

exempted prefects, mayors, and a number of other government officials and guards.[53]

Lieutenant Colonel Wittig of the Control Authority in Bourges wrote to the Armistice Commission in Wiesbaden concerning the arming of French officials and government personnel. A regional prefect advocated arming railway guards while on duty; militia members, who supported the government but were attacked by opponents of the government; and exempted people, such as mayors, of which there were 463 in the department Puy-de-Dôme alone; and the new police recruits. The pistols and revolvers would be taken from the hunting rifle depots, which was already occurring in some regions.[54]

Army Corps General Eugène Bridoux, French secretary of state for defense, wrote to Neubronn regarding the transfer to Germany of the weapons surrendered to French civilian authorities pursuant to the law of December 3, 1942. He noted that the hunting guns were not attack weapons, and that—as Admiral Platon had predicted—transfer of the guns to Germany would cause discord. Measures could be taken to keep the weapons secure.[55] In response to information on April 12, 1943, that Control Group (*Kontrollgruppe*) Châteauroux, a German authority based in the town of that name, had ordered the immediate loading of hunting guns for transport to Germany, Wittig was instructed that the negotiations regarding the hunting guns were not yet concluded, and that actions must stop until a final decision was made.[56]

Rundstedt requested that the French government list all weapons surrendered under the December decree and categorize them as military weapons, including rifles, pistols, and ammunition, and hunting guns and ammunition. The prefects should be reminded of their responsibilities to store and guard these private weapons.[57]

---

53. BA/MA, RW 34/61, Regionalpräfektur zu Clermont-Ferrand, Note für die Waffenstillstandskommission zu Royat, 31. März 1943.

54. BA/MA, RH 31/29, Brief der Kontrollinspektion der DWStK, Kontrollabteilung Nr. 500/43, an die Deutsche Waffenstillstandskommission Wiesbaden, 7. April 1943.

55. BA/MA, RH 31/29, Übersetzung eines Briefes Nr. 1220 - DN/SL des Generals und Staatssekretärs in Vichy, der mit den Beziehungen zu den deutschen und italienischen Kommandostellen beauftragt war, 9. April 1943.

56. BA/MA, RH 31/29, Aktennotiz über Ferngespräch betreffend Jagdwaffen, 12. April 1943.

57. BA/MA, RH 31/29, Brief des Oberbefehlshabers West, Oberkommando Heeresgruppe D, Arbeitsstab Frankreich, Nr. 319/43, an die französische Regierung, 17. April 1943.

On April 19, Lieutenant-General Heinrich Niehoff, commander of the army area, southern France, at Lyon, wrote to Rundstedt's quartermaster that all firearms confiscated under the French decrees of December 3 and 5 were under the control of the German army inspector, who proposed that Niehoff take over privately owned hunting guns. The Armistice Commission should proceed rapidly with the sorting of weapons fit for military use (military weapons, rifles, pistols, revolvers) and of ammunition (including bullets) from French weapons depots. Liaison officers would take over hunting-gun depots, under the supervision of the prefects, until Rundstedt issued the order to ship them to Germany. It was considered "absolutely necessary that the weapons . . . are taken out of the Army area because they could very easily be used by guerrillas, most notably in street battles."[58]

The fear was not unfounded. On April 14, French police conducted a weapons check in Grenay and stopped two men who looked like miners. When asked for his papers, one of them pulled a pistol from his left breast pocket and shot police officer Louis Guilluy, but the weapon failed to fire when he tried to shoot another officer. The second miner pulled a pistol and shot at an officer but missed. The attackers escaped unidentified.[59]

On April 15, the MBF ordered that hunting guns be available for purchase by Wehrmacht troops who held hunting permits for occupied France at the hunting-gun depot at the château of Vincennes on the eastern edge of Paris, starting on April 20. It included a list of 22 kinds of hunting guns with prices between 8 and 500 Reichsmark.[60] Soldiers could select guns each workday between 8:00 a.m. and noon; paid-for guns could be picked up in the mornings or between 2:00 p.m. and 4:00 p.m. Three-barrel guns and sporting rifles were unavailable, and the following were sold out: small caliber rifles, Browning rifles, new self-cocking double-barreled guns with ejector, self-cocking double-barreled guns with side lock and ejector, and similar guns.[61]

---

58. BA/MA, RW 34/61, Kommandant des Heeresgebietes Südfrankreich, Waffen aus französischem Privatbesitz, 19. April 1943.

59. BA/MA, RH 36/421, Tätigkeitsbericht - 5, Zweimonatsbericht der Kreiskommandantur 635, Berichtszeit 1. März bis 30. April 1943, Béthune, 6. Mai 1943.

60. BA/MA, RH 36/306, Kommandanturbefehl Nr. 46, Charleville, 29. April 1943.

61. BA/MA, RH 36/306, Kommandanturbefehl Nr. 59 der Feldkommandantur 684, Charleville, 4. Juni 1943.

As for the hunting guns surrendered to the French authorities under the December 1942 decree in the newly occupied territories, Rundstedt reminded the French government that for military security reasons these guns would be transferred to the Reich for storage. In a letter to General von Neubronn, Rundstedt's liaison officer, French Admiral Platon requested that any valuable parts of these hunting guns be returned to their owners. Maxime Ducrocq, in his role as president of the International Hunting Council (*Conseil International de la Chasse*), made the same request. After further review, the German side agreed on June 7, 1943, that the barrels and locks of hunting guns could be returned to their owners, and the stocks and triggers would be collected and stored under German control.[62]

Ducrocq wrote to Neubronn, expressing thanks for introducing him to Colonel Cullman in Vichy. After the two met in Paris and Saint-Germain, Cullman wrote Ducrocq that Rundstedt supported Laval's request concerning the weapons deposited in the formerly unoccupied territory. Rundstedt was informing the French government that he had rescinded his previous decision to transport the weapons to the Reich and instead would order them dismantled on location. The Germans expected that the dismantling and return of the barrels would take three months, and that the stocks and triggers would be stored under German control.[63]

Laval's Betrayal: The Compulsory Labor Service

A bird's-eye view of a day in the life of Pierre Laval in this period is suggested by a newspaper report of his schedule on the afternoon of June 17, when he met at the Hôtel Matignon, the official residence of the prime minister in Paris, with Messrs. Cathala, minister secretary of state for national economy and finance; Darquier de Pellepoix, commissioner for Jewish affairs; Sailly, head of economic control; Maxime Ducrocq, president of the International Hunting Council; and Prefect Lacombe, head of the wartime protection ser-

---

62. BA/MA, RH 31/29, Note des Oberbefehlshabers West an die französische Regierung, 7. Juni 1943.

63. BA/MA, RH 31/29, Brief des Conseil International de la Chasse an General von Neubronn in Vichy, 8. Juni 1943.

vice. This appeared under headlines on the Fortress Europe and Luftwaffe attacks in Sicily.[64]

In this period, Jean Moulin united the *Armée Secrète, Comte d'Action Socialiste, Francs-Tireur, Front National,* and *Liberation* under the *Conseil National de la Résistance* (National Council of the Resistance, or CNR). However, the Gestapo caught member René Hardy, who under torture revealed Moulin's hiding place. On June 21, Moulin was arrested in Caluire. He was tortured by Klaus Barbie's operation and died on July 8.[65]

But the Resistance was not dissuaded. It was, in the words of Guillain de Bénouville, "the army of an entire people which, once it had accomplished a feat of arms, disappeared again into the mass of the people. How was the enemy to know that a load of rifles lay beneath the load of hay in the farmer's horse-drawn cart?" In one instance in Toulouse, German police arrived at the house of a Monsieur Pécheur, whose trucking business was used to smuggle arms. He drew his revolver and shot one German in the head, another in the chest, and a third in the back, and then escaped with his wife.[66]

Meanwhile, through the STO, Laval was collaborating to provide Germany with compulsory labor. Jean Guéhenno wrote in his diary on June 12: "All young men in the classes of '40–'42 have to leave for Germany on July 1. The panic of a crushed anthill. Some are thinking of crossing the border into Spain. Others of hiding in the mountains, in Savoy, or in the Massif Central. But most will resign themselves to it and leave."[67]

Rundstedt wrote on June 18 to the French government that the French law of December 3 and 5, 1942, was legally effective for all of France, but in fact was applied only in southern France. That decree punished arms possession and failure to inform of another's arms possession with mandatory prison or death, with limited exemptions for French military, police, and government personnel. The previously occupied area of France remained subject to the

---

64. "Le Président Laval a de Nombreux entretiens a Paris," *Cherbourg-Eclair,* 18 juin 1943, 1. http://www.normannia.info/ark%3A/86186/wkc9.

65. See la-loupe.over-blog.net/article-moulin-jean-39630707.html.

66. de Bénouville, *Unknown Warriors,* 219, 243.

67. Guéhenno, *Diary of the Dark Years,* 209 (entry dated June 12, 1943).

German decree of December 18, 1942.[68] That decree, which related to the dissolution of the French military, prohibited French officers from carrying pistols.

As an example, Lieutenant-General Niehoff informed regional prefects that field and harvest guards were prohibited from weapons possession and must immediately surrender the hunting guns with which they were equipped. The French had authorized field and harvest guards to be armed in order to repress the poaching that had increased greatly because food was scarce.[69] Neubronn wrote to General Eugène Bridoux that any danger to the field and harvest guards was not as grave as the dangers that the guards, some four thousand strong, could pose to the Germans.[70]

Meanwhile, on July 4, the *Journal Officiel* published the amendment to the December 3, 1942, ban on all firearms and parts thereof, allowing the return of barrels and forends to their owners.[71]

According to a *New York Times* account, the barrel return policy took place at a time when the Nazis anticipated disturbances. When turning in the weapons to the police, the owners were assured that the guns would be properly oiled. The current shortage of lubricants now required return of the barrels. The policy was seen as a ruse to separate the barrels from the actions and stocks in order to render the weapons wholly inoperative.[72]

As supplemented by a circular issued by René Bousquet on July 12, the barrels and forends were to be returned to their owners within three months. The gendarmerie took the labeled barrels and returned them township by township to their owners who came to look for them at the town halls.[73] The

68. BA/MA, RH 31/29, Brief des Oberbefehlshabers West, Arbeitsstab Frankreich, Gruppe Wehrmacht Nr. [no number]/43 an die französische Regierung, 18. Juni 1943.

69. BA/MA, RH 31/29, Übersetzung eines Briefes des Generals und Staatssekretärs in Vichy, der mit den Beziehungen zu den deutschen und italienischen Kommandostellen beauftragt war, 11. Juli 1943.

70. BA/MA, RH 31/29, Brief des deutschen Generals des Oberbefehlshabers West in Vichy an den Staatssekretär für die Verteidigung, Armeekorpsgeneral Bridoux, 22. Juli 1943.

71. Loi du 3 juillet 1943 n° 381 modifiant la loi n° 1061 du 3 décembre 1942 fixant le regime des materiels de guerre, armes et munitions, *Journal Officiel*, 4 juillet 1943. See *Le Saint-Hubert*, n°4, 42e année, juillet–août 1943, 37.

72. "French Civilian Guns to be Made Useless," *New York Times*, July 10, 1943, 3.

73. de Loisey, "Le déclarations d'armes" 26, 29.

new policy on barrel returns was reported in a Paris newspaper, but it had to clarify the next day that it applied only in southern France, and not in the area occupied since 1940.[74]

While the extent to which barrels and forends were returned to their owners is unknown, what was the significance of the decision to do so? It was certainly a sincere effort by Ducrocq and his associates to help owners have at least parts of their firearms returned. Vichy could take credit for ameliorating a certain aspect of the prior deprivation, and the Germans might see a propaganda value to the measure, albeit knowing full well that the separation of basic firearm components rendered them useless as weapons. If members of resistance groups raided arms depots, they could seize only certain parts, while the other essential parts would be dispersed to unknown individuals elsewhere. Then again, determined gun owners might try and add makeshift parts to the barrels and forends to make usable weapons. Whether any did so would be subject to conjecture.

Henri Frenay Pleads for Arms for the Resistance

In July, Resistance leaders secretly left France to meet with the London French. Henri Frenay informed the exiles of the drastic need for arms inside France, and was astonished with the reply of General Henri Giraud, who was, on paper, the commander of the French forces of French North and West Africa:

"Arms, is it? Well, gentlemen, they're not indispensable, you know. One can get along without them."

We looked at one another dumfounded.

The general continued: "Gentlemen, what is of the essence in modern warfare? Of course! Air power. If you can neutralize enemy air power, you immediately have the upper hand. And what do you need to neutralize an airfield? Pebbles!"

We thought we'd heard wrong, but no, the general continued his oration: "To obstruct a hangar's sliding door and stop its aircraft from

---

74. See "La détention des canons d'armes de chasse n'est pas interdite," *Le Matin*, July 22, 1943, 2; "La détention des canons d'armes de chasse," *Le Matin*, July 23, 1943.

exiting all you need is a pebble. With another pebble you can block a plane's air shaft, causing it to turn over when it tries to land."

With the self-satisfaction of a nightclub magician Giraud rose and concluded: "You see, gentlemen, one can make war even without weapons!"

And this was the man who was going to command our armies![75]

Frenay then traveled to Algiers to meet with de Gaulle, telling him that failure of the Resistance to receive arms and funds created distrust. Meanwhile, Jean Moulin, de Gaulle's representative who had been tortured and killed, was replaced by Claude Serreules and Jacques Bingen. Bingen, operating in southern France, reported that "not a day goes by that I am not set upon by the chiefs of some organization who bitterly complain about their inability to arm their militants." He added, "The future delivery of large quantities of arms seems indispensable to me. This materiel, instead of being buried where it lands and then forgotten, should immediately be turned over to those organizations which can effectively use it."[76]

The failure of the British and Americans to supply more arms to the Resistance was based on more than scarcities, logistics, and other priorities. The *Franc-Tireur et Partisans* (FTP) was an arm of the French Communist Party, which was subject to Stalin's wishes when he signed the nonaggression pact with Hitler in 1939 and could be expected to support a Communist takeover after France was liberated. Churchill, Roosevelt, and de Gaulle were not enthusiastic about arming those they could not control. Non-Communist resistance groups suffered as a result.

The duty to denounce could lead to potentially tragic results. In Troyes, a French girl named Marie Edith Marcelle Brunclair was playing with friends when she found two rifles in her family's attic, which she immediately reported to a German post. She was interrogated by the military police. Her father said she did the right thing by doing so, suggesting that she informed without his prior knowledge. Neither she nor her father knew how they got there, but French soldiers stayed there in 1940 before fleeing, and maybe left them. But the arms were a hunting gun and an obsolete 1886 military rifle.

---

75. Frenay, *Night Will End*, 284.
76. Frenay, *Night Will End*, 290, 297.

One wonders whether the guns really belonged to the father, who the daughter might have betrayed had the Germans not believed their story.[77]

French collaborationists were often targets for attack, and the Germans entrusted some with weapons. Lieutenant-General Niehoff was responsible for all decisions on the issuance of weapons permits to French citizens, since he had taken over the relevant weapons depots. French agencies would issue permits, but the commander could review and deny them.[78] Regarding the issuance of weapons permits in southern France, the Germans became aware that the French tried to gain advantage by submitting the same matter to different German offices without informing the respective offices accordingly.[79] The French State Secretary of the Interior, René Bousquet, wrote to the regional prefects of the formerly free zone: "Any requests for issuance of individual weapons permits that you receive must be submitted to the head of the SS or the commander of the Italian Army territory. Please submit requests to me only if such requests were given approval by those offices."[80]

Karl Oberg, head of the SS, castigated Bousquet about the French people's failure to turn in their firearms in obedience to yet another amnesty, this one dated August 16, 1943. Contrary to the hope that the amnesty would deliver a large quantity of weapons, particularly those parachuted by the British and the Americans, it was lamentable that only 2,300 revolvers, 555 rifles, and 4,700 rifle cartridges were turned in. No machine gun or other parachuted weapon was delivered. Oberg concluded ominously:

> This marked insult has shown that the psychological conditions for an amnesty concerning weapons no longer exist in the French people. . . .
> If the illegal possession of weapons is now being combated with the

---

77. BA/MA, RH 36/190: Bericht des Stabsfeldwebels der Feldgendarmerie in Troyes betreffend Waffenfund, 8. August 1943.

78. BA/MA, RH 31/29, Brief der Kontrollinspektion der DWStK, Kontrollabteilung, Az. Privatwaffen, Nr. 861/43, an den deutschen General des Oberbefehlshabers West in Vichy, 24. Mai 1943.

79. BA/MA, RH 31/29, Brief des Oberbefehlshabers West, Oberkommando Heeresgruppe D, Arbeitsstab Frankreich, Gruppe Wehrmacht Nr. 1745/43 an den Befehlshaber der Sicherheitspolizei und des SD im Bereich des Militärbefehlshabers in Frankreich, 25. September 1943.

80. BA/MA, RH 31/29, Übersetzung eines Briefes des Regierungschefs, Ministers, Staatssekretärs des Inneren an die Herren Regionalpräfekten des unbesetzten Gebietes, 3. Dezember 1943.

most severe means, this is an imperative necessity for the security of the occupying force and because in any case it is necessary to detain illegal arms, based on feelings of resistance.[81]

Bousquet dutifully transmitted Oberg's missive about illegal arms possession to all of the prefects in France.[82] Once again, Vichy France had marching orders from the SS to help combat gun possession—in Oberg's words—"with the most severe means."

Despite increasing attacks on the police, the Germans allowed Paris police to be armed only with pistols with five or six rounds.[83] But the SS enhanced the ability of the *Milice* to be trained and issued with weapons.[84]

Rendevous in Switzerland

Switzerland was an important center for Allied coordination with resistance groups. From Bern, OSS operative Allen Dulles met with French resistance agent General Jules-Maurice-René Davet, who reported that code name "A.S." had available "10,000 trained troops, 3,000 of whom are armed, for Hautes Alpes, Haute-Savoie, Savoie, Isère and Drôme. . . . There are another 7,000 men who must obtain munitions and arms, presumably by parachute, if they are to be used as guerrillas or for other military action." If support could be obtained, they could destroy railway lines, attack local garrisons, and sabotage power plants and other essential services.[85]

Men fleeing the *Service du travail obligatoire* (STO, or Obligatory Labor Conscription) provided a steady stream of recruits for the Resistance. Jean Guéhenno described a difficult journey in returning to Paris: "Our train hit a

---

81. Oberg à Bousquet, Au sujet de l'amnistie concernant les armes du 16 aout 1943, 10 novembre 1943. Armes, matériel de guerre, 16W87, Archives de la Marne, Reims.

82. Bousquet à Prefects, No. 493 Pol. Cab. Cire, 22 novembre 1943. Armes, matériel de guerre, 16W87, Archives de la Marne, Reims.

83. Mitchell, *Nazi Paris*, 102.

84. Philippe Burrin, *France Under the Germans: Collaboration and Compromise*, trans. Janet Lloyd (New York: The New Press, 1993), 443–44.

85. Telegram dated September 11, 1943, in Neal H. Peterson ed., *From Hitler's Doorstep: The Wartime Intelligence Reports of Allen Dulles, 1942–1945* (University Park, PA.: Pennsylvania State University Press, 1996), 123.

bomb near Argenton. (It was the 17th attack in two weeks in this region where thousands of 'deserters' from the Work Service have taken to the Maquis.)"[86]

Invisible Executions

The STO in Paris was a target of the Resistance. Deportation of young men as workers to Germany required that the authorities have their identities. On October 14, some 65,000 files were stolen. Later, FTP and Combat members entered the office posing as a maintenance crew and set the building on fire. Léo Hamon, who led the raid, described how they escaped to their car and "crossed Paris with the barrels of two pistols pointing out of the rear window, ready to shoot at anyone who tried to follow us."[87]

Guéhenno noticed the execution of fifty "Communists" in an "invisible little paragraph" in an October 6 newspaper. "Two years ago, news like that would be printed in poster-size characters. In the meantime, they keep on shooting a few patriots every day. They do it without saying so." Now the policy had again changed. "These announcements in small print, they think, will be read by patriots and will scare them without arousing horror in the general public."[88]

"The Germans are shooting hostages or people who have been convicted, every day in Fresnes," noted Guéhenno on November 3. The word would be spread from cell to cell of each morning's executions, and as the victims would walk across the yard, the other prisoners would sing the *Marseillaise* or *Le Chant du départ* ("The Song of Departure"), which originated in the revolutionary times of 1794.[89]

Young Jewish diarist Hélène Berr reflected as she walked by a German-occupied hotel on Avenue de la Bourdonnais: "All you need is for a man to throw a bomb through that door, and twenty innocent people will be shot. . . ."[90] This illustrated the moral dilemma of individual attacks. As to the role of the French police, she recalled an inspector arresting Jewish children

86. Guéhenno, *Diary of the Dark Years*, 217 (entry dated October 4, 1943).
87. Cobb, *The Resistance*, 197.
88. Guéhenno, *Diary of the Dark Years*, 217.
89. Guéhenno, *Diary of the Dark Years*, 221–22 (entry dated November 3, 1943).
90. Berr, *Journal*, 169 (entry dated October 25, 1943).

at an orphanage excusing himself with the comment: "Sorry 'bout this, lady, I'm just doing my duty!"[91] But some police acted honorably: "There are not many Jews left in Paris, and as arrests are now being made by the Germans, we won't have much prospect of keeping out of the way, because we won't be tipped off."[92]

Arming for the Allied Invasion

Apprehension about an Allied invasion of France was rising. *Combat* advised its underground readers to obtain and hide firearms in anticipation of an Allied landing. *Défense de la France*, an underground newspaper in the northern zone, noted that "the enemy is completely incapable of searching every house and every cellar of Paris or the towns to discover if each resident has a rifle or revolver." It continued, "Every house, every cellar, must become a small fort where one will await the departure of the enemy. Everyone must obtain a weapon and carefully hide it at home. The policy in favor of stockpiling weapons is an absurdity. Arms must be distributed from now on."[93] Any arms caches could be seized if discovered, and should be spread out where they could be easily accessed.

Combat reported increased resistance activities. On the night of November 19–20, members of the *Forces Unies de la Jeunesse* (United Youth Forces) executed an operation to seize arms and munitions from barracks at Bourgoin, escaping with a truckload of a ton and a half of materiel.[94] That month, the *Groupes Francs* and the Haute-Savoie wing of the *Francs-Tireurs et Partisans* (FTP, the military arm of the National Front) conducted 310 armed attacks and acts of sabotage.[95]

But the Allies were ever slow or reluctant to provide arms. It was reported to the Americans in Geneva that just 16,000 of 69,200 men in several Resis-

---

91. Berr, *Journal*, 202 (entry dated November 9, 1943).

92. Berr, *Journal*, 229 (entry dated December 13, 1943).

93. "Consignes en cas de Débarquement," *Combat*, n° 47, 1er septembre 1943; "La Seule Attitude Possible Sera la Resistance Acharnée," *Défense de la France*, N° 40, 25 octobre 1943, reprinted in *Le Journal Défense de la France* (Paris: Presses Universitaires de France, 1961), 216.

94. "Des jeunes s'arment pour la libération," *Combat*, n°53, décembre 1943.

95. "The Resistance Front," *Combat*, no. 53, quoted in Frenay, *Night Will End*, 323.

tance groups were armed in both zones of France. This report was followed by a request for thousands of firearms.[96] Combat leader Henri Frenay noted that their delegation in Switzerland would send the Allies cables describing their activities and pleading for arms, such as the following:

> The air raid on Annecy wreaked terrible havoc. . . . The planes overshot the ball-bearing plant at an altitude of 5,000 meters. Civilian houses were destroyed. . . . Last week we sabotaged a number of transformers with explosives. . . . If you get us the arms, our groups will knock out any target you want. . . .
>
> If you get us the materiel, we can guarantee you destruction of railways, harassment of troops, wiping out of locomotive depots. To leave our men unarmed is a grave political and military error.[97]

The Germans were responding in kind. For November and December 1943, the MBF reported 123 French citizens sentenced to death: 71 for guerrilla activities, 19 for giving aid and comfort to the enemy, and 7 for weapons possession.[98] This did not include any French killed in combat with the Germans.

"I saw a German lorry piled high with corpses that weren't even covered." That was in Paris, recorded Hélène Berr, who commented, "Probably men who had been executed; no one will ever know anything about them."[99] The days of show trials and ominous newspaper warnings with details about the victims were long gone. Hélène, a young Jewish woman who helped others escape, would be arrested in March 1944 and deported to Auschwitz and then to Bergen-Belsen, where she would die just days before the camp was liberated in 1945.[100]

At a time when every French citizen should be prepared to bear arms, *Défense de la France* opined in early 1944, many sought to excuse themselves with comments such as, "We do not have any arms; how can one fight? It is not yet time. What can one do with the Germans here? Resistance is futile." Yet

---

96. de Bénouville, *Unknown Warriors*, 365, appendix 5.

97. Frenay, *Night Will End*, 310–11.

98. BA/MA, RW 35/26, Militärbefehlshaber in Frankreich, Abteilung Ia, Nr. 220/44 g.Kdos., Einsatzbericht für die Monate November und Dezember 1943, 15. Januar 1944.

99. Berr, *Journal*, 242 (entry dated January 13, 1944).

100. Berr, *Journal*, 263, 272.

arms had been thrown away—the waterways of Paris were full of discarded military rifles, revolvers, and cartridges. "If each wants at all costs to obtain arms for himself, he will find some. There are some that are still hidden, there are some on isolated Germans who go for a walk." And the struggle would not be fought in battle lines: "Our war is to render the occupation untenable for the Germans."[101]

The great tragedy of the Resistance, *Défense de la France* continued, was the lack of arms, which was sorely evident when the hour of combat came for the Maquis. Arms parachuted in by the Allies were quite insufficient. "Since the beginning of 1944, clashes between the Maquis, Germans, and Vichy police forces were sufficiently frequent and bloody that the shortage of arms was tragic."[102]

It would be unrealistic to surmise that more small arms at that time would have defeated the Germans without an Allied invasion. No one had that illusion. Resistance leaders pleaded for mortars, anti-tank guns, and other heavy weapons, but rarely got them. Frontal armed resistance against the heavily armed and experienced Wehrmacht and Waffen-SS would have been suicide. Guerrilla warfare would have been more of an option with better arms, particularly after D-Day. Whether resistance was worth it was an individual decision, as capture meant being shot on the spot. Members of the Maquis were willing to take their chances, and more and better arms would have facilitated their objectives immensely.[103]

Resistance agents in Switzerland passed on the intelligence to OSS operative Allen Dulles: "Almost totally without arms and suffering from lack of financial support, we are losing 100 men weekly; the Germans take no prisoners and slaughter all the wounded. In spite of our shortage of arms, we inflict twice as many casualties upon the enemy." The *Mouvements Unis de la Résistance* (MUR) had 22,000 men in the southern zone and 14,000 in the northern zone; half were in camps, only 10 percent of them armed, and half could be mobilized quickly. The message emphasized "the value of contri-

---

101. *Défense de la France*, N° 43, 15 janvier 1944, reprinted in *Le Journal Défense de la France* (Paris: Presses Universitaires de France, 1961), 238.

102. *Le Journal Défense de la France*, 249, n.1 (editor's comment).

103. See Peter Lieb, *Vercors 1944: Resistance in the French Alps* (Oxford, England: Osprey Publishing, 2012).

butions the Maquis can give to Allied military action through the guerrillas' dispersion throughout the whole area." But they needed money, arms, and munitions immediately.[104]

Colonel Henry Dutailly, writing about the Maquis in the Haute-Marnais, a department in the Champagne-Ardenne region of northeastern France, noted that the shortage of arms, the need to be mobile to escape German forces, and the necessity to live off the land limited the first Maquis to groups of five to ten men armed in a symbolic way: a carbine for five men in the woods of Plesnoy; a revolver, a hunting gun, and three Lebels for six men in Chantraines; and a revolver and hunting guns for six men in Mathons. Over time, the Maquis recovered weapons that had been hidden by French troops in 1940 at the time of the armistice. In 1944, a Maquis agent went to Switzerland to plead for arms from a British consul, and arms were parachuted to them in the night of June 1–2, just before D-Day. By June and July, they were attacking isolated German detachments to seize their arms and munitions.[105]

Charles de Gaulle estimated some 100,000 Maquisards in the countryside at the beginning of 1944, and the number doubled by the Battle of France. He added: "But the striking force of the resistance soldiers depended directly on the armament they received." Numbers swelled when supplies were available and shrank when they were not. The Allies never parachuted enough arms, and a significant quantity was not captured from the Germans until the summer battles.[106]

A bird's-eye view of the Maquis is represented in an interview by Jean Guéhenno of a young man who had been his student three years before. When his class was registered for forced labor the year before by the Germans, he made his way to a Resistance camp in the French Alps. They had struggled with the snow and cold, the Italians and the Gestapo, and the informers. He related:

> The Maquis lacks weapons. Weapons were dropped by parachute only a few times. It seems that England and America do not want to arm

---

104. Telegram to London, dated January 31, 1944, in Peterson, *From Hitler's Doorstep*, 209.

105. Colonel Henry Dutailly, "Les armes des Maquis Haut-Marnais," *Revue de la société des amis du musée de l'armée*, n° 109, juin 1995, 20–22.

106. de Gaulle, *War Memoirs*, 588–89.

revolutionary bands. They are beginning to see what the debate will be tomorrow. There are three distinct forces: the AS (*Armée Secrète*), organized and armed by the Anglo-Americans, tightly linked to the British Intelligence Service; the FTP (*Francs-Tireurs et Partisans*), Communists who've had weapons and experience in underground action for a long time and who call their own tune in complete independence; and finally the MUR (*Mouvements Unis de la Résistance*), ready for sacrifice and wanting to save France's autonomy; but with no doctrine and few weapons, it may well be crushed between the AS and the FTP.[107]

Eventually, the armed resistance groups were organized under the *Forces Françaises de l'Interieur* (French Forces of the Interior, or FFI). The symbol "FFI" appeared on armbands, flags, walls, and vehicles. D-Day was in the planning stage, and discussions were underway about how the Resistance could support the Allied invasion. Winston Churchill told Franklin Roosevelt about his meeting with Emmanuel d'Astier de la Vigerie, who in Haute-Savoie "has over 20,000 men all desperate, but only one in five has any weapon. If more weapons were available, very large numbers more would take to the mountains." Eisenhower foresaw armed action by the Resistance in support of the coming Normandy landings.[108]

Resistance and repression escalated dramatically. Guéhenno wrote in his diary on March 24, 1944: "Every day we learn of new horrors. Young STO evaders were hanged in Nîmes and various villages of the Midi (seventeen in Nîmes). The farms suspected of feeding the Maquis burnt, the farmers shot. Huge round-ups in Paris. Mass deportation, with the help of the Minister of Labor and National Solidarity, Déat."[109]

But the Maquis fought on. In a letter to forced laborers in Germany encouraging them to commit sabotage, a Maquis member wrote, "Even if they are pathetically few in number, our submachine guns and carbines give us a different soul from yours. Unlike you, we have the privilege of preparing

---

107. Guéhenno, *Diary of the Dark Years*, 239–40.
108. Cobb, *The Resistance*, 243, 237–38.
109. Guéhenno, *Diary of the Dark Years*, 245–46.

ourselves for the liberating fight ahead." He added that the Maquisards "are living with their weapons in their hands, like men who are *already free*."[110]

The military commander in France reported for January and February 1944 that 4,698 "terrorists" were arrested and 447 killed in battle. Numerous caches were captured and large quantities of weapons, ammunition, explosives, parachutes, and vehicles were secured.[111] Some 495 containers filled with weapons, ammunition, and explosives were seized. In addition, 21 machine guns, 511 rifles, 125 machine pistols, 234 pistols, 3 light grenade launchers, 34,356 rounds of ammunition, and 551 explosive shells were captured. The total of 267 French citizens sentenced to death reflected that far more were now being condemned for the use of arms than for mere possession: 182 for guerrilla activities, 53 for giving aid and comfort to the enemy, and 16 for illegal weapons possession.

Much Ado About Hunting Guns

But surviving Wehrmacht documents for early 1944 about arms show a major concern about hunting and hunting guns. The *Standortkommandantur* (garrison commander's office) at Angers warned of the dangers of armed poachers who had killed Wehrmacht soldiers engaged in hunting, admonishing the hunters to be on the lookout for weapons and suspicions people.[112] He further reported that all of 10,000 hunting guns that belonged to French citizens had been sold to Wehrmacht soldiers. The last sales from the Vincennes hunting-gun depot were concluded on January 1, 1944, and it was closed for good.[113] A more exact report by the MBF revealed that 11,143 hunting guns and 4,602 gun cases were sold to Wehrmacht hunters for a total of 477,855 Reichsmark (RM).[114]

---

110. Guéhenno, *Diary of the Dark Years*, 248–49.

111. BA/MA, RW 35/30, Militärbefehlshaber in Frankreich, Abteilung Ia, Nr. 1160/44 g.Kdos., Einsatzbericht für die Monate Januar und Februar 1944, 15. März 1944.

112. BA/MA, RH 34/3 Standortkommandantur Angers, Standortbefehle, 13. Dezember 1943 bis 28. Februar 1944.

113. BA/MA, RH 34/3, Standortbefehl No. 10 der Standortkommandatur Angers, 21. Februar 1944.

114. BA/MA, RW 35/297, Der Militärbefehlshaber in Frankreich, Lagebericht über Verwaltung und Wirtschaft Januar bis März 1944, mit Anlagen.

On March 9, General Bridoux, French secretary of state for defense, complained to General von Neubronn, Rundstedt's liaison officer to Vichy, that the Germans had confiscated the following hunting guns that were stored properly in the warehouse of the mayor's office in Annecy: 600 Gras rifles (an obsolete French military rifle altered for hunting mountain goats) and 200 6 mm carbines. He asked that the guns be restored, naively stating, "The French government is responsible to the rightful owners for these weapons and the operations troops may take these weapons only in exchange for a proper receipt to each individual owner."[115]

Neubronn wrote to Lieutenant-General Heinrich Niehoff, commander in southern France, suggesting that the guns were seized because of gang activity in Haute-Savoie.[116] Niehoff responded that 606 rifles (*Kugelschußgewehre*) and four double-barreled hunting guns (none of which could be disassembled) had been seized from the hunting-gun depot of the Annecy mayor's office. He denied that 100 common hunting guns were also taken, and asserted that the liaison officer of the prefect's office, Captain Bonnaire, examined the weapons and confirmed that the prefect's office was wrong. Niehoff continued that the seized firearms could not be disassembled as was required, and should not be held in French depots, particularly given current gang activities.[117]

Bridoux insisted that the confiscations of the six hundred rifles were unjustified under Rundstedt's order that percussion guns and guns that are difficult to disassemble could be safeguarded with the buttstocks of the other rifles. Some six hundred of the rifles confiscated in Annecy met this description. The two hundred 6 mm carbines were exempt parlor guns that Rundstedt ordered should be returned to their owners. Nor did the situation in Haute-Savoie warrant the seizures.[118]

---

115. BA/MA, RH 31/29, Übersetzung eines Briefes des Generals und Staatssekretärs in Vichy, der mit den Beziehungen zu der deutschen Kommandostelle beauftragt war, 9. März 1944.

116. BA/MA, RH 31/29, Brief des deutschen Generals des Oberbefehlshabers West in Vichy an den Kommandanten des Heeresgebietes Südfrankreich, 9. März 1944.

117. BA/MA, RH 31/29, Brief des Kommandanten des Heeresgebietes Südfrankreich, Lyon, an den deutschen General des Oberbefehlshabers West, 2. April 1944.

118. BA/MA, RH 31/29, Übersetzung eines Briefes des Generals und Staatssekretärs in Vichy, der mit den Beziehungen zu der deutschen Kommandostelle beauftragt war, 29. April 1944.

Niehoff agreed to order that the weapons confiscated in Annecy would be transferred to the *Milice* for safekeeping, and Bridoux approved.[119] This was collaboration at its best—the *Milice* was Vichy's attack dog against any French dissent. Obsolete guns and even parlor guns were seen as a threat.

Lack of arms left the Resistance with little means to attack German forces directly, although they could more readily assault French collaborators.[120] In the spring of 1944, they stepped up hit-and-run acts of sabotage against German vehicles and the railways. Wehrmacht units struck back aggressively.[121]

Claude Bourdet, who succeeded Henri Frenay as head of Combat, was captured in April, but a letter he previously wrote to Frenay described their plight: "The Maquis are being attacked from all directions and are daily losing men and what few arms they have." De Gaulle's government-in-exile was operating from London and Algiers, where Frenay was now in service. Maquis from France met Frenay in Algiers, reporting that "[t]he lack of arms . . . was costing many lives." They blamed those abroad for promoting resistance and then leaving the Maquis to be wiped out.[122]

Noted Simone de Beauvoir, "Paragraphs were always appearing in the papers to the effect that 'fifteen refractory elements' or 'twenty bandits' or a whole 'band of traitors' had been destroyed." No longer were warning notices posted in Paris, but instead photographs of condemned "foreign terrorists" appeared on the walls. She stared at the faces of those to be executed, observing, "Despite the crudeness of the reproductions, all these faces thus held up for our hatred were moving, beautiful even. . . ."[123]

Confident of the final victory, a Wehrmacht weapons department ordered on May 1 that hunting guns be ready for sale *after the war* to soldiers and army brass. They could be purchased only by those who had hunting licenses or were eligible to obtain them based on having previous licenses or passing a hunting exam. Previous purchasers could not acquire more. The guns would

---

119. BA/MA, RH 31/29, Übersetzung eines Briefes des Generals und Staatssekretärs in Vichy, der mit den Beziehungen zu der deutschen Kommandostelle beauftragt war, 12. Mai 1944.

120. Laub, *After the Fall*, 292.

121. Meyer, *Die deutsche Besatzung*, Chapter 7.

122. Frenay, *Night Will End*, 329, 332.

123. de Beauvoir, *Prime of Life*, 683–84.

be sold at their estimated value, but not below 30.00 Reichsmark, excluding percussion guns and French "Halifax Darne" double-barrel shotguns. Approximately 25,000 hunting guns would be provided for the field forces and kept at the army ordnance depots until the end of the war.[124]

The above expressed an uncanny, surreal assurance that Germany would win the war, just a month before the Allied D-Day invasion at Normandy on June 6. But they continued a zero-tolerance policy that left nothing to chance. This was exemplified by a *Combat* report in April that at Artemare, an old man thought to be a poacher was shot. His crime: he had a hunting shotgun.[125]

---

124. BA/MA, RH 19IV/178, Oberbefehlshaber West, Besondere Anordnungen für die Berforgung, 3. Juni 1944.

125. "Contre la terreur nazie," *Combat, organe du mouvement de libération nationale*, n°56, avril 1944.

8

Liberation

ON JUNE 5, 1944, the BBC broadcast coded messages to the Resistance to carry out sabotage and armed attacks that night to assist the D-Day invasion that would begin the next morning. Maquis in the Vercors, Mont Mouchet, and Limousin attacked two Wehrmacht divisions.[1] Open resistance by fighters donning the FFI (*Forces Françaises de l'Intérieur*, or French Forces of the Interior) armband replaced underground resistance. Sabotage of the rail system supplemented Allied arial attacks to impede German troop transports sent to meet the Allies in battle.[2]

In the coming days, with Wehrmacht forces rushing to defend the Atlantic Wall against the Allied onslaught, Resistance forces struck, liberating parts of France. The Germans fought back bitterly, wiping out FFI forces, executing prisoners, and massacring civilians in the area.

"Oradour-sur-Glane. That was the pretty name of a little village near Limoges," wrote Jean Guéhenno. "A German officer was killed there. . . . They razed the village and machine-gunned the assembled population until no one was breathing or screaming anymore."[3] Numerically, this massacre of 642 men, women, and children on June 10 was the worst German atrocity of its kind committed in Western Europe during the entire war. Troops of Der Führer Regiment of the 2nd Waffen-SS Panzer Division, Das Reich, avenged the killing of Wehrmacht soldiers by Resistance fighters by shooting

---

1. Michel, *Shadow War*, 290.
2. Cobb, *The Resistance*, 245–46.
3. Guéhenno, *Diary of the Dark Years*, 258.

all the men in the village and, after forcing all the women and children into the church, setting fire to the church and burning them alive.[4]

The Waffen-SS commander in charge, Sturmbannführer Adolf Diekmann, reported that his unit "occupied the village and immediately conducted an intensive search of the houses. . . . [L]arge quantities of weapons and ammunition were found. Therefore, all the men of the village were shot, who were surely Maquisards." He added that while the women and children were locked into the church and the village set on fire, hidden ammunition in most houses and in the church's roof caused the burning to death of the women and children in the church.[5]

However, witnesses later testified in war crimes trials that no evidence existed of arms or ammunition in the village.[6] A participant in the massacre, Untersturmführer Heinz Barth, testified at his trial in 1983 that no arms, ammunition, or explosives were discovered at the village.[7]

The same day as the above, the Wehrmacht attacked some 2,500 Maquisards at Mont Mouchet in the forested Auvergne region. The Germans conquered the area within three days, killing 125 partisans. While the Maquis were defeated, this illustrated how they helped to tie up German forces. "The Resistance rose up too soon and the repression is appalling," opined Guéhenno.[8]

On July 21, the Germans committed 10,000 troops to attack the Maquisards in the mountainous Vercors, in the Grenoble region. US Flying Fortresses had parachuted 1,700 rifles and 1,400 Sten guns to them, but half the fighters were still unarmed, and they received no heavy weapons. After several days of fighting, SS troops landed in gliders to turn the tide in the Germans' favor. While 500 Maquisards and civilians were killed, many escaped to fight another day.[9]

4. Meyer, *Die deutsche Besatzung*, Chapter 8. See also Lieb, *Konventioneller Krieg oder NS-Weltanschauungskrieg?*, 368–69.

5. Otto Weidinger, *Comrades to the End*, quoted in www.oradour.info/ruined/chapter6.htm.

6. Michael Williams, *In a Ruined State: The Full Story of Oradour-sur-Glane 10th June 1944* (2011), www.oradour.info/ruined/chapter7.htm.

7. Williams, *In a Ruined State,* www.oradour.info/ruined/chapter5.htm; Meyer, *Die deutsche Besatzung*, 166.

8. Cobb, *The Resistance*, 250–53; Guéhenno, *Diary of the Dark Years*, 258.

9. Cobb, *The Resistance*, 251–53.

In the Vercors and in the Tarentaise, the FFI forces prematurely attacked and sought to defend against superior, better trained and equipped German forces, instead of engaging in hit-and-run guerilla tactics. They could not hold the territory they liberated. Still, notes historian Peter Lieb, "the FFI in the Alps helped the Allied troops to pave the ground for the liberation of their country on a tactical level by delivering invaluable intelligence, carrying out diversionary attacks, and cutting the German lines of retreat."[10]

In this period, American operatives were seeking to procure arms in Switzerland for the Resistance. OSS operative Allen Dulles reported from Bern, "We now have the chance to obtain a number of modern arms by completely legitimate means, ostensibly for storing here but actually we intend to use them chiefly in French and Italian Maquis, especially to arm escapees and internees who have come back. . . ." He added that codename "520" (U.S. Brigadier General Barnwell Legge, who was the military attaché to Switzerland) "can legitimately and openly buy a number of arms, after which, with his assistance, I can get them out."[11]

By now, the Germans began to mistrust the French police with whom they had previously collaborated so closely. Garrison headquarters Limoges, on July 18, reported that the higher SS and police leaders ordered that seized and confiscated arms held by the French police be surrendered to the German order police (*Ordnungspolizei*). Some of these weapons held by French police had been stolen by terrorists. To prevent these incidents, such arms were to be turned in to the nearest SD or Wehrmacht department.[12]

Indeed, some French police were joining the Resistance. The Communist journal *En avant* decried the lack of weapons but urged resourcefulness in obtaining revolvers, rifles, and hunting guns to be used to attack and disarm Germans. It added, "There are many policemen and gendarmes who have decided to contribute their arms or to join the ranks of our militias. We must denounce those who keep their weapons and refuse to distribute them to those who fight to wipe out the boches and assume the liberation of our homeland."[13]

---

10. Lieb, *Vercors 1944*, 91.

11. Telegram dated August 7, 1944, in Peterson, *From Hitler's Doorstep*, 357.

12. BA/MA RH 34/342, Standortkommandantur Limoges, Standortbefehle Nr. 59–88, Februar – August 1944.

13. "Comment armer les milices," *En avant, organe régional des jeunesses communistes du Nord*, août 1944.

The Anti-Hitler Conspiracy in the Wehrmacht

By this point, Wehrmacht officers at the highest level were conspiring to assassinate Hitler. On July 20, Colonel Claus von Stauffenberg planted a bomb under a table right by the Führer at Wolf's Lair, excused himself, heard it explode, flew back to Berlin, and set the coup d'état in motion. But fate intervened—someone moved the briefcase with the bomb over where a portion of the table shielded the blast and Hitler survived.[14]

Exposed to constant shelling and bomb attacks from both sides since D-Day, Normandy resident Marie-Louise Osmont heard the news and wrote in her diary: "Dynamite attack against Hitler, who is burned and shaken up . . . an indication of disintegration. Speech by the Führer—police measures. May this first crack be followed by a collapse that would stop this war, which is going to destroy everything in France."[15]

None other than Carl-Heinrich von Stülpnagel led the plot in Paris. He directed Wehrmacht troops to arrest SS personnel, including Karl Oberg, the senior SS and police leader. But news arrived that fate saved the Führer, and the conspiracy collapsed. Implicated in the plot, Stülpnagel was ordered to Berlin. Along the way, he shot himself in the head, but survived, only to be tried by the people's court and hung with piano wire. Hitler enjoyed himself watching films of the conspirators' hangings.[16]

Uprising in Paris

But the days of the occupation of Paris were numbered. On August 15, the Paris police went on strike to protest the disarming of police in the suburbs. On the 19th, insurrection broke out. Policemen joined with hundreds of armed civilians to seize the prefecture of police, located just across from Notre Dame. A detachment of the *Forces Françaises de l'Intérieur* (FFI) fired on a German

---

14. The most thorough account is in Peter Hoffmann, *The History of the German Resistance, 1933–1945*, 3rd ed. (Montreal: McGill–Queen's University Press, 1996).

15. Marie-Louise Osmont, *The Normandy Diary of Marie-Louise Osmont, 1940–1944*, trans. George L. Newman (New York: Random House, 1994), 100.

16. For a fascinating account by one of the conspirators, see Wilhelm von Schramm, *Conspiracy Among Generals*, trans. R.T. Clark (New York: Charles Scribner's Sons, 1956); see also Laub, *After the Fall*, 282–86.

convoy on the Pont Neuf. German vehicles were set on fire, barricades went up, and government offices were seized.[17]

Original film footage shows the street fighting, with snipers shooting Germans and seizing their rifles and citizens building barricades.[18] Jean Galtier-Boissière, a participant, noted that "one comes home to lunch carrying one's rifle; the whole neighborhood is at the windows to have a look and to applaud; the milkman, the greengrocer, and the man in the bistro won't chalk anything up on the slate [keep a tab]."[19] Photographs of the struggle depict civilians with revolvers (even the obsolete model 1873), semiautomatic pistols, and rifles shooting from buildings or at the barricades. As usual, insufficient arms inhibited the struggle.[20]

Jean Guéhenno saw two German sentries on the bridge of the rue Manin: "With their grenades in their belt, their submachine guns in their hands, they were terrified, waiting for an inevitable death—the passerby with an indifferent air who would fire a revolver at them through his pocket almost at point-blank range." When he passed by again later, the soldiers were dead. Guéhenno almost felt sorry for them, but resisted: "All my heart is with those boys of Paris who are fighting almost without weapons, and my pity is reserved for them."[21]

Some 20,000 German soldiers remained in Paris, along with 80 Panzers and 60 pieces of artillery. They were arrayed against partisans armed with an estimated 600 handguns and an unknown number armed with who knows what.[22] De Gaulle wrote that the partisans numbered some 25,000 armed men of autonomous groups operating in the neighborhoods, unsubordinated to hierarchal orders from above.[23]

17. Larry Collins and Dominique Lapierre, *Is Paris Burning?* (New York: Simon & Schuster, 1965), 107–8; de Beauvoir, *Prime of Life*, 715; Cobb, *The Resistance*, 259–60.

18. *La Libération de Paris.* Available at https://archive.org/download/LaLiberationde Paris1944/LaLiberationdeParis1944.mp4.

19. Pryce-Jones, *Paris in the Third Reich*, 204.

20. Christine Levisse-Touzé, *Paris libéré, Paris Retrouvé* (Paris: Gallimard Découvertes, 1994), 3; "Le Journal de la Libération de la France," *L'Événement du Jeudi*, August 18–24, 1994, 21, 25, 30; Venner, *Armes de la Résistance*, 156; Cobb, *The Resistance*, 264.

21. Guéhenno, *Diary of the Dark Years*, 269 (entry dated August 19, 1944).

22. Cobb, *The Resistance*, 261.

23. de Gaulle, *War Memoirs*, 633.

Simone de Beauvoir described FFI ambushes on August 21: "Men were hidden behind the balustrades along the *quais*, . . . and there were more in the neighboring apartment blocks, and yet more in the Place Saint-Michel, on the steps leading down to the Métro station." She saw two German soldiers drive by and be killed twenty yards later. "F.F.I. men cycled up and down the *quais* asking invisible combatants if they had enough ammunition." The FFI had also taken over the printing presses and newspaper offices, allowing *Combat* and *Libération* to be sold in the streets. Every time armored cars left the Sénat, they were greeted with a hail of bullets.[24] The Sénat was housed in the Luxembourg Palace, which was a German strong point for defending Paris.

On August 22, as described by Jean Guéhenno, "[t]he town halls of each arrondissement and the ministries were occupied by the FFI and Vichy vanished like a puff of smoke. The Germans no longer control life in Paris. They only hold the points where they have dug in. There is fighting all over. Place de la République, Place du Panthéon, on the Île de la Cité, and in front of the Senate." "They're fighting all over Paris this morning," continued Guéhenno the next day. "The Resistance had occupied the Grand Palais and the Germans attacked and set fire to it."[25]

Wanting to continue the fight against major German forces, the Allied Command had opposed diverting forces to Paris, but that became politically impossible. The French 2nd Armored Division, consisting of 16,000 soldiers and 200 tanks, was sent to help, arriving on the 24th and 25th and being joined by an American infantry division. German forces put up a violent resistance but were overcome.[26]

On the morning of the 24th, Guéhenno continued, "American radio was announcing yesterday that the FFI had liberated Paris, and this morning that General Leclerc entered the city at the head of his army." But he considered the actual facts to be far broader, in that "Paris is no longer accepting German control: it has given itself free institutions, and that simple affirmation is being paid for every minute with a great deal of blood." Fighting continued at the Île de la Cité, on rue Manin, and at the Porte des Lilas. "They're building

---

24. de Beauvoir, *Prime of Life*, 717–18.
25. Guéhenno, *Diary of the Dark Years*, 270–71.
26. Cobb, *The Resistance*, 265–67. See Lieb, *Konventioneller Krieg oder NS-Weltanschauungskrieg?*, 480.

barricades that they don't have the weapons to hold."[27] De Gaulle verified that "since morning, groups of partisans with only the most meager weapons had bravely assisted the regular troops in mopping up the nests of German resistance."[28]

General Dietrich von Choltitz had assumed his post as the commander of Greater Paris on August 9, 1944, with orders not to surrender Paris without the Führer's directive.[29] When the occupation began to collapse, Hitler ordered him to torch the city. To his credit, Choltitz refused to carry out the order and capitulated on the 25th. The ordeal is depicted in the book and film *Is Paris Burning? (Paris brûle-t-il?)*.[30]

An estimated two thousand Parisians, eight hundred FFI and police, and more than one hundred Free French and American soldiers died to liberate Paris.[31] As Guéhenno concluded his diary, "Freedom—France is beginning again."[32]

Toward Victory

The liberation of Paris was only another step toward victory. The continuing struggle involved both great and small incidents, leading to both triumph and tragedy. In a letter to me, Marcel Demnet related how, in the evening of August 15 in Vierzon, two German soldiers, quartered in the Château of the rue Etienne-Dolet, quietly talked over a bottle of wine at the Café de l'Eglise.[33] Two FFI Maquis entered the café and sat down. They hatched a plan to retrieve their guns from their car, then to pretend being cooks who would serve the Germans, then seize their arms and take them prisoner. The plan worked.

27. Guéhenno, *Diary of the Dark Years*, 271–72 (entry dated August 28, 1944).

28. de Gaulle, *War Memoirs*, 647.

29. Laub, *After the Fall*, 287; Mitchell, *Nazi Paris*, 149.

30. *Is Paris Burning?* and *Paris brûle-t-il?* directed by René Clément (Hollywood, CA: Paramount Pictures, 1966). The script was based on Larry Collins and Dominique Lapierre, *Is Paris Burning?* (New York: Simon & Schuster, 1965).

31. Cobb, *The Resistance*, 270.

32. Guéhenno, *Diary of the Dark Years*, 272.

33. "Rafle du Cafe de l'Eglise aux Forges," document attached to letter from Marcel Demnet to author, November 13, 2002.

202 | *Gun Control in Nazi-Occupied France*

The following day, after searches for the two missing soldiers proved unsuccessful, the Germans rounded up several citizens of Vierzon. After identities were checked, all were released except four who were kept as hostages. They were taken away by the Gestapo in cars in the direction of Bourges, a nearby town. The hostages included Madame Rolland, mother of the cafe's owner; Madeleine Chantelat, her employee; Alice Curdled, café manager; and Camille Lurat, a bus driver. They simply vanished. Post-war research revealed nothing of their fate. Of the two Maquis who captured the Germans, Charles Hemel was caught and executed, the other one escaped.

In another incident, Jewish partisans ambushed a German train. Maurice Bernsohn recalled:

> We pounced on them, I tearing a revolver from the belt of a German major (I have that gun to this day) and shouting: "*Wir sind Juden! Wir sind Juden!*" ("We are Jews!") They turned quite white. We made them line up, and they were sure we were going to kill them right then and there. But we only made prisoners of them.[34]

The Maquis obstructed German routes through the Vosges and in the Ardennes. In October, 60,000 FFI Maquis surrounded Wehrmacht units at La Rochelle, Royan, and Verdon. Some 140,000 Maquis were absorbed into the Free French army.[35]

By fall 1944, with much of France liberated, a new government was in power with de Gaulle giving orders. Of the paramilitary Resistance groups, de Gaulle related in his memoirs, "I induced the government to decree the formal dissolution of the militias," which passed on October 28. The National Council of the Resistance objected—de Gaulle met with them, but "I could answer only by complete refusal." It was not the Communists who were vocal: "The most ardent in their protest were those who represented the moderate factions."[36] One can imagine the resentment and sense of mistrust felt by the partisans who fought and died in France while de Gaulle sojourned in London and Algiers.

---

34. Latour, *Jewish Resistance*, 49.
35. Michel, *Shadow War*, 344.
36. de Gaulle, *War Memoirs*, 712.

A French Gun Decree

On October 31, the Council of Ministers decreed that "any force which was not a part of the Army or the police was to be dissolved at once. . . ." But the following measure went much further: "Any armament in the possession of private citizens was to be turned in within a week to the police commissariats or the *gendarmerie* brigades."[37] Was this a new version of a prohibition on firearm possession by citizens, with a week to turn them in instead of twenty-four hours, and the punishment being something less than the death penalty?

There is no reliable data on the number of firearms in France before the Nazi invasion. Handguns and certain rifles were required to be registered (those of possible military use were banned), but hunting guns were not. Registered firearms were more likely to be surrendered when the Germans so decreed, as the owners would be known.

There were three million hunting guns in France in 1939, according to the *Saint-Hubert-Club de France*, a hunting association. After the Nazi takeover and occupation in 1940–44, some 715,000 were surrendered by their owners in the occupied zone. In the zone that was not occupied until 1942, 120,000 hunting guns were turned in to French authorities. The hunting guns not surrendered were, if not lost or stolen, hidden by their owners and in some cases used by the Resistance.[38]

That means that only 835,000 of three million hunting guns—less than one-third—were turned in by French citizens threatened with the death penalty for not doing so. That is an incredible testament to the inefficacy of gun control in the most extreme circumstances.

What was the fate of the surrendered hunting guns? In the occupied zone, those in German custody were mostly destroyed, sent to Germany, or loaned or sold to Wehrmacht soldiers for hunting in France. A few, mostly in Vincennes, were abandoned by the Germans as they retreated. In the free zone, most of the arms surrendered to the French authorities were not shipped to Germany. Other than hunting guns, in both zones "war weapons," pistols,

---

37. de Gaulle, *War Memoirs*, 712.
38. *Le Saint-Hubert*, n°1, janvier–février 1945, 1.

revolvers, and rifled hunting carbines (*carabines rayées de chasse*) were completely removed or destroyed by the Germans.

When the Germans retreated, of the surrendered arms, all rifled hunting carbines and all of the best shotguns, with rare exceptions, disappeared. In the vicinity of Paris, the château of Vincennes had about 14,000 centerfire guns (*fusils à percussion centrale*) in poor condition, 7,000 pinfire rifles (*vieux fusils à broche*), and 4,000 percussion muskets (*fusils à piston*), mostly unusable. Of these 25,000 guns, about 4,000 had labels with the name and address of the owner.[39]

While it will never be known how many French citizens surrendered and had their firearms confiscated, far more significant is how many French lost their lives for possession of firearms, how the mere uncertainty of arms not surrendered tied up more German forces, and how private ownership of firearms contributed to the Resistance.

Trials of Those Who Denounced Gun Owners

After the liberation, collaborators were held accountable. Informal justice and revenge were meted out to the worst offenders, who were summarily executed, as well as to those who simply got too close to the Germans, such as the women who were punished by shaving their heads.

One of the most pernicious degradations during the occupation was the practice of denunciations based on greed, revenge, or other base motive. Hélène Berr wrote in her diary that "Mme P. spoke to me about her plans to take revenge on the disgusting cowards who denounce other people and pillage their homes when they are arrested. . . ."[40] Many were denounced for hiding firearms.

The courts of justice tried many for such denunciations. A municipal employee was sentenced to twenty years of hard labor because he denounced a young man to the Gestapo for hiding revolvers in his cellar. A wife denounced her seventy-five-year-old husband to the Gestapo, but the rifle found was so old that he was released; the man forgave his wife.[41]

---

39. *Le Saint-Hubert*, n°2, mars–avril 1945, 9.

40. Berr, *Journal*, 242 (entry dated January 13, 1944).

41. André Halimi, *La Délation Sous L'Occupation* (Paris: Éditions Alain Moreau, 1983), 252–53.

A man was sentenced to forced labor for life for denouncing a neighbor for listening to the English radio, after which a rifle was found, leading to his execution. The death penalty was given to a landlord who denounced a tenant to the Gestapo for possession of a pistol, who was executed.[42] A worker was condemned to death for denouncing coworkers to the Gestapo for possession of some automatic pistols, leading to one worker being executed by the Germans.[43] A man was sentenced to twenty years' imprisonment for denouncing his neighbors for possessing firearms.[44]

A woman got ten years of hard labor for denouncing her boss, an industrialist. A man got twenty years of hard labor for denouncing a neighbor for possession of military firearms. Another man got fifteen years' hard labor for denouncing a firearm owner.[45] A woman was sentenced to five years' imprisonment for denouncing her ex-husband to the German military authority for possession of firearms.[46]

A particularly revolting case concerned a woman who in December 1940 denounced her husband and son to the Germans for possessing firearms. The husband was imprisoned for nine months and the son for three months. Two years later, the husband was turned over to the Gestapo by a rural guard who the FFI resistance group shot during the liberation. Condemned the second time as a recidivist, the husband was sent to a deportation camp where he died. The wife informer was sentenced to just ten months' imprisonment.[47]

Accounting for Gun Owners Who Were Executed or Deported

Marcel Demnet, born in 1921 in Vierzon-Forges (Cher), was employed in the town hall from 1934 to 1979. After the war, he took charge of assisting both military and civilian victims of the war, and published a compilation about members of the Resistance and the victims of Nazi barbarism in the

---

42. Halimi, *La Délation*, 257–58.
43. Halimi, *La Délation*, 260.
44. Halimi, *La Délation*, 264.
45. Halimi, *La Délation*, 279–80.
46. Halimi, *La Délation*, 297.
47. Halimi, *La Délation*, 289.

department of Cher.[48] He would become president of the *Fédération Natio-nale des Déportés et Enternés, Résistants et Patriotes* (National Federation of Deportees and Externs, Resistants, and Patriots, or FNDIRP).[49]

In response to my questionnaire, Demnet provided a document entitled "Civilian Arrests During the Occupation in the Department of Cher for Possession of Arms (June 20, 1940–September 4, 1944)."[50] The following shows some of the listings, beginning with the name of the town in italics and then the person arrested:

Bourges. Camille Vincent, arrested July 24, 1942, possession of hunting gun, died in deportation (S.A.R.).[51]

Chassy. Georges Pitrau, arrested July 24, 1942, possession of hunting gun, deported in October 1942 to Inzert, Diez, and Breslau, died in deportation April 21, 1943.

Gracay. Chalandre, woodworker, arrested in November 1942 for keeping and hiding abandoned weapons from the debacle of June 1940 (S.A.R.)

Gron. Raymond Blondeau, possession of a revolver, arrested June 16, 1944, would have been executed the same day.

Lignieres. Raymond Mahiet, arrested at the demarcation line at Cher in possession of a weapon where he would have died (S.A.R.)

Vierzon. Stanislaw Szymanski, arrested October 27, 1942, possession of a revolver and a cane gun (S.A.R.)

Vierzon. Marcel Mass, notorious poacher (I knew him well), arrested November 22, 1940, confined at the Bourges Jail, freed January 29, 1941. Conviction: Possession of hunting gun and hunting without

---

48. Marcel Demnet, *Livre-mémorial des résistants, patriotes et civils vierzonnais raflés, victimes de la barbarie nazie, "morts pour la France" 1942–1945* (Vierzon: la Gaucherie, 2005).

49. "Déportés politiques à Auschwitz, le convoy du 6 juillet 1942," politique-auschwitz.blogspot.com/2010/12/lanoue-moise-lucien-alexis.html.

50. "Civils Arrêtés dans le Departement du Cher pour Detention D'Armes sous l'Occupation (20 juin 1940 – 4 septembre 1944)," document attached to letter to author from Marcel Demnet, November 13, 2002.

51. Unknown abbreviation.

authorization (and for reason!). If my memory is correct, he was arrested by the gendarmes of Vierzon for poaching and would have been judged by French Justice (it was not the first). He therefore did not need to be sent to the Germans.

Ivoy-le-Pre. Edouard Habert, arrested September 23, 1943, for hiding parachuted arms. Deported to Buchenwald, Dora, and Bergen-Belsen.

• • •

Calculating how many French were executed, deported, or imprisoned for all offenses, from possession of a firearm and spreading anti-German propaganda to listening to the BBC and sabotage, would be a difficult if not impossible task. De Gaulle wrote, "With the co-operation of a considerable number of officials and a mass of informers, 60,000 persons had been executed and more than 200,000 deported of whom a bare 50,000 survived. Further, 35,000 men and women had been condemned by the Vichy tribunals. . . ."[52] The numbers killed, whether as Maquis, Jews, or as noncombatants who were massacred for whatever reason, were exceedingly higher.

It would be difficult to provide even a rough estimate of the number of people arrested, imprisoned, executed, or deported specifically for firearm possession. Wehrmacht districts regularly reported statistics in their *Lagebericht* on the numbers of people arrested for firearm offenses. The reports are voluminous but incomplete. Newspapers published the names of some people executed for firearm possession by order of the military commander, but not every case.

Statistical reports on and identification of gun violators and other offenders were greatly reduced when the SS took over security functions and as a result of *Nacht und Nebel,* under which people disappeared without explanation. The Vichy police would have kept their own records of gun arrestees, although the extent to which records thereon survived is unclear. Suffice it to say that large numbers of French citizens were arrested and punished by imprisonment, execution, or deportation for gun possession.

---

52. de Gaulle, *War Memoirs*, 789.

The Fate of the Vichy Collaborators

This story would not be complete without relating the fate of the Vichy collaborators who made it all possible. As the Allies and the Resistance were pushing the Germans back during the summer of 1944, Pierre Laval hatched a plan to try and convince the Germans to allow the National Assembly to reconvene and to restore full powers to Pétain. Laval may have fantasized that the Americans would prefer an interim government of his own rather than of de Gaulle. Laval went to Paris just days before the battle there began in order to negotiate with the Germans, who instead took him into custody and transported him, along with Pétain who had been fetched from Vichy, to the more secure city of Belfort.[53]

The Germans wanted to maintain their puppet government, but at this point neither Laval nor Pétain wished to continue playing the game. Ultra-collaborationist Fernand de Brinon stepped forward to propose a new government with himself at its head. With the Allies advancing, the French entourage was transferred to Germany where they remained until the Nazi regime collapsed in April 1945. Pétain then returned to France, de Brinon surrendered to the Americans, and Laval fled to Spain, which after a brief sojourn delivered him to the Americans, who passed him on to the French.[54]

In the trials that followed of members of the Vichy government for their crimes during the occupation, Pétain was sentenced to life imprisonment—it would not do to execute an old senile World War I hero who had been beloved by many. De Brinon was condemned to death and shot.[55] Laval received the same fate, but a few more details are in order.

Whether out of arrogance or delusion, Laval thought that he could persuade the jury that he protected France as best anyone could. He wrote a testament to justify his every act to save France from a worse fate.[56] But as Albert Lebrun, the Third Republic's last president, testified in Laval's trial, "It would have been better for France . . . that the country be administered directly by a

---

53. Warner, *Pierre Laval*, 400–404.

54. Warner, *Pierre Laval*, 404–7.

55. Henry Rousso, *Les années noires: Vivre sous l'Occupation* (Paris: Gallimard, 1992), 123–24.

56. Laval, *Diary*.

Gauleiter [Nazi administrative official] than by a French government, which was not going to have any power any longer *except in appearance* and whose essential role would consist, in sum, in guaranteeing all the decisions of the occupation authorities."[57]

Given that general perception, it was no wonder that only a show trial would ensue, as Laval's guilt and sentence had already been decided before it began.[58] Given the mood of many French based on Laval's crimes, he was lucky not to have simply been shot and hung upside down in public like Mussolini. The judicial formalities having been met, on October 15, 1945, Laval was tied to a stake in a courtyard at the Fresnes prison, south of Paris—where his Nazi partners had previously imprisoned and tortured countless French— and shot.[59]

57. Shirer, *Collapse of the Third Republic*, 891–92 (emphasis in original).

58. See J. Kenneth Brody, *The Trial of Pierre Laval* (New Brunswick, NJ: Transaction Publishers, 2010).

59. Warner, *Pierre Laval*, 408–16.

Concluding Thoughts

PIERRE LAVAL'S 1935 executive action decreeing firearm registration and tightening up the ban on military-style firearms was touted in what today might be called a common-sense gun safety measure. After all, there was violence in the streets, and there were radical groups in society that might disrupt the social order. That only some law-abiding citizens would obey the decree and that many would ignore it, and that actual criminals and subversives definitely would not, did not seem to matter. What did matter was to enhance the power of the government over the citizens.

Little did anyone anticipate that, just five years later, France would be conquered by Nazi Germany, that under the armistice the French government would enforce German occupation policy, that the Wehrmacht would decree the death penalty for anyone who failed to surrender his or her firearms within twenty-four hours, that the French police would have the gun registration records with the identities of those who had been gullible enough to comply, that countless French citizens would face firing squads for not surrendering their firearms, and that lack of firearms would greatly impede an effective French Resistance. And who would have thought that one and the same Pierre Laval would become the chief collaborator to harness the people and resources of France to the needs of the German war machine?

Fortunately, not every French farmer or city dweller had registered their firearms in 1935—ignoring diktats from Paris is a wonderful French tradition. If the French government mistrusted gun owners, many gun owners mistrusted the French government. Moreover, they hid their hunting guns and revolvers when the Germans overran France in 1940, and in the ensuing four years of occupation braved the death penalty for doing so. The civil disobedience to Nazi gun control was so pervasive that one Wehrmacht district reported in exasperation, "Illegal weapons possession still represents the core of criminal activities of the French. It appears almost impossible to get rid of it."[1]

What was an occupier to do? After shooting so many for not turning in their guns, offer amnesty to those now willing to do so? Threaten to execute people for not denouncing others who had guns? Since the existence of unknown gun owners in the country threatened the security of the German occupation, and required extra security forces that could be deployed elsewhere, harsh measures were in order to achieve a "gun-free" France.

That was all the more the case as the Resistance grew and its members armed to protect themselves from capture, particularly when committing sabotage, raiding installations, gaining intelligence, and finally fighting back in groups such as the Maquis.

The value of an armed citizenry to resist tyranny, either domestic or foreign, can be debated. Guarantees of the right to keep and bear arms were demanded by the Third Estate in France and were considered, but not adopted, in the French Declaration of Rights of 1789. No constitutional tradition existed in France of a right of commoners to possess arms. Without such a tradition, it appears to have been relatively easy for the Laval government simply to decree draconian gun control measures. Yet many French ignored the threat of imprisonment imposed by those measures, and later disregarded the threat of the death penalty. A large number paid with their lives. This is a telling phenomenon regarding the enforceability of gun registration and prohibition.

The value of the armed forces of a nation state to resist invasion can also be debated. The Wehrmacht's blitzkrieg crushed the French army in just a few weeks. And that is where the role of the armed citizen became relevant. The "shadow army," as Henri Michel dubbed the resistance groups that rose all over occupied Europe to fight the enemy, contributed to the defeat of Nazism.[2] Guerrilla warfare helped the regular armies by wearing down and demoralizing the Germans. Michel noted, "If the regular armies are initially

---

1. BA/MA, RW 35/1264, Lagebericht des Militärverwaltungsbezirks B, Südwestfrankreich, für die Zeit vom 16. November 1941 bis 15. Januar 1942, 19. November 1942.

2. Michel, *Shadow War*, 15.

defeated, guerrillas can play a major part in defensive strategy; once these same regular armies have been reconstituted, guerrillas can assist their offensive operations."[3] He further observed:

> When an army dissolves its war is over, for it will take years to reconstitute and can only be of use if the situation takes a favourable turn—this was what the men of Vichy thought and it was the tragedy of the French Armistice Army. The "shadow army," on the other hand, can melt away if the enemy offensive becomes too hot; it will do so only to recover its strength through contact with its country and its people. . . .[4]

It is telling that the only armed resistance in France until D-Day was conducted by civilians, from the politically motivated men and women who organized into urban cells to the young men who fled labor conscription to fight with the Maquis in the mountains. While they could not liberate France without the help of foreign armies, they helped pave the way for the Allied invasion. Once the Allied armies hit the beaches of Normandy, the Resistance would fight with them to the final victory.

The phenomena of occupied France during World War II involve countless historical factors, of which gun control in the prewar and occupation periods is only one of many (albeit one that has been wholly ignored by historians). The extent to which the negative experiences of gun control in those periods are remembered today in France or other European countries is unclear and maybe dubious. The European Union appears to have an agenda to disarm the populations to the fullest extent possible.

But France's experiences did sway public opinion in the United States, where opposition to firearm registration and prohibition was influenced not just by the National Rifle Association but more so by the major media. As shown in this work, the *New York Times* regularly published the names of French citizens who were executed for gun possession. While memories about the details have faded, the laws in most of the United States reflect a robust protection for lawful gun ownership and for the right to keep and bear arms.

---

3. Michel, *Shadow War*, 290–91.
4. Michel, *Shadow War*, 357.

The extent to which the pendulum should swing between gun control and gun ownership continues to be debated in Europe, the United States, and the rest of the world. In response to terrorist attacks in France, Belgium, Germany, and elsewhere, the European Union appears to be hell bent to register and prohibit possession of firearms by law-abiding citizens. It is said that those who do not learn from history are apt to repeat it. Whether there are lessons to be learned on this issue from the experiences of the France of Pierre Laval and the Nazis with whom he collaborated is for the reader to decide. Yet it cannot be questioned that France's nightmare in that era with firearm registration, prohibition, and confiscation, enforced by the firing squad, suggests a telling lesson: be careful what you wish for.

The defeat of its forces in 1940 and its occupation were not proud moments for France. Yet there was an element of French society that could be remembered as its "greatest generation." That would be those who refused to submit, who refused to turn in their guns, and who fought back. Many died for those very reasons, and their courage should never be forgotten, as they helped ensure the fulfillment of their slogan: "*Vive la France libre!*"

Bibliography

Archives

Archives de la Marne, Reims
Archives de la Préfecture de Police
Archives des Ardennes
Archives Nationales
Bibliothèque Nationale de France
Bundesarchiv Lichterfelde
Bundesarchiv-Militärachiv (BA/MA)

Books

Archives Parlementaires de 1787 a 1860: Recueil Complet des Débats Législatifs & Politiques des Chambres Françaises. Première série (1787 à 1799). Paris: Librairie Administrative de Paul DuPont, 1867–1879.

Arnaud, Patrice, and Fabien Théofilakis, eds. *Gestapo & Polices Allemandes: France, Europe de l'Ouest 1939–1945.* Paris: CNRS Éditions, 2017.

Barbier, Henri. *Le Délit de Port D'Armes Prohibées.* Paris: Éditions Littéraires de France, 1939.

Berr, Hélène. *The Journal of Hélène Berr.* New York: Weinstein Books, 2008.

Berlière, Jean-Marc, and Franck Liaigre. *Le Sang des communistes: les Bataillons de la jeunesse dans la lutte armée, automne 1941.* Paris: Fayard, 2004.

Best, Werner. *Dänemark in Hitlers Hand: Der Bericht des Reichsbevollmächtigten Werner Best.* Edited by Siegfried Matlok. Husum, Germany: Husum Druck GmbH, 1988.

Bevans, Charles I., comp. *Treaties and Other International Agreements of the United States of America 1776–1949.* Vol. 1. Washington, DC: US Government Printing Office, 1968.

Brody, J. Kenneth. *The Trial of Pierre Laval.* New Brunswick, NJ: Transaction Publishers, 2010.

Burrin, Philippe. *La France à l'heure allemande, 1940–1944.* Paris, Seuil: 1995.

Burrin, Philippe. *France Under the Germans: Collaboration and Compromise.* Translated by Janet Lloyd. The New Press: New York Press, 1993.

Cobb, Matthew. *The Resistance: The French Fight Against the Nazis.* London: Simon & Schuster, 2009.

Collins, Larry, and Dominique Lapierre. *Is Paris Burning?* New York: Simon & Schuster, 1965.

Dams, Carsten, and Michael Stolle. *The Gestapo: Power and Terror in the Third Reich.* Translated by Charlotte Ryland. New York: Oxford University Press, 2014.

de Beauvoir, Simone. *The Prime of Life.* Translated by Peter Green. New York: Lancer Books, 1966.

de Bénouville, Guillain. *The Unknown Warriors.* Translated by Lawrence G. Blochman. New York: Simon & Schuster, 1949.

de Brinon, Fernand. *Mémoires.* Paris: L.L.C., 1949; Déterna, 2001.

de Gaulle, Charles. *The Complete War Memoirs of Charles de Gaulle.* New York: Carroll & Graf, 1998.

Demnet, Marcel. *Livre-mémorial des résistants, patriotes et civils vierzonnais raflés, victimes de la barbarie nazie, "morts pour la France" 1942–1945.* Vierzon: la Gaucherie, 2005.

Federal Firearms Legislation: Hearings Before the Subcommittee to Investigate Juvenile Delinquency. Senate Committee on the Judiciary, 90th Cong., 2nd Sess. 1968.

Flender, Harold. *Rescue in Denmark.* Princeton University Press, 1963, reprinted by Washington, DC: Holocaust Library, n.d.

Frenay, Henri. *The Night Will End: Memoirs of a Revolutionary.* Translated by Dan Hofstadter. New York: McGraw-Hill, 1976.

Gildea, Robert. *Marianne in Chains.* New York: Henry Holt and Company, 2002.

Guéhenno, Jean. *Diary of the Dark Years, 1940–1944: Collaboration, Resistance, and Daily Life in Occupied Paris.* Translated by David Ball. New York: Oxford University Press, 2014.

Halbrook, Stephen P. *The Founders' Second Amendment: Origins of the Right to Bear Arms.* Chicago: Ivan R. Dee, Independent Institute, 2008.

———. *Gun Control in the Third Reich: Disarming the Jews and "Enemies of the State."* Oakland, CA: Independent Institute, 2013.

———. *Target Switzerland.* New York: Sarpedon, 1998.

Halimi, André. *La Délation Sous L'Occupation.* Paris: Alain Moreau, 1983.

Hennig, Eike, ed. *Hessen unterm Hakenkreuz.* Frankfurt am Main: Insel Verlag, 1983.

Herbert, Ulrich. *Best: Biographische Studien über Radikalismus, Weltanschauung und Vernunft, 1903–1989.* Bonn: J. H. W. Dietz Nachfolger, 1996.

Hitler's Secret Conversations. Translated by Norman Cameron and R. H. Stevens. New York: Signet Books, 1961.

Hitlers Tischgespräche im Führerhauptquartier 1941–1942. Stuttgart: Seewald Verlag, 1963.

Hoffmann, Peter. *The History of the German Resistance, 1933–1945.* 3rd ed. Montreal: McGill–Queen's University Press, 1996.

Hogg, Ian V., and John Weeks. *Military Small Arms of the 20th Century.* Northfield, IL: DBI Books, 1985.

Humbert, Agnès. *Résistance: A Woman's Journal of Struggle and Defiance in Occupied France.* Translated by Barbara Mellor. New York: Bloomsbury, 2008.

Jaurès, Jean. *Democracy & Military Service.* Edited by C. G. Coulton. London: Simpkin, Marshall, Hamilton, Kent & Co., 1916. http://www.marxists.org/archive/jaures/1907/military-service/index.htm.

———. *L'Armée Nouvelle.* Paris: l'Humanité, 1915.

Jucker, Ninetta. *Curfew in Paris: A Record of the German Occupation.* London: The Hogarth Press, 1960.

Kaul, Friedrich Karl. *Der Fall des Herschel Grynszpan.* Berlin: Akademie-Verlag, 1965.

Kersaudy, François. *Norway 1940.* Lincoln, NE: University of Nebraska Press, 1990.

Kladstrup, Don and Petie. *Wine & War: The French, the Nazis, and the Battle for France's Greatest Treasure.* New York: Random House, 2001.

Latour, Anny. *The Jewish Resistance in France (1940–1944).* New York: Holocaust Library, 1970.

Laub, Thomas J. *After the Fall: German Policy in Occupied France, 1940–1944.* New York: Oxford University Press, 2010.

Lecler, Philippe. "Les auxiliares français de la police allemande: L'exemple du département des Ardennes." Chap. 4 in Patrice Arnaud and Fabien Théofilakis, eds., *Gestapo & Polices Allemandes: France, Europe de l'Ouest 1939-1945.* Paris: CNRS Éditions, 2017.

Lecornu, Bernard. *Un Préfet sous l'Occupation allemande: Chateaubriant, Saint-Nazaire, Tulle.* Paris: France-Empire, 1984.

Le Journal Défense de la France. Paris: Les Presses universitaires de France, 1961.

Le Moigne, Jean-Paul. *Le contrôle administratif de la détention des armes à feu par les particuliers.* Université Reims Champagne-Ardenne, Faculté de Droit et de

Science Politique: Mémoire de D.E.A., 1999–2000. Unpublished doctoral thesis in *Droit public.*

Lévy, Gilles. *Drames et secrets de la Résistance* (Paris: Presses de la Cité, 1984).

———. *Guide des Maquis et hauts-lieux de la Résistance d'Auvergne* (Paris: Presses de la Cité, 1986).

Lieb, Peter. *Konventioneller Krieg oder NS-Weltanschauungskrieg? Kriegführung und Partisanenbekämpfung in Frankreich 1943/44.* Munich: R. Oldenbourg Verlag, 2007.

———. *Vercors 1944: Resistance in the French Alps.* Oxford, England: Osprey Publishing, 2012.

Maler, Juan [Reinhard Kops]. *Frieden, Krieg und "Frieden."* Buenos Aires: J. Maler, 1987.

Martens, Stefan, ed. *Frankreich und Belgien unter deutscher Besatzung 1940–1944. Die Bestände des Bundesarchiv-Militärarchivs Freiburg.* Sebastian Remus compl. Stuttgart: Thorbecke, 2002.

Mazower, Mark. *Hitler's Empire: How the Nazis Ruled Europe.* New York: Penguin Press, 2008.

Meyer, Ahlrich. *Die deutsche Besatzung in Frankreich 1940–1944: Widerstandsbekämpfung und Judenverfolgung.* Darmstadt, Germany: Wissenschaftliche Buchgesellschaft, 2000.

Michel, Henri. *The Shadow War: European Resistance 1939–1945.* Translated by Richard Barry. New York: Harper & Row, 1972.

Miller, Russell. *The Resistance: World War II.* Chicago: Time-Life Books Inc., 1985.

Mitchell, Allan. *The Devil's Captain: Ernst Jünger in Nazi Paris, 1941–1944.* New York: Berghahn Books, 2011.

———. *Nazi Paris: The History of an Occupation, 1940–1944.* New York: Berghahn Books, 2010.

Musée de l'Ordre de la Libération, *Cinquantenaire de l'Ordre de la Libération.* Paris: Musée de l'Ordre de la Libération, 1990.

Nazi Conspiracy and Aggression. Vol. 1. Washington, DC: U.S. Government Printing Office, 1946. Available at https://archive.org/stream/naziconspiracyag01unit /naziconspiracyag01unit_djvu.txt.

Nicholas, Lynn H. *The Rape of Europa.* New York: Random House, 1994.

Noguères, Henri. *Histoire de la Résistance.* Vol. 1 : *La Première Année, Juin 1940–Juin 1941.* Paris: Robert Laffont, 1967.

Osmont, Marie-Louise. *The Normandy Diary of Marie-Louise Osmont, 1940–1944.* Translated by George L. Newman. New York: Random House, 1994.

Ousby, Ian. *Occupation: The Ordeal of France, 1940–44.* New York: Cooper Square Press, 2000.

Paxton, Robert O. *Vichy France: Old Guard and New Order, 1940–1944.* New York: Alfred A. Knopf, 1972.

Peterson, Neal H., ed., *From Hitler's Doorstep: The Wartime Intelligence Reports of Allen Dulles, 1942–1945.* University Park, PA: Pennsylvania State University Press, 1996.

Porter, Roy P. *Uncensored France.* New York: Dial Press, 1942.

Pryce-Jones, David. *Paris in the Third Reich: A History of the German Occupation, 1940–1944.* New York: Holt, Rinehart and Winston, 1981.

Reynaud, Paul. *In the Thick of the Fight, 1930–1945.* New York: Simon & Schuster, 1955.

Roberts, J. M. ed. *French Revolution Documents.* Oxford, England: Basil Blackwell, 1966.

Rotem (Kazik), Simha. *Memoirs of a Warsaw Ghetto Fighter and the Past Within Me.* New Haven, CT: Yale University Press, 1994.

Rousso, Henry. *Les années noires: Vivre sous l'Occupation.* Paris: Gallimard, 1992.

Schuker, Stephen A. "Seeking a Scapegoat: Intelligence and Grand Strategy in France, 1919–1940." Chap. 3 in Jonathan Haslam and Karina Urbach, eds., *Secret Intelligence in the European States System, 1918–1989.* Stanford, CA: University Press Scholarship Online, 2014.

Schwab, Gerald. *The Day the Holocaust Began: The Odyssey of Herschel Grynszpan.* New York: Praeger, 1990.

Sémelin, Jacques. *Unarmed Against Hitler: Civilian Resistance in Europe, 1939–1943,* trans. Suzan Husserl-Kapit. Westport, CT: Praeger, 1993.

Shirer, William L. *The Collapse of the Third Republic: An Inquiry into the Fall of France in 1940.* New York: Simon & Schuster, 1969.

Soucy, Robert. *French Fascism: The Second Wave, 1933–1939.* New Haven, CT: Yale University Press, 1995.

Stamm, Luzi, Johannes Hofmann, Stefanie Frey, and Lotti Wanner, eds., *Liberty, Independence, Neutrality.* Lenzburg, Switzerland: Verlag Merker im Effingerhof, 2006.

Levisse-Touzé, Christine. *Paris libéré, Paris Retrouvé.* Paris: Gallimard Découvertes, 1994.

Trial of the Major War Criminals before the International Military Tribunal: Nuremberg January 22–February 4, 1946 (Buffalo, New York: William S. Hein & Co.,1995), Vols. 6 and 7. 1946. avalon.law.yale.edu/subject_menus/imt.asp.

Umbreit, Hans. *Der Militärbefehlshaber in Frankreich 1940–1944.* Boppard am Rhein: Harald Boldt Verlag, 1968.

U.S. Department of State, *Documents on German Foreign Policy 1918–1945,* Series D. Washington, DC: U.S. Government Printing Office, 1956, 1964.

van der Geest, Jack. *Was God on Vacation? A WWII Autobiography.* Highlands Ranch, CO: Van der Geest Publishing, 1999.

Venner, Dominique. *Les Armes de la Résistance.* Paris: Pensée Moderne, 1976.

von Schramm, Wilhelm. *Conspiracy Among Generals.* Translated by R. T. Clark. New York: Charles Scribner's Sons, 1956.

Warner, Geoffrey. *Pierre Laval and the Eclipse of France.* New York: Macmillan, 1968.

Articles. See also Newspapers.

"1947: Fernand de Brinon, Vichy minister with a Jewish wife." April 15, 2008. www .executedtoday.com/2008/04/15/1947-fernand-de-brinon-vichy-minister-with-a -jewish-wife/.

"An American Diplomat in Vichy France." 1986. adst.org/2013/07/an-american -diplomat-in-vichy-france/.

Best, Werner. "Die deutsche Militärverwaltung in Frankreich." *Reich, Volksordnung, Lebensraum,* Vol. 1, 29-76. 1941.

"Cohors-Asturies," https://fr.wikipedia.org/wiki/Cohors-Asturies.

"Comment armer les milices," *En avant, organe régional des jeunesses communistes du Nord,* août 1944.

Conan, Eric. "Jean-Pierre Ingrand: Les regrets d'un serviteur de Vichy." *L'Express,* August 8, 1991. www.lexpress.fr/actualite/politique/les-regrets-d-un-serviteur -de-vichy_492450.html.

"Contre la terreur nazie." *Combat, organe du mouvement de libération nationale,* N° 56, avril 1944.

de Loisey, Phillibert. "Le déclarations d'armes de 1942–43," *Gazette des armes,* Mai 2004.

"Déportés politiques à Auschwitz, le convoi du 6 juillet 1942." politique-auschwitz. blogspot.com/2010/12/lanoue-moise-lucien-alexis.html.

Dutailly, Colonel Henry. "Les armes des Maquis Haut-Marnais." *Revue de la société des amis du musée de l'armée,* n° 109 (juin 1995).

"Francesc Macià," www.catalangovernment.eu/pres_gov/government/en/president /presidents/macia.html.

"German Weapon Registry to Take Effect in 2013." *Deutsche Welle.* December 18, 2012. http://www.dw.de/german-weapon-registry-to-take-effect-in-2013/a-16461910.

Halbrook, Stephen P., "Congress Interprets the Second Amendment: Declarations by a Co-Equal Branch on the Individual Right to Keep and Bear Arms," *Tennessee Law Review* 62:597 (Spring 1995).

———. "Why Can't We Be Like France? How the Right to Bear Arms Got Left Out of the Declaration of Rights and How Gun Registration was Decreed Just in Time for the Nazi Occupation," *Fordham Urban Law Journal*, no. 5, 39:1637-94 (October 2012).

James, Garry. "French Model 1873 Revolver." *American Rifleman*, November 2012, 130.

Kahn, Jeffrey. "'Protection and Empire': The Martens Clause, State Sovereignty, and Individual Rights." 56 *Virginia Journal of International Law* 56:1-49 (2016).

"La restitution des armes de chasse déposées aux autorités allemandes." *Le Saint-Hubert*, n° 4, 40e année, juillet-août 1941, 37.

"Le Journal de la Libération de la France." *L'Evenement du Jeudi*, August 18–24, 1994.

Le Moigne, Jean-Paul and Stéphane Nerrant. "Commentaire critique et comparé de la Proposition de loi n°2773 du 30 juillet 2010." *Gazette des Armes*, 14 août 2010. www.armes-ufa.com/spip.php?article678.

"Le Président Laval a de Nombreux entretiens a Paris. *Cherbourg-Eclair*, 18 Juin 1943. http://www.normannia.info/ark%3A/86186/wkc9.

"Léon Bérard," www.assemblee-nationale.fr/sycomore/_fiche_14-19.asp?num_dept =650.

Lévy, Général Gilles. "Les Maquis d'Auvergne dans la Résistance: Pourquoi le Mont-Mouchet?" lesamitiesdelaresistance.fr/lien1-maquis.php.

"Morts au Champ d'Honneur. France." *Combat*, n° 36, novembre 1942.

"Morts pour la France." *Combat*, août 1942.

"The Nazi Deadline." *American Rifleman*, February 1942, 7.

"NBC Tells France." *Time*, May 26, 1941. http://www.time.com/time/magazine /article/0,9171,765661,00.html.

"Ni Allemands, ni Russes, ni Anglais." *Défense de la France*, N° 3, 20 novembre 1941, reprinted in *Le Journal Défense de la France* (Paris: Presses universitaires de France, 1961).

"Prominent Rabbi Calls on Europe to Allow Jews to Carry Guns." www.israelnational news.com/News/News.aspx/189932#.VLas7Xtlbm6.

"Réseau Cohors-Asturies." sgmcaen.free.fr/resistance/reseau-cohors-asturies.htm.

Ridgeway, Greg. *Summary of Select Firearm Violence Prevention Strategies*. Washington, D.C.: National Institute of Justice, 2013. http://www.firearmsandliberty .com/PDF-News/nij-gun-policy-memo.pdf.

"Troisième République." http://www.histoire-france-web.fr/republique_3/lebrun.

Weidinger, Otto. *Comrades to the End.* Quoted in www.oradour.info/ruined/chapter 6.htm.

Williams, Michael. *In a Ruined State: The Full Story of Oradour-sur-Glane 10th June 1944.* 2011. www.oradour.info/ruined/chapter7.htm.

Correspondence

Charmeau, Louis Maurice, président de l'Union Départementale des Combattants Volontaires de la Résistance. Bordeaux, France. Letter to author, June 10, 2003.

"Civils Arrêtés dans le Departement du Cher pour Detention D'Armes sous l'Occupation (20 Juin 1940–4 Septembre 1944)." Document attached to letter to author from Marcel Demnet, November 13, 2002.

Créau, Noël, ancien président national, Amicales des Anciens Parachutistes S.A.S. et des Anciens Commandos de la France Libre. Neuilly-sur-Seine, France. Letter to author, February 4, 2002. For more details on Noël Créau, see www.francais libres.net/liste/fiche.php?index=62760.

Daguier, Maurice, president, Ceux de la Libération. Response to author's questionnaire, February 27, 2002.

Demange, Jacques, vice-président de l'association d'anciens combattants du village. Mont-sur-Meurthe, France. Letter to author, June 3, 2003.

Demnet, Marcel. Response to author's questionnaire, November 13, 2002.

Faisant, Guy. Rennes, France. Response to author's questionnaire, undated (circa 2000).

Lenogré, Yves. Périgueux, France. Letter to author, January 15, 2000.

Lévy, Gilles. Saint Maur des Fossés, France. Response to author's questionnaire, October 4, 1999.

Marchiset, André. Raddon Haute-Saône, France. Response to author's questionnaire, undated (circa 2000).

Michel, Général Pierre. Paris, France. Response to author's questionnaire, October 18, 1999.

"Rafle du Cafe de l'Eglise aux Forges," document attached to letter from Marcel Demnet, November 13, 2002.

Newspapers

Der Bund (Bern)
Gazette nationale ou le Moniteur universel
L'Echo de paris

L'Homme Libre
Le Figaro
Le Matin
Le Saint-Hubert
Le Temps
Neue Zürcher Zeitung
New York Times
Reichsgesetzblatt
The Times (London)
Völkische Beobachter

United States Legal Citations

18 United States Code §§ 922(t)(2), 926(a).
Congressional Record
Property Requisition Act, Pub. L. 274, 55 U.S. Statutes 742. 1941.
United States v. Goering, 6 Federal Rules Decisions 69. International Military Tribunal in Session at Nuremberg 1946–47.

French Legal Citations

1ère séance du 6 décembre 1935, *Journal Officiel* (J.O.). débats parlementaires, 7 décembre 1935.
Declaration of the Rights of Man and of the Citizen (French), Art. 2. 1789.
Décret ayant pour objet d'augmenter les effectifs de la garde républicaine mobile, 23 Octobre 1935. lecahiertoulousain.free.fr/Textes/decret_1935_effectif.html.
Décret-loi du 18 avril 1939 fixant le régime des matériels de guerre, armes et munitions, *Journal Officiel*, 13 juin 1939, 7463-7466.
Décret-loi du 23 octobre 1935 portant réglementation des mesures relatives au renforcement du maintien de l'ordre public. https://www.legifrance.gouv.fr/affichTexte.do?cidTexte=LEGITEXT000006071320&dateTexte=vig.
Décret portant réglementation de l'importation, de la fabrication, du commerce et de la détention des armes, *Journal Officiel*, 24 octobre 1935.
Journal Officiel, Lois et Décrets, 25 October 1935, 11202-4.
Loi du 4 septembre 1942 relative à l'utilisation et à l'orientation de la main-d'œuvre. https://www.legifrance.gouv.fr/affichTexte.do?cidTexte=JORFTEXT000000882881&categorieLien=id.
Loi N° 773 du 7 août 1942 punissant de la peine de mort la détention d'explosifs et les dépôts d'armes, *Journal Officiel*, N° 189, 8 août 1942.

Loi N° 1005 du 31 décembre 1942 modifiant la loi du 3 décembre 1942 fixant le régime des matériels de guerre, armes et munitions, *Journal Officiel*, N° 21, 24 janvier 1943.

Loi N° 1061 du 3 décembre 1942 modifiant le décret du 18 avril 1939 fixant le régime des matériels de guerre, armes et munitions, *Journal Officiel*, N° 290, 4 décembre 1942.

Loi N° 1065 du 5 décembre 1942 modifiant la loi N° 1061 du 3 décembre 1942 fixant le régime des matériels de guerre, armes et munitions, *Journal Officiel*, N° 292, 6 décembre 1942.

Loi du 3 juillet 1943 n° 381 modifiant la loi n° 1061 du 3 décembre 1942 fixant le regime des materiels de guerre, armes et munitions, *Journal Officiel*, 4 juillet 1943.

Ordonnance concernant la détention d'armes et de radio-émetteurs dans les territoires occupés, on display at the *Musée de l'Ordre de la Libération*, Paris.

Ordonnance du 5 juni 1942 modifiant l'ordonnance du 10 mai 1940, concernant la détention des armes en territoire occupé de la France, Verordnungsblatt des Militärbefehlshabers in Frankreich (VOBIF), No. 64, 5 juni 1942, 385.

Ordonnance du 10 mai 1940 sur la détention d'armes en territoire occupé, *Verordnungsblatt für die besetzten französischen Gebiete*, n° 1, 4 juillet 1940.

Film

Die Deutsche Wochenschau. No. 506, 15 May 1940, UfA, Ton-Woche. Reproduced by International Historic Films, vol. 2, disk 1. Available at ihffilm.com/22902 .html. Newsreel.

Is Paris Burning? Directed by René Clément. Hollywood, CA: Paramount Pictures, 1966.

La Libération de Paris. A documentary film written by Pierre Bost. Paris: Le Comité de Libération du Cinéma Français, France Libre Actualités. 1944.https://archive .org/download/LaLiberationdeParis1944/LaLiberationdeParis1944.mp4.

La Mer à l'Aube (*Calm at Sea*). Directed by Volker Schlöndorff. Cergy-Pontoise Cedex, France: Arte Éditions, 2012. DVD.

Paris brûle-t-il? Directed by René Clément. Hollywood, CA: Paramount Pictures, 1966.

Credits for Illustrations

The following photos/images are published with the permission of the listed entities.

Bundesarchiv

On May 10, 1940, Germany launched...Poster Ordinance... (Bundesarchiv, Transit Film GmbH)

French troops of the 14th regimen... (Bundesarchiv, Bild 101I-126-0311-14 / Heinz Fremke)

Wehrmacht troops march into Paris, June 14,1940... (Bundesarchiv, Bild 146-1994-036-09A / Horst Sturm)

The carriage at Compiègne, June 22, 1940... (Bundesarchiv, Bild 146-1982-089-18 / Horst Sturm)

Laval with Karl Oberg...1943... (Bundesarchiv, Bild 183-H25719 / Horst Sturm)

Archives Ardennes

"Firearms, Munitions, and Explosives: Very Important Notice"... (Armes a feu, 1919-1946, 4Mb, Occupation Allemande. Archives départementales, Département des Ardennes, Charleville-Mézières)

The Image Works

An anti-government demonstration in Paris...1934... (ERVL0016203©Roger-Viollet)

Collaborators: F. de Brinon and General O. von Stülpnagel...1941... (ERVL0208506 ©LAPI/Roger-Viollet)

Ullstein Bilderdienst

French Foreign Minister Pierre Laval signs accord...1935... (Keystone, Ullstein Bilderdienst, 01022355)

Le Saint Hubert Club de France
A German arms depot storing 60,000 hunting guns… (*Le Saint-Hubert*, Juillet-Août 1941, 37. Le Saint Hubert Club de France)

Musée de l'ordre de la Libération
Ordonnance / Decree Concerning the Possession of Arms and Radio Transmitters in the Occupied Territories… (Musée de l'Ordre de la Libération, Paris)

Bildarchiv Preußischer Kulturbesitz
Vichy France meets with the Führer… 1942… (Bildarchiv Preußischer Kulturbesitz, Art Resource, NY, ART540476 / Heinrich Hoffmann)

Franz Stock
A Wehrmacht execution squad shoots members of the Manouchian resistance group… 1944… (Les Amis de Franz Stock)

Dominique Venner
Citizens with hunting guns…surrender their arms… (Dominique Venner, *Les Armes de la Résistance* (Paris: Pensée Moderne, 1976), 146.)

Bridgeman Images
Rifle instruction for members of the Maquis… (Training young Resistance fighters, 1944 / Bridgeman Images)

National Museum of the U.S. Navy
At the barricades with pistols and rifles in the liberation of Paris…1944… (National Museum of the U.S. Navy, Lot 4568-4)

Associated Press
The execution of Pierre Laval, found guilty of treason…1945… (Associated Press, 451015062)

Index

and the defeatist mentality, 50–51
exempted weapons, 115
French authorities' cooperation with Germans, 45, 50
German decrees about, 50–51, 69 (*see also* Decree of May 10, 1940, on the Possession of Arms in the Occupied Territory)
gun registration records' role in, xii, 45 (*see also* registration of arms)
vs. hiding guns, 51–53, 66, 86, 143, 166–167, 211–212
hunting guns, 8, 45, 47–48, 52, 72–73, 117
identities of owners, 45, 69
misunderstood duty to surrender arms, 104–105
in Paris, 120
perceived as cowardly, 46, 49
of private vs. military origin, 174–175
receipts for, 134–135, 138, 141, 166, 192
retaliation/prosecution for resisting, 73–74
safeguarding and return of firearms, 134, 138, 141, 162, 166–167
Otto von Stülpnagel's Last Deadline for Surrendering Arms, 108–110
types of guns surrendered, 47
Vichy's arms concealment program, 163–164
witnesses' accounts of, 46–48
See also weapons possession
Switzerland
armaments buildup by, 19
French Resistance aided by, 169, 184–185, 197
militia army of, 18–19
Resistance agents in, 188–189
Resistance aided by, 99
Szymanski, Stanislaw, 206

Teitgen, P.-H., 78
terrorist attacks, 6, 214
Thierfelder, Rudolf, 84, 167
Third Republic (France, 1870–1940), 9
Thorez, Maurice, 25
Those of the Liberation (*Ceux de la Libération*), 105–108
Tillon, Charles, 87, 94
Tirole, Henry, 112
La Toucheférond, 107–108
Tribouillois, Sylvain-André, 104
Tuffery, Hubert, 110
Tyler, Royall, 128

l'Union Fédérale des Sociétés de Tir aux Armes de Chasse, 69
United Movements of the Resistance. See *Mouvements Unis de la Résistance*
United States
firearm prohibitions in, 1–2, 213–214
firearm registration in, 4–6, 213–214
Maquis aided by, 196
right to bear arms in, 2, 4, 213
See also Allies
United Youth Forces (*Forces Unies de la Jeunesse*), 186

Vallat, Xavier, 88
van der Geest, Jack, 42–43
Venner, Dominique, 33–34
Verdier, Judge, 16
Versailles Treaty (1919), 116
Vichy France. *See* occupation and collaboration
Vierzon-Forges (France), 66–67, 201–202
Vildé, Boris, 132–133
Vincent, Camille, 206
"*Vive la France libre!*" 214
Vogt, Specialist, 139
Völkische Beobachter, 43

Wagner, Eduard, 113–114
Wannsee conference, 147
weapons ban. *See* bans on arms
weapons possession, 91–123
amnesty for, 102–104, 122 (*see also* amnesty vs. execution)
Communists' awakening re, 94–96
in criminal court cases, 147–148
denunciation, death penalty for failure of, 122–123, 129–131, 136, 152, 165–166
denunciation incentives, 111, 116–117
escalation of gun seizures and executions, 97–99
executions for, and looting of arms, 114–120, 119*t*
and executions of hostages, 91–97, 100–102, 110–115 (*see also under* amnesty vs. execution)
by French military officers, 167
by gun dealers, 93, 156, 173
Hitler on, 92
impossibility of eliminating, xii, 122–123, 212
Jews arrested for, 94

About the Author

STEPHEN P. HALBROOK is a Senior Fellow at the Independent Institute. He has taught legal and political philosophy at George Mason University, Howard University, and Tuskegee Institute, and he received his J.D. from the Georgetown University Law Center and Ph.D. in social philosophy from Florida State University.

The winner of three cases before the U.S. Supreme Court (*Printz v. United States, United States v. Thompson/Center Arms Company*, and *Castillo v. United States*), he has testified before the Subcommittee on the Constitution of the Senate Judiciary Committee, Senate Subcommittee on the Constitution, Subcommittee on Crime of the House Judiciary Committee, Senate Governmental Affairs Committee, and House Committee on the District of Columbia.

A contributor to numerous scholarly volumes, he is the author of the books, *Gun Control in the Third Reich: Disarming the Jews and "Enemies of the State"*; *The Founders' Second Amendment: Origins of the Right to Bear Arms*; *That Every Man Be Armed: Evolution of a Constitutional Right*; *A Right to Bear Arms*; *Firearms Law Deskbook: Federal and State Criminal Practice*; *Securing Civil Rights: Freedmen, the Fourteenth Amendment, and the Right to Bear Arms*; *State and Federal Bills of Rights and Constitutional Guaranties*; and *Target Switzerland: Swiss Armed Neutrality in World War II*. Dr. Halbrook's scholarly articles have appeared in such journals as the *Arizona Journal of International and Comparative Law, Drug Law Report, George Mason University Law Review, Journal of Air Law and Commerce, Journal of Law and Policy, Law & Contemporary Problems, National Law Journal, Northern Kentucky Law Review, St. John's*

Journal of Legal Commentary; Seton Hall Constitutional Law Journal, Tennessee Law Review, University of Dayton Law Review, Valparaiso University Law Review, Vermont Law Review, and *William & Mary Bill of Rights Journal.*

Dr. Halbrook's popular articles have appeared in such publications as *The Wall Street Journal, Newsday, San Francisco Chronicle, USA Today, Washington Times, National Review, Investor's Business Daily, Kansas City Star, Washington Examiner, Shreveport Times, Sacramento Bee, Providence Journal, Tampa Tribune, Pittsburgh Tribune-Review, History News Network, San Antonio Express-News, The Daily Caller, Detroit News, Honolulu Star Advertiser, Birmingham News,* and *Environmental Forum.* He has also appeared on numerous national TV/radio programs on CNN, Fox News Network, Fox Business Channel, Court TV, NewsMax TV, CBN, Voice of America, and C-SPAN. He has also appeared on numerous national TV/radio programs on CNN, Fox News Network, Fox Business Channel, Court TV, NewsMax TV, CBN, Voice of America, and C-SPAN.

Independent Institute Studies in Political Economy

Independent Institute Studies in Political Economy

INDEPENDENT
I N S T I T U T E

100 SWAN WAY, OAKLAND, CA 94621-1428

For further information:
510-632-1366 • orders@independent.org • http://www.independent.org/publications/books/